WAR AND PEACE IN
SOUTHERN AFRICA

ROBERT I. ROTBERG AND GREG MILLS
Editors

WAR AND PEACE IN SOUTHERN AFRICA

Crime, Drugs, Armies, and Trade

BROOKINGS INSTITUTION PRESS
Washington, D.C.

THE WORLD PEACE FOUNDATION
Cambridge, Massachusetts

Library of Congress Cataloging-in-Publication Data

War and peace in Southern Africa : crime, drugs, armies, and trade /
   [edited by] Robert I. Rotberg and Greg Mills.
      p. cm.
   Includes bibliographical references and index.
      ISBN 0-8157-7584-9 (cloth : alk paper). — ISBN 0-8157-7585-7
   (pbk. : alk paper)
      1. Crime—Africa, Southern. 2. Africa, Southern—Emigration and
   immigration. I. Rotberg, Robert I. II. Mills, Greg.
   HV7150.W37 1998
   364.968—dc21   97-45312
                                                                       CIP

                              9 8 7 6 5 4 3 2 1

The paper used in this publication meets the minimum requirements of the American National Standard for Information Sciences— Permanence of Paper for Printed Library Materials. ANSI Z39.48-1984

                              Typeset in Bembo
                        Composition by Linda Humphrey
                             Arlington, Virginia
                     Printed by R. R. Donnelley and Sons Co.
                           Harrisonburg, Virginia

Contents

Robert I. Rotberg

Preface

THE END of apartheid in South Africa heralded more than the onset of black rule. Together with the coming of President Nelson Mandela's Government of National Unity and the disruption of the old social order arrived major new expectations and a variety of anticipated and unanticipated perils. The regimentation of 40 million South Africans by whites, a process effectively in retreat for a decade before 1994, ceased. Black South Africans came into their own in all endeavors; they embraced both the challenges as well as the opportunities inherent in the nation that they had reclaimed. Many of those new opportunities were in the criminal sphere. A once tightly controlled society had been opened, and entrepreneurs of all kinds naturally entered.

Crime has become the painful Achilles' heel of the rapid development of both South Africa and the surrounding smaller states of southern Africa. Not only has the pre-independence level of criminal activity by indigenous South Africans multiplied manyfold. Now criminal endeavors are better organized, more widespread (not just confined to Soweto and the other ghetto locations of the apartheid era), and much more brutal.

As South Africa and southern Africa attempt to uplift themselves, to achieve Asian Tiger-like rapid economic growth, to create masses of jobs, and to deliver social services and social safety nets to long deprived populations, high levels of crime, and the perception of those high levels, continue to frustrate such efforts. The behavior of foreign investors and local corporations cannot help but be influenced adversely by reports of crime and its reality. Every mugging and every carjacking has reverberations far beyond the incidents and the statistics. Criminal activity eats away at the viability of law-abiding communities, no matter how poor. When the state cannot deliver political goods, especially security, the fabric of the state, as well as its prospects for political and economic growth, is threatened.

The crime scene in southern Africa is multidimensional. The problem is not merely its enormous volume, nor the manner in which it has overwhelmed the security forces in South Africa and the other states of the region. South Africa, as measured by its murder rate and its hanging rate, was always regarded as a violent society. But the sheer number of killings, and the vastly increased number of killings that accompany robberies, carjackings, and drug-trafficking incidents, has traumatized black and white working and professional classes, and energized governments to rethink their policing methods and security priorities, including the use of the armed forces against crime. These issues are introduced, with recent statistics, in the chapters by Greg Mills, Mark Shaw, and Joan Wardrop. Escalated murder and crime rates have also led white and black communities to take the maintenance of order into their own hands. Vigilantism is on the rise, keeping pace with more common forms of lawlessness.

Beyond escalations of violence, the myriad modern dimensions of crime in southern Africa encompass drug trafficking, arms smuggling, illegal immigration, profiteering syndicates, and the thoroughgoing involvement of foreigners. As the chapters by Ambassador Robert Gelbard and Colonel C. J. D. Venter make perfectly clear, South Africa (and by extension southern Africa) is an integral center of the worldwide trade in heroin, cocaine, and marijuana, as well as a local entrepôt for Mandrax (Quaaludes) shipments and a supplier of locally grown marijuana to the region and to Europe. Heroin transits South Africa from Asia to Europe, and cocaine transits southern Africa from South America to Europe and the Middle East. Marijuana goes in many directions. Some of each illicit commodity stays in southern Africa, too, where addiction levels are growing.

If this activity were confined, passively, to a transit trade, drug trafficking might worry southern African authorities less than it does. But international drug-trafficking syndicates now operate viciously in southern Africa, selling locally, competing with one another, and becoming engaged in ancillary criminal activities. The growth of drug-trafficking activity in the hitherto inexperienced states of the region, and across their porous borders, has been rapid and alarming. A large proportion of domestic crime is attributable to, or is a fallout from, drug rivalries and drug-trafficking competition. In addition, the over-whelmed local authorities are new to intercepting couriers, airlifts and sealifts of smuggled drugs, and money laundering. That they are also easily corrupted greatly inhibits policing of all manner of crime—not just drug-infected crime.

In early 1997, South Africa began to focus more effectively than before on all of these manifestations of the worsened crime scene. A successful private industrialist was persuaded to assume administrative control of police activities; greater attention was being paid to com-batting carjacking, particularly in troubled Gauteng; and the South African authorities started cooperating more closely with international police authorities and drug-interdiction actions. On the ground, former New York City Police Commissioner William Bratton's obser-vation that South African policing was invisible—that cops were not walking the beat—still remained true. Rosebank Station, in the heart of the wealthy northern suburbs of Johannesburg, had an official estab-lishment for four shifts of 131 persons. Yet, in May 1997, only 37 persons could be mustered there. Morale was low in Rosebank, and everywhere else. Bratton's criticisms (offered at the conference in August 1996 that preceded this book) still rang true, but the govern-ment of South Africa was conscious of his suggestions, and was busily attempting to make improvements in the national response to bur-geoning crime.

But the government had little chance of closing the door on the mas-sive trade in illegal and unregistered arms—from revolvers to AK-47s—that had contributed mortally for several years to South and southern Africa's escalating rates of crime and killings in the course of crimes. In 1996 alone, 196,000 licenses to carry weapons were granted, and almost an equal number of guns were lost or stolen from official police and military armories. The minister of safety and security admitted in early 1997 that at least 20,000 criminals had mistakenly been given approval to carry guns, but what the minister could not say was that—

whether criminals purchased their weapons legally or illegally—the country was awash with potent firearms, and that conventional weapons of all kinds continued to cascade across regional borders, almost without hindrance. The chapters by Jacklyn Cock and Glenn Oosthuysen provide the detailed dimensions of this bitter and almost unstoppable trade.

In addition to drugs and arms, people constitute the other massive movement across the region's borders. Since the end of apartheid, the comparative wealth of South Africa has pulled large numbers of economic migrants—skilled and unskilled, professional and lesser–white collar—out of their home countries and into South Africa. In 1997, it was estimated that South Africa's 41 million citizens had been joined by 8 million aliens—a full 12 percent of the total population. (Illegal immigrants account for only about 4 percent of the population of the United States.)

The chapters by Katherine Marshall and Hussein Solomon indicate that South Africa was attracting migrants partly because it was hostile to open trade from its neighbors. Zimbabweans were exporting persons instead of such items as foodstuffs and textiles, which were blocked by tariff and quota barriers to trade. Mozambique was also exporting large numbers of people who could not hope to be employed at home until new South African investments there created employment opportunities. Marshall's chapter also discusses the interlocking nature of southern Africa's trade domain, and some of the myriad political obstacles to the more open regional trade that will doubtless come.

The different parts of this book are deeply interrelated. Just as trade flows, or their absence, affect the direction and intensity of population movements, so the easy availability of arms, the proliferated drug trafficking, and the cross-border market for second-hand luxury cars motivates crime and intensifies crime rates. The demobilization of military forces throughout the region—discussed in the chapters by Mark Malan and Steven Metz (who also focuses on the ethos of the new South African defense force)—has influenced rising crime rates and arms proliferation. It has also encouraged governments and their critics to consider deploying retrained military units for policing purposes both inside and outside national borders for peacekeeping purposes. Jeffrey Herbst's chapter and Malan's chapter consider the roles that could be played externally, and under what kinds of circumstances, by the reorganized armies that are described by Metz.

As Marshall makes clear, South Africa's population of 41 million is less than one-third of the southern African region's 140 million people (the Democratic Congo adds another 50 million), but its gross domestic product (GDP) of $131 billion is 79 percent of the $165 billion total of the region, and over 22 times that of Zimbabwe's $5.9 billion GDP. Once South Africa begins to grow rapidly—in Tiger fashion (its annual growth rate per capita was about 2 percent in 1997)—its growth could fuel the growth of the entire region, uplift the poorer (but more rapidly growing) countries like Malawi and Mozambique, and play an essential part in substituting increased trade flows for cross-border migrations. Growth would permit South Africa to spend more of its scarce budgetary resources on combatting crime and drug trafficking, as well as engaging in more regional peacekeeping.

This book contains lessons about the need for politicians and governments to accept the existing integration—and the inescapable globalization—of southern Africa. None of the region's countries can afford, henceforth, to think of itself as isolated. There can be no escape into autarky. International drug- and arms-trafficking syndicates ignore national borders, and so does crime. The more rapidly and the more thoroughly South Africa can embrace free trade for the region, and help convert the Southern African Customs Union (SACU)—and even the Southern African Development Community (SADC)—into a zone of tariff-less commerce, the better will it be for growth (despite painful and temporary transitional issues), and for a concerted attack on crime and the smuggling of drugs and weapons. A new era of mutual cooperation after the indignities of apartheid could well be what President Mandela's government makes of its options.

Greg Mills and I, as well as the chapter authors, were greatly assisted by Ed Freedman's careful and thoughtful editing of our prose. We are also grateful to Emily Edson and Maeve McNally, of the Foundation, for their continuing contributions to the development and production of this book. The conference which preceded the book was generously supported by the Trustees of the World Peace Foundation, the South African Institute for International Affairs, the South African Institute for Security Studies, the U.S. Department of State's Bureau of International Narcotics and Law Enforcement Affairs, and the U.S. Army War College.

1

Greg Mills

Introduction

EVEN AFTER the end of the Cold War and the collapse of apartheid, the lives of many southern Africans are, to approximate Hobbes's state of nature, "solitary, nasty, brutish and short." The creation and mainte-nance of peace in southern Africa is part of a development process, which involves the demilitarization and demobilization of police and military forces, the understanding of the causes and effects of popula-tion movements, and, where necessary, the intervention of forces in peace-support operations. It also hinges on the application of effective strategies for policing. All of these areas of activity are crucial for eco-nomic development. In this complex synergy, economic growth also depends on a package of macroeconomic reforms.[1]

In September 1996, President Nelson Mandela admitted for the first time that crime in South Africa was "out of control." Arguing that his government was "getting on top of the situation," he realized that the eradication of poverty would lay the basis for a long-term strat-egy against criminal behavior: "Although we are using short-term

This introduction is an abbreviated and updated version of Greg Mills, *War and Peace in Southern Africa: Crime, Drugs, Armies, and Trade*, WPF Reports 13 (Cambridge, Mass., 1996), 1-39. For details about the conference that pre-ceded the book, see that Report.

tactics to deal with crime, we must address poverty. The government's macro-economic plan," he noted, "is an important document in this regard."[2]

Despite the end of apartheid, southern Africans are unhappy about social conditions. In South Africa, a recent study on crime, violence, and investment showed that more than 45 percent of people questioned called crime South Africa's biggest problem. Unemployment, which affects between 33 percent and 45 percent of the workforce, came in only a distant second (18 percent), followed by lack of housing (4 percent) and poor education (2 percent). In 1996, the estimated cost of all forms of crime was a minimum of R31 billion, equivalent to about 18 percent of the national budget (or 5.6 percent of 1996 GDP)—an amount completely unsustainable in a developing economy.[3]

Crime also remains a deterrent to new investment, particularly foreign direct investment (FDI) but, interestingly, investors rank it behind economic growth potential or political and social stability in importance. Just as political turmoil, as in areas of KwaZulu/Natal and in Gauteng's East Rand townships, often provides a useful smoke screen for criminals, so can criminal activity undermine political stability.

The advent of democracy in southern Africa has served to make criminal activity all the more visible. In 1995, South Africa had 21,000 crime-related deaths. It had double the number of road-accident victims, and six times the per capita murder rate of the United States. According to Interpol, South Africa has an average of 53.4 murders per 100,000 people; the international average is 5.5. It has the most reported rapes (99.7 per 100,000) and the eleventh most aggravated assaults, even though many such crimes go unreported. Not only has the incidence of crime—especially car hijacking, which is seemingly peculiar to South Africa—had an impact on investment; it is also driving many skilled South Africans out of the country. In the first nine months of 1996 alone, 7,811 South Africans, mainly white, left for greener pastures abroad, almost double the number of immigrants (4,603) during the same period. Others are arming themselves, in a new form of post-apartheid siege mentality. In the two years before the 1994 elections, applications for gun licenses averaged more than 20,000 a month. Although these fell to about 12,000 per month in 1995, their numbers soared again in 1996—to 16,300 per month. Licensed weapons are only the tip of the iceberg, as large numbers of illegal smuggled weapons continue to pour over the borders from Mozambique and elsewhere.[4]

The end of South Africa's isolation and its consequent political and economic integration have added another alarming dimension to the spate of criminal activity. South Africa, with its sophisticated transport and banking infrastructure and relatively poor border controls, is emerging as one of the global centers of the drug trade. An estimated 136 drug networks operate in the country, many of them controlled by Nigerians. In total, the South African Police Services (SAPS) are aware of 481 crime syndicates operating within the country, including those involved in vehicle theft (112) and commercial crime (85), of which 187 operate internationally and 125 in sub-Saharan Africa.[5]

The police and the criminal justice system are feeling the strain. Undermanning is always cited as a problem, although the number of police officers in South Africa (140,000) compares favorably on a per capita basis with other international averages. A shortage of skilled, motivated detectives would appear to be a greater hurdle.

To combat these problems, the South African government has devised a coordinated twenty-five-year National Crime Prevention Strategy (NCPS). Closer police-justice cooperation is inevitably warranted. It is estimated that although 45 percent of crimes are reported, 23 percent are solved, 10 percent prosecuted, 7.7 percent convicted, and 3.6 percent of the perpetrators imprisoned. It is calculated that only 8 of every 1,000 crimes result in convictions of two years or more.[6]

The experience of the United States and other countries shows that even though economic causes often lie at the root of criminal activity, crime can be controlled by effective policing. A combination of strategies will need to be followed in South and southern Africa; democratic governments must answer to constituencies whose lives have not improved under democratic rule as they had expected and were, indeed, promised.

Policing the Cities

Mark Shaw, the coordinator of the Crime Policing Project at the Institute for Security Studies, highlights the importance of coordinating crime-fighting strategies under NCPS. Policymakers need to heed trends abroad and to focus on crime prevention at the city level, while provincial and national bodies concentrate on countering organized and white-collar crime. The NCPS did not make adequate provision for city or major metro participation. Shaw criticizes the city councils in South Africa for being too reliant on the national initiative. He draws attention to the successful "broken window" initiative in New York city, which resulted in a marked decline of most crime in the world's former crime capital.

To Shaw, a city's crime prevention approach is the logical outcome of locally developed forms of partnership policing, such as the Business Against Crime initiative. He stresses the importance of targeting organized crime and white-collar crime, and the requirement for tailored solutions and investigative strategies, since evidence from other states in transition suggests that the power of organized crime can rival that of the state itself if left unchecked. South Africa is not comparatively underpoliced, but police concentrate strongly on the "front-end" of the criminal justice system; little progress has been made by the new order to encourage crime detection. A major overhaul of the detective branch is probably in order. In the past, promotion in the old South African Police force was achieved through service in the Security Branch; in the future, the Detective Branch might be the path for career advancement. As mentioned above, the number of police personnel (140,000 in total) compares favorably with international figures when measured on a per capita basis—328 people per police officer, compared with an international average of 1,014.

Joan Wardrop of Curtin University, Perth, Australia, offers a closer perspective on the "invisible" crime situation in Soweto. Criminal activity against black residents within the townships (before 1986) was largely ignored by the politically and economically dominant minority. Wardrop stresses the impact of the repeal of the Influx Control Act (1986), which, along with the collapse of the homelands, led to a rise in unemployment and an explosion in criminal activities outside the Johannesburg townships in the 1990s. She notes the dissonance between the national crime statistics and what she has herself observed. She questions how such precise organized-crime-syndicate numbers could have been found, contending that they must be "largely speculative." Wardrop, who worked with the Soweto Flying Squad and Dog Unit and has interviewed scores of gangsters since 1994, estimates that more than 400 gangs operate in Soweto, some of which have been in existence since the 1940s.

A typical gang has an uncomplicated structure centered around a kingpin. Normally working through a small inner circle of extremely loyal functionaries, these "businesses" sometimes are family-run affairs that recruit thousands of youngsters to learn specific tasks, such as car stripping, *dagga* (marijuana) selling, passing counterfeit money, transporting gold and diamonds, robbing or stealing vehicles or other property, and trafficking in firearms.

New recruits can expect to earn between R500 and R5,000 per "ordered" stolen car, which can be stripped and made ready almost anywhere. An elaborate "clearing" system makes the apprehension of suspects extremely difficult. Organized syndicates, using gangs to steal their required commodities, prepare the goods for shipment to other provinces, or to any destination on the globe. The black-taxi industry provides a large market for illicit spare parts/vehicles and the means to launder the easily gained cash.

In an environment with a tremendous influx of illegal immigrants and plenty of firearms, the preventive side of policing is at an extreme disadvantage. Nevertheless, recent initiatives—including the use of satellite tracking by private companies, the deployment of spotter aircraft, and the Highway Patrol Scheme—are beginning to have a positive effect.

Wardrop emphasizes the importance of distinguishing between basic structural variables (such as unemployment, opportunities for employment, and socioeconomic conditions) that cannot be altered easily, and those variables that are more amenable to change to alleviate crime, as well as the importance of identifying the criminal activities that pose the greatest danger to society and thus contain the greatest cost benefit for policing. Resources have to be allocated accordingly. Violent crime must be examined by neighborhood, not even by city or by district. In this regard, there is also an important link between demography and criminal activity. For example, people over twenty-five years of age are less likely to be involved in crime; in the United States, for example, those under twenty-five tend to be concentrated geographically. Policing strategies can be developed and applied with such trends in mind.

South Africa has tended to fixate, not surprisingly, on its own operations against criminal activity at the expense of alternative preventive strategies elsewhere, especially regarding the so-called "crimes of shame" (particularly rape), and white-collar crime. The SAPS reported that, in 1995, commercial crime cost the South African economy an estimated R2.6 billion. White-collar crime, often a by-product of society in transition, escalated not only in South Africa, but also in Eastern Europe and the former Soviet Union.

The effective utilization of scarce resources in South Africa is key for a successful crime-fighting strategy. Resources have to be allocated where intelligence is best and where maximum impact and benefit can be derived.

Preventing Weapons Proliferation

Crime in South Africa is a complex, interrelated phenomenon. Organized crime syndicates link smuggling channels and networks of drugs, arms, ivory, vehicles, gems, and money. South Africa's long and porous borders, as well as its developed banking system, make it an easy and profitable operating environment. Compared with, for example, Zimbabwe, which has only seven border crossing points, South Africa has fifty-two, including thirty-six airports classified as "international," though many are without air-traffic control, regular policing, customs, or immigration checks. Illegal imports cost the country an estimated R2 billion annually in lost customs revenues, partly the result of corruption, but also the paucity of immigration and customs officials and loopholes resulting from the South African Customs Union (SACU). Of all the cross-border crimes, weapon smuggling has sparked the most concern about poor border security and controls in South Africa.

Glenn Oosthuysen discusses the southern African region on a country-by-country basis, examining the weapons-control measures in terms of internal legislation and the success attained in eliminating illegal weaponry. "Small arms" or "light weapons"—defined as those weapons that can be carried physically by individuals without the need for mechanized or other platforms (rifles, revolvers, pistols, shotguns, explosives, etc.)—have come to play a significant role in the shaping of southern Africa. This influence has not diminished even though the major inter- and intrastate conflicts have either ended or diminished.

In his review of the extent and consequences of small-arms proliferation in southern Africa, Oosthuysen examines present controls employed in the region. Both Mozambique and Angola provide informative case studies as to how demobilization and demilitarization within a UN context can be applied successfully to peace-building efforts. The United Nations Operation in Mozambique (UNOMOZ) supervised the demobilization and disarmament of the Front for the Liberation of Mozambique (FRELIMO) and the Mozambique National Resistance (RENAMO) troops, as well as their integration into the new national defense force and into society. Combatants were required to hand in their arms upon registration at assembly areas, a process that yielded 167,758 weapons. Approximately 104,000 of these weapons were small arms—a figure far short of even the most conservative estimate of 1.5 million in circulation. It was contended that UNOMOZ disarmament strategies in Mozambique were a failure. UNOMOZ might have been slightly more successful without the operational limitations imposed on it by the Mozambican Ceasefire Commission, the UN Security Council mandate, and its own finite resources. Much of the disarmament effort was wasted; large numbers of the weapons handed in to UNOMOZ were lost or stolen from UN armories and store houses. Weapons were often simply abandoned and later stolen to be used for nefarious purposes. Some of the weapons found their way into South Africa.

In South Africa, legal, or licensed, weapons are subject to the provisions of the Arms and Ammunition Act, which regulates the licensing procedure. In 1993, there were 3,717,463 weapons in South Africa; 256,989 applications were received that year, of which 248,976 were granted. In 1995, these figures increased to 4,100,015 licensed firearms, and 145,932 licenses granted. All told, there were 1,944,066 gun owners in South Africa in 1995.

Ironically, South Africa's increase in armed crime not only has been fueled by the importation of weapons from across South Africa's borders; it has also been a result of the rise in licensed weapons. The incidence of licensed firearms being reported as stolen or lost continues to increase in South Africa: In 1994, at least 16,110 licensed firearms were reported as lost/stolen, and in 1995, this figure rose to at least 17,617. Between April 1990 and 12 September 1995, the SAP itself "lost" 7,261 firearms, and the South African National Defense Force (SANDF) lost 1,324. The former homeland-states security forces have also accounted for considerable losses. For example, in 1995 in the former Transkei, 2,120 (38 percent) of the 5,634 weapons supposedly under police control could not be located. Given the SAPS's estimate that it recovers approximately 10 percent of all weapons entering the country illegally, the number of illegal weapons in South Africa has increased by more than 417,000 since 1993. In 1995, 2,916 rifles (including 1,392 AK-47s), 7,200 pistols, 2,842 revolvers, and 2,624 home-made weapons were seized.

These statistics concerning the proliferation of light weaponry in South Africa have met with some skepticism. Indeed, difficulties in ascertaining the exact numbers of illegal weapons create obstacles to determining how to reduce the level of small arms in South and southern Africa. Without accurate statistical evidence, it is impossible to implement effective countermeasures, whether these be more stringent licensing requirements, more effective policing, or tighter border controls.

As the southern African region has moved to reestablish normal relations and to improve the flow of regional trade, so too has the cross-border flow of people, goods, and vehicles intensified, thus facilitating the illicit trafficking in weapons. An examination of regional border-security conditions shows why it is possible for weapons to be smuggled with relative impunity into South Africa. Long borders and limited resources—including undermanned and poorly equipped policing forces—combine to make southern Africa's borders extremely porous.

According to Oosthuysen, the result is an increase in criminal activity throughout southern Africa, with dire consequences for sociopolitical stability. Given South Africa's centrality as an "engine for growth" in southern Africa, for the long term, illegal weapons have to be removed from the hands of criminals, which will require creative policing and enforcement measures. In the short term, South Africa has to revert to boosting its first line of defense—to improve border inspection capabilities at South Africa's borders and formalize agreements with neighboring states to provide for the repatriation and extradition of those who are involved in illegal activities and for the maximum penalty to be attached to cross-border trafficking in weapons.

Jacklyn Cock of the University of the Witwatersrand perceives the problem of small arms to be a social issue, which cannot be controlled through border security. She argues instead for the need to map the social conditions that have led to the proliferation of light weaponry. In this regard, she uncovers a "commercialization" of violence in South Africa, with a culture of macho stereotypes and ethnic identities at its heart. The Afrikaner and his gun and the right of the Zulu to carry weapons are cases in point. The symbolism attached to the AK-47 as an icon of liberation, coupled with a strategy of dehumanization of enemies in society also contributes to armed violence in South Africa. Understanding the requirement for arms-control measures means going to the root of these social tensions. Control measures also have to focus on the domestic armaments industries in South Africa, as well as on the importation of weapons.

Southern Africa's problems pale (in statistical terms) when compared to the issue of light-weapons proliferation in the United States, where there are an estimated 50 to 80 million handguns, part of an overall figure of 220 million small arms. However, the social conditions in southern Africa make weapons much more dangerous; people use them to ensure both their personal security and their livelihoods.

The ability of governments to appreciate the extent of the crisis remains a fundamental concern, as does the method of accurately assessing the effectiveness of control strategies. Weaponry might be best understood as a commodity. If controls are successful, the prices of weapons will rise. If not, the prices will drop. Novel as it may be, market analysis is one way to evaluate the effectiveness of governmental control.

Population Flows and Regional Trade

What is the relationship between crime and illegal immigrants? What is the extent of illegal immigration from the region into South Africa today? What is the cost, if any, of these "illegal aliens" to South Africa?

With these questions in mind, Hussein Solomon identifies five main types of contemporary migration: intrastate, east to west, south to north, north to south, and south to south population movements. Solomon classifies migrants in regional terms in order to understand the relationships between these different categories, which include the "contract labor migrants," incorporating 165,825 southern Africans working in South African mines and another 100,000 employed in the South African agricultural sector. Another category, "asylum seeker," pays lip service to a quasi-legal process in which "one state grants protection to a national or nationals of another state."

Solomon presents two sub-categories of legal migrants. The first comprises the "brain drain" of South African professionals and business people emigrating to Europe, North America, Australia, and New Zealand. In 1994, 10,235 citizens left the Republic. The second comprises the brain drain of African professionals and business people from the rest of the continent into South Africa: In 1994, 25.4 percent of all immigrants into South Africa came from other regions of Africa. In 1996, more than 200,000 neighboring southern Africans applied for permanent residence in South Africa. In 1991 alone, 200 medical doctors left Zimbabwe to settle in South Africa and Botswana. This trend held serious "long-term consequences for [neighboring] economies."

Eight components enter into the spatial movement of people into South Africa: sociocultural factors; communications and technology; geographical proximity; precedent; demographic influences, including population growth; environmental conditions; economic opportunities, which, although originally local, have become increasingly global; and political issues. In identifying and examining the reasons for illegal immigration into South Africa, Solomon notes the financial and social effects of so large and prominent a group of illegal aliens in the country. In 1994, it cost South Africa R1.9 billion to house alien migrant populations. Social costs may have accrued in the form of disease and epidemic potential, particularly the link between immigration and the spread of AIDS, malaria, cholera, and tuberculosis. A functional relationship "also existed between illegal aliens and the crime rate" in South Africa. During 1993, for example, 4,969 illegal aliens were arrested in South Africa in connection with serious crimes (rape, murder, theft, burglary, etc.); and the number went up to 12,403 in 1994. The SAPS contend that 14 percent of crime involves illegal aliens.

Illegal immigrants in the South African economy are involved principally in agriculture, hotels and restaurants, construction, domestic services, and informal trading. How then to manage mass migrations? If illegal immigration places a tremendous burden on the South African government and its people, clearly the influx of illegal aliens must be curbed. Solomon argues, however, that Pretoria's responses have generally been reactive, ad hoc, and short term, ranging from control measures (enforced repatriation, greater presence of police and army personnel on the borders, and so on) to accommodation (for example, the South African cabinet's decision to legalize the status of illegal immigrants who had resided in the country for longer than five years, found gainful employment, married a South African, or established no criminal record). "What is needed is the adoption of a strategic perspective to deal with the problem of clandestine migration." A long-term vision is required, which, "unlike the control and accommodation measures," stresses state intervention to address the root causes that give rise to population movements.

Although South Africa must engage southern Africa in economic development as a long-term deterrent to illegal immigration, this approach could take up to fifty years to implement. The merit of this approach is that "it bridges the concerns of illegal aliens and the state." This bilateral strategy should cover the issues not only of entry, residence, and departure, but also occupational and social rights, including participation in trade unions and social-security schemes. Thus, governments could address the insecurities of illegal immigrants who have no choice but to leave the countries of their birth due to "push" factors, and relieve the burden that illegal immigrants inevitably cause host states.

Economic development within the region has an obvious impact on population flows. Katherine Marshall of the World Bank provides a "regional portrait" of southern African trade and economics. In spite of the unprecedented hope in the region for the establishment of a common market, as well as the unprecedented synergy, she concedes that there is potential trouble ahead. The process of regional integration is complicated by the redefinition of the functions, structures, and roles of many southern African organizations. There are also questions about whether countries with massive disparities in social and economic development, as in southern Africa, can work together. Drought, AIDS, competition in the type of products produced by these states, and both intrastate and intraregional inequalities all create difficult development problems. The question in southern Africa is simply, How does one persuade these countries to cope effectively with issues of regional cooperation and growth?

Globalization (or the opening up) of markets and trade is leading to an accelerated pace of change, and accelerated demands on states having to undergo and cope with such change. The point is not to try to prevent change from taking place, or to change rates of urbanization or cross-border migrancy, but instead to cope with and manage such alterations. If inequalities continue in southern Africa, South Africa will continue to attract migrant workers. In 1996, the per capita income of South Africa was $2,560, compared with Mozambique's $100, and Zimbabwe's $650. It is ten times the sub-Saharan average of c. $280.

The World Bank estimates the number of illegal immigrants in South Africa to be about 5 million (or 12 percent of the population), although some put the figure as high as 8 million (20 percent). With regard to legal mine workers, the region is highly dependent on South Africa: Swaziland has approximately 20,000 migrant workers in South Africa; approximately one-quarter of Lesotho's labor force is abroad at any one time, and remittances from migrants account for half of its GDP. South Africa receives approximately 20,000 migrant mine workers from Botswana, and Mozambique's mine workers in South Africa constitute c. 20 percent of Mozambican employment, while miners' earnings account for 33 percent of foreign exchange earnings.

The starting point for southern Africa's improvement rests in faster rates of economic growth—between 5 and 6 percent—which requires "sensible" economic policies. First, sensible "household economics"— low inflation, freed-up exchange rates, and a deregulated banking sector—have to be implemented. Economic reform cannot be imposed; it has to be accepted by countries as an "economic fact of life." Second, although there is little consensus about trade policy in southern African countries, there is increasing international clarity of what it takes to improve an economy to the point that 5 to 6 percent growth is attained. Yet, debate still rages about the "sequencing" of trade reforms. Does a country "phase in" trade liberalization, or does it go "cold turkey"? Finally, issues concerning land ownership remain a central challenge that might have an underlying destabilizing tendency.

Clearly, it is much more difficult to manage economic policies and the liberalization of economies in accordance with a global consensus where extreme wealth inequalities prevail. The southern African community is not monolithic. In Mozambique, for example, two-thirds of the government budget originates from outside sources, thus yielding much power to outside institutions in terms of government policy.

Clearer and more accurate statistical information about labor movements and the effects of regional free-trade arrangements is needed. It is impossible to consider the effects of the free movement of labor in southern Africa upon South Africa without accurate assessments of the numbers involved. Obtaining correct statistical information is problematic in a region where many states do not regard the movement of migrants as "legal." Instead, many view the colonial borders that cut across communities, rather than the movement of populations, as the foreign factor. However, the reality in South Africa is that its population is not in favor of the free movement of people. There is also a fundamental, potential contradiction between a state's ability to assert its borders in the face of such movement and its capacity to liberalize and reduce state intervention in other areas of activity.[7]

"Formal movers," those who enter South Africa illegally from Asia, China, Europe, and elsewhere, also cause concern. Illegal job seekers from the United Kingdom (alleged to number 66,000, although the number of UK passport holders in southern Africa probably exceeds 1 million) are cited, in particular, as a grouping that takes jobs away from South Africans. Although the proposed South African Development Community (SADC) Free Movement of Persons protocol—based on the European Union's (EU) Schengen Agreement—purports to restrict migration from outside the region while relaxing internal controls, the ineffective external controls of many SADC states might not be able to prevent large-scale immigration from African states to the north.

Stanching the Flow of Drugs

Robert Gelbard, then U.S. Assistant Secretary of State for International Narcotics and Law Enforcement Affairs, declares drug trafficking in southern Africa as a global threat to an ordered civil society. Today's threats are no longer confined to the geopolitical or military–political spheres; the criminal or personalized issues surrounding the flow of drugs and weapons, money laundering, and other criminal activities have tremendous international consequences. According to Gelbard, the most significant development in the drug trade has been the rise of the Nigerian drug traffickers into a global force.

The end of isolation has resulted in the opening up of South Africa to such problems. Not only has South Africa's political transition opened the door to international criminals, its geography no longer offers protection and, with the increase in international flight traffic (the number of foreign airlines flying into South Africa has increased from twenty-one in 1990 to fifty-four in 1996), the Republic has become a favorite transshipment point for international drug syndicates.

C. J. D.Venter, assistant commissioner of the SAPS, points out that South Africa's emergence from international isolation has brought increased exposure to both the trafficking and the marketing of a wide range of popular and "designer" drugs. South Africa today has an estimated 135 drug syndicates, along with its 112 "vehicle-related syndicates," 85 commercial/fraud rackets, and 71 diamond- and gold-related syndicates.

This problem obviously demands international solutions. There is a peculiar southern African-Brazil-Nigerian nexus that requires policing. Brazil is a "cocaine source country for Nigerian traffickers" who ply their trade to, inter alia, Cape Verde, Portugal, Angola, Mozambique, and South Africa. Gelbard notes the seizure of 98 kgs of cocaine in Cape Verde, from March 1995 to May 1995, mainly from West Africans; 40 kgs of cocaine in Portugal from November 1994 to February 1995, en route from South Africa to Mozambique; and 18.5 kgs of cocaine in Angola during 1994. "Currently, cocaine is the most serious drug problem that South African authorities face," says Gelbard. "Nigerians, who acquire the drug in Brazil and Argentina and smuggle it via Angola and Namibia, manage most of the trade." He also notes that "from 1993 to 1995, Brazilian authorities arrested 42 Nigerians in possession of a total of 266 kgs of cocaine. Brazil is the primary staging area for Nigerian cocaine shipments because of its close historic ties to Africa and its large ethnic African population. In 1993," he continues, "Nigerians were responsible for more than half the cocaine that was seized in South Africa, and that percentage may be rising."

The drug-trafficking situation in South Africa eventually became so bad that in late 1996, public anger finally exploded. A well-organized crowd of several hundred armed Muslims from the movement known as People Against Gangsterism and Drugs (PAGAD), a community pressure group established at the end of 1995, gathered in Cape Town outside the home of a suspected drug dealer and shot one of their targets dead during a 15-minute gun battle.

Although one of slogans of the ruling African National Congress (ANC) at the November 1995 local elections in South Africa was "tough on crime, tough on the causes of crime," in the eyes of the communities worst affected by such violence, little has been done to redress these problems. Gang warfare has raged intermittently for many years in the suburbs of South Africa's biggest towns, fueled by deprivation, poverty, unemployment, the political struggle against apartheid, and social dislocation—interrelated, in many instances, with the flow of drugs. With its sophisticated transport and banking infrastructure and relatively poor border controls, South Africa is emerging as one of the global centers of the drugs trade.

Gelbard maintains that South Africa requires three "I"s to combat the increase in drug smuggling: *improvement* in information and intelligence gathering, with linkages established at the subregional, continental, and international levels; *institution* building among the police, judiciary, and prosecutors and, indeed, within the entire legal framework, for which the Vienna Convention provides a suitable starting point; and *international* cooperation.

Drug trafficking can flourish in nondemocratic environments— Nigeria and Burma being two pertinent examples. That South Africa has obtained little cooperation from Nigerian authorities in the fight against drug trafficking does not help in the struggles against syndicates that are active throughout the sub-continent: The well-oiled and well-disciplined organizations in Kenya, Ethiopia, Egypt, and Tanzania have proved difficult to counter. To combat such operations, customs services throughout the sub-continent need to act not just as revenue-collection agencies, but also as proactive law-enforcement agencies. The United States has been willing to offer assistance to South and southern Africa in the form of training programs to establish strong institutional mechanisms, and the opening of a Drug Enforcement Agency (DEA) and FBI offices in Johannesburg to facilitate improved relations with South Africa and assist in the fight against international drug trafficking.[8]

Drug trafficking is only a subset of South Africa's National Crime Prevention Strategy. Effective policing, however, will require far more than just greater resources. Because many South Africans are dependent on drugs, particularly marijuana, as a means of subsistence farming, crop-substitution programs must parallel policing efforts.

Demobilization and Demilitarization of Armies and Police in Southern Africa

Southern Africa is faced with many new opportunities and challenges in the post–Cold War and post-apartheid world. Although there is great potential to ease interstate tensions and implement demilitarization, including the reduction in size of armed forces, demilitarization and demobilization entail more than military restructuring; they also portend social, political, and cultural changes.

Steven Metz, of the U.S. Army War College, stresses the importance of demilitarization (and in another form, demobilization) as a crucial process in the stages of economic and social development. Demobilization can contribute to economic growth by lowering budgets, and also by easing social tensions. The mechanical questions regarding the reintegration of forces into society and the actual phased process of demobilization are important, but the psychological dimensions—such as the notion of "military ethos"—are not to be overlooked. An ethos grows from a nation's history and its culture, generally referring to the values associated with certain relationships and describing the hierarchy of loyalties.

Metz identifies several factors that will play major roles in the attempt to create and sustain a new ethos in the South African National Defense Force, which previously was dominated by a combination of British and Afrikaner military traditions: the new body of civilian expertise with a "hands-on" managerial function and supervisory capacity; the creation of disincentives for breaking the new ethos; the revision of officer training, putting officer education at the forefront of the armed forces; and the building of a post-apartheid culture within wider society. On this last point, should defense forces, for example, establish a greater presence within civilian society, emphasizing an occupational rather than an institutional function? The extension of the SANDF's role also raises the question whether the armed forces should themselves be the instigators of demobilization or social integration via demilitarization.

The process of demilitarization has not only affected the defense forces of southern Africa; it has also helped to reshape the culture of the SAPS. Prior to the 1994 election, South Africa possessed no less than eleven policing agencies. On the one hand, stood the old South Africa Police;

on the other, the forces of the so-called homelands, numbering c. 25,000. As a result of a decision in accord with the broader notions of reconciliation in South African society, every member of these eleven forces was invited to join the new force. Thus the period since 1994 has seen an increase in the budgetary allocation for policing. However, the current SAPS force of 140,000 members does not meet the demand. Demobilization has not affected the police in the same way as it has the SANDF.

Yet, the ethos of the police force—which, prior to 1994, was similar to the old South African Defense Force (SADF) intentional view of "an enemy out there"—has changed dramatically. The difficulty with the old SAP, unlike the SADF, was how to subject the organization to a wider influence through which to effect organizational change. As a result, the demilitarization of the SAPS has been a planned one. Political control over the police force has been reestablished, with attention to proactive and community-needs policing strategies, including the demilitarization, inter alia, of rank structures and uniforms. Civilian supervisory mechanisms have also been created in order to make the SAPS more accountable and efficient: a secretariat, an independent complaints unit (under the Police Act) to look into allegations of police misconduct, a Human Rights Commission (HRC), various parliamentary committees, and a Community Policing Forum.

Demilitarization is a noble goal in South Africa; it complements broader democratic tendencies. But questions still exist about the viability of demilitarizing security forces—whether these be the army or the police forces—in a society with a heavily armed and violent populace. Thus, these measures relate to the effectiveness of both deterrence and prosecution of criminal activity; they speak not only to levels of militarization and perceptions of culture and ethos within the security forces, but also (in the South African environment) to the judiciary's capacity to run the criminal justice system. In addition, the relationship between the police forces and the military vis-à-vis border security and internal policing tasks needs rethinking. Since the SANDF is commissioned annually by the president to assist the SAPS—its role determined by the Minister of Safety and Security—South Africa requires no new legislation to involve the SANDF in police functions. It is merely a matter of finding the political will.

The "peace dividend" in southern Africa is expected to accrue little financial reward. Any saving on defense spending in South Africa has already been "spent and squandered." In 1989, defense expenditure accounted for 4.3 percent of GDP; this figure was down to 1.9 percent in 1996. The peace dividend now can come only in the form of improved social conditions, and, in Angola and Mozambique, through the removal of land mines. Paradoxically, the development of private security forces and the failure to accommodate members of South Africa's Self Defense Units (SDUs) in the integration process have kept levels of militarization and tension high. The SDUs need further examination, given that some 15,000 remain in South Africa.

Police demilitarization involves delegating policing responsibilities through decentralization, collaboration in decision making, and extension of accountability to police officers. Police forces throughout southern Africa should move away from the all-too-familiar strategy of "hit, kick and deal with it."

Employing Southern African Defense Forces in Regional Peacekeeping Activities

There is no doubt that Africa has become increasingly marginalized in Western and, especially, U.S. foreign-policy eyes. This disengagement both weakens the leverage and undermines the interests of Western powers, leaving Africa largely to its own devices in preventing and ending armed conflicts. In 1994, African nations contributed around 11 percent of the troops used in UN peacekeeping missions in Africa. Given its preeminent continental military capacity, South Africa will be expected to assume a leading part in the future.

The SANDF currently possesses only a limited peacekeeping projection capacity. The SANDF (numbering 90,000 in 1996) could probably muster a peacekeeping force of 8,000 troops for a limited period (three to four months), and for a longer term sustain a combat group of 2,500 or so. Clearly though, questions of why, where, how, and when it should contribute will have to be answered. The justification for involvement can include the attempt to earn foreign exchange, to enhance a sense of military professionalism and pride, to provide a rationale for maintaining a technologically sophisticated and well-equipped defense force, or simply "to do the right thing." The South African public is in favor of a peacekeeping role for the SANDF: A poll commissioned in 1995 showed that about two-thirds of respondents wanted the country to have a force for the express purpose of helping other countries maintain the peace.

Yet, southern Africa should consider whether there are African solutions to African problems in the realm of peacekeeping. Conventional wisdom would have it that key criteria—such as those presented in President Clinton's Presidential Decision Directive Number 25 (PDD-25)—would have to be fulfilled prior to intervention. These would include clear entrance and exit strategies (a limited time frame for involvement), the allocation of sufficient personnel and equipment to do the job, consent of the conflicting parties, and international (UN) authorization. Yet, as Jeffrey Herbst of Princeton University argues, if African peacekeeping operations are to be a success, certain "rules of intervention"—potentially contradicting this conventional wisdom—have to be established.

First, the intervening powers have to be as serious as the domestic stakeholders. They at least have to understand the factors that lie at the heart of the problem that gives rise to the intervention in the first place. Second, any peacekeeping force has to alter the balance of power in societies where they intervene, requiring the disarmament or reconciliation of the conflicting groups, the allocation of sufficient resources, and the political commitment of the peacekeeping troops to carry out these responsibilities. Third, intervention has to take place within a realistic time frame—not that, for example, set by President Bush who wished to be "out of Somalia in six weeks" when the U.S. forces were not even *there* in six weeks. Fourth, exit strategies may well be an impediment to peacekeeping operations. Exit strategies imposed prior to departure of peacekeeping missions could make the occupying forces seem less than serious about finishing what they started, giving warring parties an incentive to wait out interventions.

Fifth, peacekeeping operations seldom have the consent of all parties involved. It is a myth that such operations are neutral, when they are obviously part of the "political equation." In this regard, the involvement of African armies would bring "considerable baggage" when neighbors are involved in such operations. Finally, a technically appropriate force structure for peacekeeping would have to be established in Africa. "A lot of lift" is required, and "force-multiplier" units, such as those involved in civil affairs, are often "absolutely vital." The balance of power in peacekeeping has been altered substantially by the wide-spread availability of weaponry, demanding the application of considerable military power by intervening forces.

In the African context, preventive diplomacy has not stemmed the tide of state failure. Today there is only "an illusion" of sovereignty in many African states. Part of the problem in Africa is that many of the existing states, given their artificiality and facade of independence, which were bolstered by the Cold War, are incapable today of addressing the problems of drugs, crime, and migration.

Peace support/keeping has to be viewed as a process, not as an event. Peacekeeping and development are "two sides of the same coin," requiring the establishment of institutional capacity and operational competence. However, progress in setting up African peacekeeping institutions has been "slow, disappointing, and largely at the level of rhetoric." As a result, focus has now shifted from the nominally continental (OAU) to subregional capacity-building. The SADC Organ on Politics, Defense, and Security and the evolution of the Inter-State Defense and Security Committee (ISDSC), as part of the function of the SADC Organ, should be seen in this light.

Effective use and involvement of peacekeeping forces demands a regional vision and, indeed, a vision of what exactly constitutes the "southern African" region. Moreover, training must reflect a reorientation from counter-insurgency (COIN) and counter-terrorism–type strategies to peacekeeping initiatives, and nongovernmental organizations (NGOs) must continue in both peace-support operations and conflict-prevention efforts.

The chapters that follow examine the interrelationship between crime, population movement, trade and investment strategies, issues of demobilization and demilitarization, the capacity of southern African defense forces to keep the peace, and policing strategies in the southern African region. The critical points are clear:

First, security (broadly defined) is a prerequisite for economic development in southern Africa. Second, the problem areas of crime and security—hence economic development in southern Africa—demand a thorough, situational approach. Statistics alone—no matter how accurate—will not provide solutions, particularly in the cases of light-weapon proliferation and illegal population movement.

Third, the global nature of criminal activity, as exemplified by the proliferation of crime syndicates throughout southern Africa and the use of South Africa as a trans-shipment point for international drug operations, highlights the importance of international cooperation. Such cooperation is also at issue concerning peacekeeping operations in the region.

Fourth, action to redress the problems of security and development in South Africa is necessary, not only at the international level but also at the national and regional levels. Decentralization must extend to provincial structures, as well as to various local entities, including cities.

A number of paradoxes seem to surround the debate about security and its relationship to economic development. For one, many areas on the African sub-continent are experiencing a collapse of state capacity; yet the support of such failing capacity is often justified by a bias for state survival at any price. Moreover, southern Africa is pursuing a policy of "development integration" as a means to ensure growth, contrary to the prevailing international wisdom that market integration is the priority for economic prosperity.

Hence, the SADC's stated objective of creating a southern African free trade area was dubiously conceived. First, it will involve the attempted integration of vastly unequal states and economies. Mexico's integration with the United States (and Canada) through the North American Free Trade Agreement (NAFTA) has sometimes proved difficult because Mexico's economy is ten times smaller in terms of GDP than that of the United States. South Africa's economy is twenty times the size of the next largest, Zimbabwe's. In fact, South Africa's economy is nearly four times as large as that of the other eleven members together. There is a danger—if not an inevitability—that South Africa will swallow up the entire region.

Second, although a free trade area would help to increase southern Africa intraregional trade beyond its current 8 to 10 percent of total trade, much of the region's exports are commodities required by markets outside of the SADC, irrespective of the nature of tariffs.

Third, South Africa is in a difficult position with regard to committing itself to both a specific SADC plan for a free trade area, given the state of its own negotiations with the EU and the ongoing discussions about the reconstitution of the Southern African Customs Union (SACU). The fundamental question with regard to the SADC's approach is, How can development integration live with market integration when the globalization of markets and businesses is the consensus worldwide? Furthermore, how can South Africa negotiate a free trade area with both the SADC and the EU or negotiate a more rapid reduction of tariffs under the World Trade Organization under these circumstances? Clearly, this is a matter for South Africa's Department of Foreign Affairs (DFA) and the Department of Trade and Industry (DTI) to resolve between them.

Yet another paradox concerning economic development and security is that, although job creation and prosperity in South Africa may be the only recourse against crime in the long term, failure to prevent criminal activity is wreaking havoc on economic investment and growth in the Republic. This situation would seem to demand a balanced approach between effective policing and the implementation of sustainable development strategies, which, in a world of emerging agreement about political and economic liberalization, implicates such reforms as privatization, deregulation, and the removal of exchange controls. Effective policing (as the experience of New York City has shown) can be achieved through a combination of dynamic leadership and a focus on every area of criminal activity—from petty crime to murder to international syndication.

As a "way station" between the first and third worlds, South Africa's criminal policing initiatives could carry important lessons elsewhere. The transformation from years of debilitating civil war and economic decay will not only enhance political and social stability throughout the region, including South Africa, but could set southern Africa apart as a growth pole and example of success for the rest of the African continent.

Notes for Chapter One

1. Thomas Hobbes quoted in Karl Deutsch, *Politics and Government: How People Decide Their Fate* (Boston, 1980), 78.
2. *The Sunday Independent*, 1 Sept. 1996.
3. *Financial Mail*, 6 Sept. 1996.
4. *Ibid.*; *The Citizen*, 22 Feb. 1997.
5. The figure of 481 crime syndicates operating in South Africa came from Safety and Security Minister Sydney Mufamadi on June 20, 1996. In this volume, Mark Shaw uses the same number, but Joan Wardrop puts the official

number at 412, citing a "widely publicized" figure "given legitimacy by both the national police commissioner and the Gauteng member of the Executive Council for Safety and Security during the Sword and Shield operation, June–July 1996." However, Wardrop herself claims that, "whether measured by police or criminals, the number of groups, gangs, or syndicates . . . far exceeds 412."

6. *Financial Mail*, 6 Sept. 1996.

7. An opinion survey conducted in October 1995 by the South African Communications Service found that 68% of respondents thought that the South African authorities should act more strictly regarding "illegal aliens."

8. For the problem of drug trafficking in Burma, see David I. Steinberg, *Burma: Prospects for Political and Economic Reconstruction*, WPF Reports 15 (Cambridge, Mass., 1997).

2

Mark Shaw

South Africa

Crime and Policing in Post-Apartheid South Africa

POLITICAL AND SOCIAL transformation have affected South Africa profoundly. New, and nonracial, forms of democratic government have been established at the national, provincial, and local level, and reconstruction and development has (slowly) begun. But the process has been far from painless: Political violence has ended, except in parts of KwaZulu/Natal, but the transition to democracy has been characterized by rising levels of crime.

There is a clear and crucial link between South Africa's transition and the growth in crime that has accompanied it. But it would be dangerously simplistic to argue that crime is purely a consequence of the transition. Indeed, strong evidence suggests that the roots of crime lie in the apartheid system that the transition sought to leave behind. Nonetheless, the increase in criminality from 1990—and in the decade before—cannot be divorced from the political, social, and economic changes that ended apartheid.

South Africa's increases in crime are consistent with those of other

This chapter is an updated and revised version of the original conference paper and the essay "Crime in Transition," which appeared in *Policing the Transformation*, Institute for Security Studies Monograph Series, 12 (April 1997), 7-27.

countries undergoing transition to democracy: As change proceeds, society and its instruments of social control—formal and informal— are reshaped. As a result, new areas for the development of crime, which are bolstered by the legacies of the past, open up.

Inevitably, newspaper headlines, police reports, and the experiences of citizens have brought the issue of crime to the public agenda. Many people regard the problem as a crisis. Both political elites and the media see crime as a threat to the stability of the new democracy and a deterrent to investment. As Tokyo Sexwale, the populist Premier of Gauteng, has declared, "Crime is the soft underbelly of the Reconstruction and Development Program." As such, it is a central test of the government's capacity to rule and the new democracy to consolidate.[1]

The transition has not brought with it a system of criminal justice that can respond to these challenges immediately. The institutions of criminal justice remain weighed down with the public perception that they are tools to enforce the rule of the minority, rather than to deliver protection to all. Moreover, the state security apparatus, though monstrously efficient in defending white rule through "insertion" or "fire force" policing, is too underresourced and underskilled to assume conventional policing functions; and the new government—given its desire to control the pace of transformation—has sought to retain policing as a central function, despite growing evidence that a centralized approach to crime control and prevention fails to address local problems. Pretoria-centric controls undermine the establishment of clear accountability links between local communities and the police, reinforcing perceptions that the South African Police Service (SAPS) remains oblivious and unresponsive to citizen needs.

Citizens have not always reacted to growing levels of crime by demanding that politicians do something about it. Rising crime has prompted South Africans to create substitute policing institutions, a trend that has strengthened through 1996. The private-security industry continues to grow while vigilante groups have consolidated their positions. The dangers of the growth of alternative forms of policing are obvious: They represent initiatives outside of and uncontrolled by state authority, able (and often willing) to replace the formal public policing apparatus.

The challenges that await the new order should not be underestimated; nor are they to be easily resolved. The new government is faced with a dilemma: Failure to act reinforces public perceptions that government is weak; overreaction—by characteristic "fire force" policing—leaves the impression that not much has changed. Unfortunately, South Africa has little comparative experience to consult elsewhere. Most countries emerging from transition (many with less of a socio-economic divide than South Africa) have not yet been able to reduce their crime rates significantly. The country has much to learn from its own experience, but, to date, the lessons have been few.

A Criminal Society

Crime and politics in South Africa have been closely intertwined. During the era of race domination, apartheid offenses were classified as crimes, and those people engaged in "the struggle," particularly after the mid-1980s, justified certain forms of violence against the system as fully warranted. Instability prompted a growing number of South Africans to acquire weapons. The use of guns to settle personal and family disputes became more common. Onto this complex mix was grafted the violence in KwaZulu/Natal that began in the mid-1980s, and on the Rand in 1990. Actions that could have been seen strictly as violent crimes were interpreted as a legitimate retaliations against political "enemies." The result was a society in which the use of violence to achieve political and personal aims became endemic.

Measuring crime during apartheid's last decade reveals contradictory trends. At the height of political conflict during the 1980s, increases in certain crimes appeared to have stalled. Political liberalization in South Africa brought a crime explosion, as in other societies (like the states of Eastern Europe and those emerging from the former Soviet Union) undergoing sustained periods of democratic transition. The loosening of social controls opens spaces that allow growth in criminal activity; and, in developing countries attempting to make the transition, fewer resources mean that the cost in growth in crime can be extremely high (even if rates of increase are comparatively small).[2]

At the outset, any understanding of criminality in South Africa is complicated by the difficulty of measuring the extent of lawlessness, or its costs. Recording crime relies on a two-stage process: victims or bystanders submitting reports and the police recording them. However, only a fraction of offenses make it that far. In South Africa, the collection of statistics has been hampered by the historic divide between people and police and the vagaries of apartheid record keeping. SAPS figures, for example, historically excluded those of the homelands; statistics show all recorded crime in KwaZulu/Natal, for example, as occurring in the "white" Natal section, implying that the "dark figure" of unrecorded crime in the country is substantial.

Barring a comprehensive survey of victimization in South Africa, official crime statistics are the only ones available. If they are to be useful, they should not be analyzed for minutiae and rejected out of hand, but probed for broad trends. The common perception, for example, is that crime in South Africa only began to increase after 1990 in conjunction with political transition. But most serious crime—notably murder, robbery, and housebreaking—began to increase in the mid-1980s.

South Africa's crime problem is not recent; the society, given levels of inequality and political conflict, has always been "crimo-generic." The decade 1980 to 1990, in which the apartheid state was most strongly challenged, showed significant increases in crime. According to police figures, serious offenses rose by 22 percent, and less serious ones by 17 percent; murders increased by 32 percent, rape by 24 percent, and burglary by 31 percent.[3]

Crime increased dramatically in 1990—the year when the political transition began. Recorded levels of almost every type of crime showed absolute increases for the period 1990 to 1994. Although the murder rate declined by 7 percent—consistent with declining levels of political violence (from 16,042 fatalities in 1990 to 14,920 in 1994)—several other crimes increased dramatically: assault by 18 percent, rape by 42 percent, robbery by 40 percent, vehicle theft by 34 percent, and burglary by 20 percent. Crime against the affluent also increased. Although no accurate figures are available, commercial crimes increased significantly during this period. Trends throughout the country were not uniform; the greatest increases occurred in the urban complexes around Johannesburg, Durban, and Cape Town.

The problems related to the recording of crime suggest that government needs to continue managing perceptions of increasing levels of crime for the next decade. If police reform succeeds, and wealth becomes distributed more evenly throughout society, recorded levels of crime will continue to rise, particularly property crime. Greater numbers of cars and telephones, as well as a more developed insurance industry and a more accessible police service (through, for example, a single emergency phone system) will translate into higher levels of reporting. The government will have responsibility for managing this growing volume of records—a task that the Ministry of Safety and Security, by its own admission, does not perform very well.

This problem of compiling will apply mainly to less serious crimes. Given the greater likelihood of reporting, figures for such crimes as murder may become more accurate. South Africa has a large proportion of citizens killed in crime-related instances. The figure for the first six months of 1996—30 citizens killed per 100,000 head of population— is nearly four times that of the United States. Hospital records (which are often more accurate than crime statistics) show that everyday 2,500 South Africans require treatment as a result of stabbings, beatings, and shootings. Figures for the first part of 1996 continue to show dramatic increases in levels of reports of assaults, domestic violence, and rape.[4]

The growth in organized crime in the new democratic order has also been dramatic. There are now said to be 481 criminal organizations in the country (although police definitions of "organization" remain unclear), which are engaged in smuggling weapons, drugs, and vehicles. Countering crime before it can organize is now a priority. Evidence from other states in transition suggests that unless organized crime operations are stopped quickly after their formation, they have the potential to harden, penetrate the state, and form parallel and competing centers of power. The rise of criminal enterprises in parts of Eastern Europe, the former Soviet Union, and West Africa illustrate these developments.[5]

The impact of crime on the country is not uniform; increases appear to affect different parts of South African society in different ways. Hence, since not all South Africans are exposed to equal dangers, different strategies to curb crime should be used in different areas. Although crime in general has increased during the past decade, not all types of crime have; nor do all areas of the country suffer equally. An examination of statistics over time shows that the Northern province displays high levels of crime against property, but a comparatively low figure for crimes of violence. KwaZulu/Natal suffers high levels of property and violence-related offenses. The Northern and Western Cape have high assault figures, yet comparatively lower readings for theft and housebreaking. The Free State consistently reports the lowest rate for all categories of crime.

These variations suggest that national crime figures may be deceptive, since levels of victimization and forms of criminality are not the same in all provinces. For instance, although vehicle hijacking is feared nationally, almost all cases occur in Gauteng. Local police-station figures reveal that categories of crime vary considerably even between station areas. A detailed examination of crime totals for various magisterial districts in Gauteng shows that districts with very high crime rates and those with very low crime rates are often contiguous.[6]

These findings are hardly surprising. It is an established truth in policing that the causes and consequences of crime are often locally specific and, as such, require local solutions. Although this understanding is generally accepted in South Africa, in light of the political imperatives of a country in transition, policymakers do not necessarily subscribe to it. The result is a messy breakdown of police functions and levels of accountability that serve to hinder police effectiveness.

One serious defect is the lack of any connection between elected local government and police agencies. Community Police Forums (CPFs), designed to give local communities a say in policing priorities, have been written into national legislation, but their entry into the system has not been smooth. Such structures, given their volunteer nature, are seldom representative. In addition, since CPFs can do little to influence the operational priorities of the police—depending on the personalities involved—they are often little more than "toy telephones."

In any event, local station commissioners, who report straight through the police command structure to the National Commissioner in Pretoria, have little incentive to respond to community needs. Promotions and transfers depend on the hierarchy in Pretoria, not on the community's input. The problem of accountability is compounded at the provincial level. Under the new constitution, provincial members of the Executive Councils (MECS) for Safety and Security are supposed to monitor and supervise police functions, but, in effect, they have little say (beyond political influence) over operational policing issues in their provinces.

Local policing priorities are often (although not always) subsumed under a complex bureaucratic structure directed from Pretoria. The centralization of police functions is based on a political imperative to maintain the control of the coercive apparatus of the state from the center. Breaking up the police agency, the argument goes, could invite exploitation and abuse from the provinces and even at the local level. There is also doubt about the capacity of many local structures and station commanders to take full responsibility for policing in their areas. Proponents of centralized policing contend that delegating police functions would mean good services in some areas and poor ones in others. On the contrary, the continuation of such critical police duties as public order and organized crime investigations at the national level would prevent local abuse from occurring. The key to better policing is to allow communities to take responsibility for safety and security rather than assuming that they are incapable.

Colonialism required a centralized police agency, as did apartheid, with its desire to control and suppress opposition. Ironically, the post-apartheid government, in seeking to establish order in society and transform the policing functions of the state, also wants to retain centralized control of the police. The results are increasing levels of disorder in many communities and little democratic participation to ensure accountable forms of policing at the local level.

Criminal Justice in Crisis

Beyond its policing function, South Africa's criminal justice system is in crisis. If its ability to prevent, process, and deter crime is any indication of its effectiveness, then reforming the system should not only be a necessity but a national priority. Unfortunately, the system cannot easily be fixed; it does not suffer from a single problem but from multiple blockages, many of which cause delays in other parts of the criminal justice pipeline. Nor has the system, which stretches across the departments of Safety and Security, Justice, and Correctional Services, ever been a unified one. The links between the various departments are weak, and the involvement of other departments, such as Welfare, Education, and Health—which should contribute heavily to crime prevention—is minimal.[7]

An effective system should consist of both proactive and reactive components. Proactive crime-prevention strategies are essential to the long-term reduction of crime in South Africa, but they depend on strong institutions to process (and rehabilitate) convicted offenders. In the short to medium term, the focus will have to rest on transforming the reactive components of the criminal justice system, which should still permit significant scope for the development of proactive strategies—rehabilitation being the most obvious.

Inevitably, reform efforts after 1994 concentrated almost exclusively on the front end of the criminal justice system—the most visible component of policing. Community policing has been the watchword of police efforts to sell themselves to the South African public; the idea has been as important for transforming citizens' views of the police as for changing the ethos of the police officers themselves. The transformation of the most publicly visible component of the criminal justice system is still far from complete, and equally serious problems beset the system further along—primarily in the areas of detection, prosecution, and incarceration.

The issue of detecting crime has been virtually ignored by policymakers in the new order, and the consequences have been severe. In 1995, only 25 percent of all robberies were resolved, 20 percent of all house breakings, 10 percent of all vehicle thefts, and about 50 percent of all murders. Hardly surprisingly, South Africa's detectives have always been a threatened breed. Under apartheid, the quick road to promotion for bright and ambitious officers was through the security branch; in the new order, the fast track is uniform, or visible, policing. This trend has been exacerbated in the past year by the large numbers of experienced detectives leaving the services for the more handsome pickings of the private sector and by the difficulty of recruiting more detectives.[8]

There are currently few incentives for detective work. Uniform officers work four days and then take fours days off. Good detectives often work seven days a week with no overtime, under dangerous conditions and with little support, carrying as many as fifty dockets at once. Only about half of them have received any detective training and only 13 percent of them have more than six years of experience—these being mostly in specialized units. Since there is no formal mentoring or assistance program, the vast majority of new detectives are thrown in at the deep end.

The situation has been aggravated over time by structural changes. Specialized units were created to replace station-level detectives who were seen as ineffective. The removal of these experienced officers resulted in loss of morale among ordinary street-level detectives. The SAPS recently has been considering an academy to train detectives and pass skills from specialized units to station-level officers.

The Department of Justice is not blameless. Most public prosecutors have little experience, and courts are often badly managed. Constant postponements frustrate witnesses, who often fail to appear when cases are finally heard. Most problematical, however, is the interface between detectives and public prosecutors. Greater cooperation and coordination between justice and police officials would ensure a higher rate of prosecutions. At the moment, prosecutors and investigating officers in the lower courts often meet each other for the first time only when detectives are in the witness box.

Both departments protest that systems are in place to ensure smooth operations, but what appears to be a common problem is a lack of skilled (and motivated) middle management. Old-order civil servants are disillusioned, and new or recently promoted officials have little experience and (often deliberately) receive no support.

South Africa's prisons are also in dire need of reform. Ironically, the prisons are not as full as they have been. In the mid-1980s, more than 4 in every 1,000 citizens spent time in jail, but apparently, the jails were better managed. Staff shortages, prisoner and warder unrest, and increasing corruption are bringing the crisis to a head. The majority of escapes seem to stem from the bribing of prison officials. The Department is known to its employees as the Department of Corruptional Services.

South African prison conditions are almost Victorian. The announcement that Correctional Services would begin issuing condoms—as an attempt to protect unwilling prisoners forced into sexual intercourse from AIDS—has brought the issue into sharp relief. Most prisons are dank and dark, and maintenance budgets are severely limited. Internally, some jail areas are controlled not by warders but by prisoners.

To be fair, the problems are not all of Correctional Services' making. One-quarter of South Africa's 130,000 inmates are still awaiting trial. In effect, Correctional Services must cater to those whose passage through the criminal justice system is blocked at the point where crime is investigated and processed through the courts. Since those prisoners awaiting trial merely being held by Correctional Services pending the outcome of their court cases are not considered as full-fledged convicts, they are not subject to the usual (albeit limited) privileges, such as prison clothes and recreational services.

The clearest indication that the system is failing lies in the fact that more than half of those imprisoned commit crimes again after their release. Rehabilitation in South Africa's prisons (admittedly, as in most other countries in the world) is a farce, and the likelihood of future improvements is slim. Any new budgetary allocations are likely to go toward more prisons and the staff to guard them. Public opinion is also geared more to the ending of crime than the rehabilitation of prisoners (although the two are closely linked), and convicts are widely viewed as deserving of the conditions under which they live. For example, Business Against Crime, a prominent private-sector initiative aimed at ending lawlessness, supplies resources to the front end of the criminal justice pipeline where criminals are caught but displays little interest in the backwaters where crime often gets started. SAPS officers refer to prisons as "universities."

At least part of the problem lies in the rigidity of the South African penal system. Alternative forms of sentencing are virtually unavailable, and magistrates (influenced by public perceptions that the system is criminal friendly) seem unwilling to use them when they are. In Europe and North America, parole and correctional supervision have often become viable alternatives to shutting people away. In certain parts of the United States, as many as 80 percent of convicted prisoners are on probation or parole; in South Africa the figure is 20 percent. Moreover, since the granting of parole in South African prisons is in the hands of the Department of Correctional Services itself, it is an open invitation for bribery and an easy (but inappropriate) mechanism for releasing pressure on the prison system.[9]

In effect, the Department has the power to alter sentences established by an independent judiciary. What is urgently needed is an investigation into community forms of sentencing for some offenders, which would mean the appointment of a greater number of supervisors (as opposed to prison wardens). There are now only 1,100 supervisors for the 33,340 convicted offenders (including those who have been granted parole) who are serving their sentences outside prison. The enlisting of business and government support to ensure alternatives to prison sentencing would also be a step in the right direction.

Although few figures are available, corruption throughout the criminal justice system is said to be pervasive. The current prosecution rate can only be the tip of the iceberg. Corruption—bred by declining morale, as well as by poor controls, management, and training within the system itself—is a symptom rather than a cause, but its effect on public perception of the criminal justice system is severe. The dilemma is that any large crackdown on corruption is bound to undermine already flagging public confidence, but so will any denial of the problem, particularly if the corruptibility of the police, the courts, and the correctional officials becomes common knowledge. The only short-term alternative is unattractive—namely, selective high-profile prosecutions.

Government Initiatives

The growing weakness of the criminal justice system has not escaped the government. The recently released National Crime Prevention Strategy—a compact, eighty-eight page document—has as its central task the consolidation of departments involved in crime control and prevention—Correctional Services, Defense, Intelligence, Justice, Safety and Security, and Welfare—and the coordination of their activities. But the greatest strength of the crime prevention strategy—its inclusiveness and comprehensiveness—also holds the potential to be its greatest weakness. The very complexity and expansiveness of the strategy suggests that coordination and leadership will be critical factors in its success or failure.

Although the strategy provides vision for a society that has begun to confront the problem of criminality eating at its core, the actual work of restructuring the criminal justice system, and in the longer term, creating more effective crime-prevention programs still remains to be done. At a different level, the strategy indicates another significant shift in the discourse of safety and security in South Africa, from "community policing" (which is barely mentioned in the document) to "crime prevention" and the building of "partner-

The South African security industry shows some unique traits mix between sophisticated electronics and the use of armed guards. is also distinguished by its reliance on the reactive side. Traditionally, both in South Africa and elsewhere, security companies had a proactive function: Guards, modeled on the concept of the "bobby on the beat," patrolled defined areas, but now in South Africa armed response has become more in evidence. Panic buttons relay electronic signals via a control room to security officers patrolling in cars, who perform functions similar to those of the traditional police.

The growth in the South African security industry does not reflect broader trends. Indeed, it seems to be implicated in an inverse relationship with the rest of the economy, tending to thrive in poor economic conditions. During the pre-election months, when most business in the country stagnated, security reflected record growth. It has stabilized to some extent since the 1994 election, but the recent crime wave is boosting the security companies again. Nonetheless, parts of the market, like guarding, are showing more and more signs of saturation.

The development of the private security sector in South Africa has not been untroubled. Attempts to obtain more power for certain kinds of security guards are likely to fall on deaf ears if the consensus is that private security officers are untrained and act unprofessionally. Public perceptions, whether the industry likes it or not, are shaped by individual instances of abuse—for example, the deaths of sixteen people in a stampede caused by security guards armed with electric batons at Tembisa, northeast of Johannesburg in 1996, or the shooting deaths of forty-one alleged burglars over a number of years by "Lious" van Schoor.

The danger of replicating the Tembisa incident is real. Private security companies are operating more and more in the so-called private–public sphere—that is, private property that is open for public usage, such as shopping malls or university campuses. Moreover, the trend of enlisting private police in urban neighborhoods or central business districts is growing. Private firms have been known to handle such public-order activities as clearing squatters.

Heavy dependence on the private security industry does not necessarily release the public police from pressure. The private industry employs mechanisms—guards, alarms, and detection devices—to gather information that can be fed to police. Rather than decreasing

ships" with both government agencies and external organizations in civil society.[10]

The document provides a detailed accurate analysis of the many interconnected factors that have contributed to the growth of crime in South Africa and outlines steps underway in various government departments to counter them. Outside repair of the criminal justice process, three key areas are identified as critical for intervention to reduce crime—environmental design, education, and transnational crime. In addition, the strategy presents eighteen national programs for implementation, involving such plans as improving information systems (poor information transfer being at the heart of the system's problems), empowering and supporting victims, and devising mechanisms to deter organized crime. It also includes various initiatives in line-function departments and provisions for forging partnerships with outsiders.

Notably absent from the list of new programs are specific preventive strategies related to drug use, the proliferation of small arms, and the gang problem in certain parts of the country. Although each is covered directly or indirectly within various sections of the document, it would have been worthwhile to merge current initiatives and develop specific strategies to form two or three additional, conspicuous prevention programs, since these particular criminal activities have the potential to spawn wider forms of criminality.

The issue of increasing drug usage, for instance, is critical. Government response to the drug problem has historically been fragmented and poorly funded, with no coordination between reactive and proactive approaches. What needs to be explored is the establishment of a law-enforcement body separate from the current police and intelligence structures that would provide leadership in the areas of both prevention and enforcement.

It is regrettable that the strategy does not allot more space to initiatives by local government. International experience suggests that the key to crime prevention lies in the cities. The strategy could have advanced the process and stimulated local debate had it emphasized the issue of crime prevention at the metropolitan level. Other countries have established city forums to compare experiences and determine joint guidelines for crime prevention.

Nor have South African city authorities been idle. Many are beginning to work on crime prevention plans and establish local-authority police agencies. But central government has dragged its heels on these developments. No framework yet exists for local government policing or crime-prevention strategies, and, if current developments mean anything, local governments will run ahead of the national authorities in this sphere. Many cities, including crime-ridden Johannesburg, are in the process of formulating plans for city police services designed to supplement the SAPS.

The National Crime Prevention Strategy correctly maintains that local-level initiatives should be able to tailor individual programs for local-level conditions and circumstances. But it is not clear what the consequences will be if local authorities stray outside the vague boundaries delineated by the strategy. The document could have suggested guidelines to contain or, where necessary, focus any such initiatives.

The key to the strategy's success is coordination. Without it, the strategy simply becomes a reflection of a wide variety of programs that might have been possible in one form or the other. A related problem with such a large and complex national initiative is that it is virtually immune to measurement. The danger is that success will be equated with a flurry of activity (in this case, committee meetings) rather than any actual decreases in crime.

The document makes allowance for monitoring departments and programs, but the extent to which the whole enterprise will be subject to review is not clear. Although the difficulty of interpreting crime statistics runs counter to exact prediction, program goals need to be better defined. Despite the fact that it is a guide for implementation, the strategy contains virtually no time frames for the completion of the various initiatives, although some may be forthcoming.

Management is by committee. An interministerial committee, comprised of the ministers of Safety and Security, Defense, Justice, Correctional Services, Welfare, and Intelligence, will supplement the cabinet Committee on Security and Intelligence. It will meet quarterly, or convene on an ad hoc basis if necessary. Under the ministerial committee will be the committee of directors-general, which will also be chaired by the lead department, Safety and Security.

With no deadlines to meet, the committees, which have apparently already assembled, have made little progress. A publicly released set of

objectives and deadlines would have provided some basis to j progress. Without them, the plan could seem like another paper s egy, creating expectations that the government will not be abl honor.

Frustration has already occurred. Media coverage of specific cri nal activities has turned the spotlight once again on the issue of cri Government responses that these activities are just isolated instances media fabrications fundamentally misunderstand the role of the pr Unless government law-enforcement agencies establish themselves the ground—in the short term—where most citizens experien crime, no amount of strategies formulated in Pretoria will bring relie On the contrary, if every fresh outburst of crime provokes only wor without visible counteraction, disillusionment with proactive crim prevention, which is indispensable to the long-term solution of disor der in South African society, will grow, further encouraging reactive self-help, and increasingly violent solutions to crime.

Citizen Responses

The increasing failure of the criminal justice system to deter or punish offenders has led many citizens to take the law into their own hands. None of their options are new; all of them were available in some form under apartheid rule. What is new is the growth of extra-state mechanisms of law and order in conjunction with declining public confidence in the ability of the police to secure a safe environment. Forms of protection vary; the wealthier members of society can afford to contract with the private security sector, whereas those in less fortunate communities are more likely to take their own initiative.

Unlike that in Europe and North America, the South African private security industry has not attracted much study. It has grown rapidly since 1980; it initially expanded at a rate of 30 percent per year, slowing to 10 to 15 percent in the last five years. Since the late 1970s, the estimated annual average growth rate has been 18 percent. The exact value of the industry is difficult to quantify. A recent estimate suggested that the guarding industry alone was worth around R3.6 billion. Private security officers outnumber the public police by about 2 to 1.[11]

demands on the public force, private security may overburden it in some areas. In KwaZulu/Natal, between January and April 1996, the SAPS traveled 170,000 km in response to electronic alarm activations—accounting for 40 percent of all complaints in the province—of which 99 percent were false alarms.[12]

To argue, as the industry does, that private security serves as a useful complement to state structures ignores their differing goals. The private companies seek to protect the interests of their clients, whereas the police theoretically defend the rights of citizens. In the main (and barring certain private investigations), private companies are more concerned with the prevention of loss than the apprehension of offenders; the exercise of discretion by private security personnel is often more influenced by the needs of their immediate employers than by any generalized concern for the public interest. Thus, private agents will bring offenders to justice only if doing so is in their clients' interests. Public and private policing do not fit together as neatly as first assumed.

If the public activities of private security companies continue to grow, what are the policy alternatives? Greater regulation, beyond that offered by the Security Officers Board, a statutory body staffed and funded by the industry itself, would not be enforceable in South Africa. Another option is the establishment of a publicly accessible, independent body to hear complaints and supervise the industry—over and above citizens' ordinary recourse under the law. But, with or without such a mechanism, the industry will remain contract driven—responsible in the final analysis to individual clients rather than the public at large.

While the wealthier segments of society seek to buy safety, the less fortunate are forced to confront the problem of crime more directly. Although by no means the first of such movements, the campaign by the vigilante group, People Against Gangsterism and Drugs (PAGAD), in the Western Cape—which maintains an armed presence in some Cape townships and was responsible for the public murder of an alleged drug dealer—has brought the issue of citizen action to a head. But there are genuine risks to the new order should such initiatives become a permanent feature of community action in South Africa.[13]

South Africa is beginning to display characteristics similar to the crime-wracked states of Latin America. In Brazil, where the army has

been summoned to control crime in major urban areas, vigilante policing is nothing new, especially in the crowded urban complexes around
Rio and São Paulo (and increasingly in the small towns of the interior),
because of the inefficiency of Brazil's established judicial institutions.

The experience in Latin America carries profound lessons for South
Africa. Ironically, vigilante action, which (at least in the rhetoric of its
proponents) is an attempt to strengthen state institutions, often has the
opposite effect, through the creation of alternative centers of power (and
by definition coercion) outside the state security apparatus. Vigilante
actions against criminals are the result when a violent culture responds
to a state's inability to maintain control. The conclusion is easy for citizens to draw: If a state cannot deter criminals, it cannot deter vigilantes
either. In Latin America, for example, states attempt to coopt rather than
confront vigilantism. Police Commissioner George Fivaz's expressed
desire to work in "partnership" with vigilante groups (not to be con-
strued as an endorsement) in the Western Cape is a classic response.

What vigilante behavior achieves is not necessarily useful. Vigilante
action is reactive, seeking (violently) to suppress, and it tends to be ad
hoc. Even though the violation of formal legal boundaries may be supported by the majority of the community (as in São Paulo and on the
Cape Flats), vigilantism is disorderly and unpredictable. It often solid-
ifies the opposition that it aims to undercut. Not for nothing did the
gangs on the Cape Flats resolve their differences; they had to find a way
to counter the common threat.

When law-enforcement officials participate in vigilantism—either
directly or indirectly—the moral validity (or the remains of it) of the
formal system of laws is compromised. One of the most serious developments concerning vigilante violence in the Western Cape is the
widespread public perception that the police (frustrated by their own
inability) have allowed "natural justice" to take its course. The greatest
danger of vigilante action is that it will spread and become institutionalized—an accepted mechanism for policing what is increasingly
viewed as unpoliceable. New complexities are imminent. Police who
are viewed to be in cahoots with criminals, for instance, could become
targets for attack, escalating and complicating the conflict.

Vigilante actions in South Africa, though their causes and aims may
differ, are nothing new. The use of vigilantism to achieve political ends
was a common feature of the last decade of apartheid, as well as of the

transition to democracy. The difference was that such forms as the "wit doeke" on the Cape Flats and the "impis" in KwaZulu/Natal enjoyed state support. Nonetheless, the principle of using violent action outside the formal institutions of the state is well established in South Africa.

The growth of self- and private policing provides a ready base from which violent vigilante actions can grow. In Soweto, for example, groups like Youth Against Crime—a motley collection of youngsters who patrol sections of the township—can easily mutate into violent vigilante groups. Indeed, the groups in Soweto watched the events in the Western Cape with great interest. Although their organizing principles are not as strong as those of PAGAD, they contain the potential for violent action.

Given the dangers of vigilante action, what are the solutions? The most effective solution would be the most difficult one to achieve—the establishment of a powerful and competent criminal justice system. That should be the national priority. The South African state, despite its problems in this area, still retains the capacity for enacting such a reform. Seeking to coopt vigilante leaders and placate criminals, though it may bring peace in the short term, will eventually undermine the last shreds of public confidence in the criminal justice system.

Crime and Democracy

Just as the transition affects crime, so crime affects the transition. Not long ago, the new government's willingness to compromise politically—and the affluent minority's willingness to compromise in turn—in the interests of racial accommodation seemed to bode well for democratic prospects. Ironically, however, this unexpected success could be nullified by the emergence of crime as a—if not *the*—central determinant of attitudes toward the new democracy on the part of local affluent minorities, and, perhaps, international investors.

Crime affects all South Africans, but its effects in the new democracy appear to vary between racial groups. For affluent, suburban whites, whose mobility is high and whose commitment to majority rule conditional, growing evidence suggests that crime is the main threat to confidence in the new order and the factor most likely to prompt continued emigration. Since skills and resources are disproportionately concentrated in this group, its flight from attacks on persons and property would weaken democracy's economic foundation. The predominantly white residents of the suburbs also show the inclination to isolate themselves physically from the mainly black poor who are seen as the criminal element. A decided move in that direction would entrench a form of social distance, thereby impeding attempts to create a common South African loyalty.

For much of the black majority, exit is neither a feasible nor a desired option. Since this section of society has been living with high rates of violent crime for decades, concern about a relative increase is far outweighed by enthusiasm for a new order in which black people are full citizens: There is no visible evidence yet that crime is substantially denting black confidence in democracy. Recent research suggests that black citizens see crime as a symptom of social and economic inequality rather than a product of democracy's "weakness." Survey evidence reveals that the positions of white and black citizens about increasing crime and the state's responses to it are diametrically opposed. What whites view as a breakdown of policing standards and the weakness of the new order, blacks view as the sign of an unfinished democracy.[14]

This state of affairs will not last. Indeed, the outlook of important constituencies in the growing black middle classes is beginning to converge with that of their white compatriots. If the personal safety of black citizens declines further, enthusiasm for measures to "restore order" that ignore democratic liberties could grow. Perhaps tellingly, the majority of black South Africans (and even African National Congress [ANC] members) now support a return to capital punishment.[15]

The idea that achieving safer communities is beyond the means of the state or the attitude that the best response to threat is social isolation could ensure declining political participation. The indications—although not all of them are a response to crime—are already noticeable. Recent survey evidence suggests that the ANC has lost 10 percent of its support, but not to any of the other parties in the political system. The perception that an elected government cannot perform the most fundamental duty of state authority—protecting the persons of its citizens—could reduce faith in the new democracy.[16]

What are the prospects that crime will decline significantly? In South Africa, as elsewhere, the roots and cures of crime are far too complex to permit definitive predictions. The conventional wisdom is divided: Crime will decline as soon as development takes off, or as soon as the police can assume their "rightful" place. Neither claim is substantiated or likely to be for some time. Even if crime stabilizes, reported crime will probably rise, possibly masking any progress.

An underemphasized constraint on the reduction of crime, particularly its violent variety, is a grim legacy of the transition period—the ready availability of weaponry, which also erodes one of the key prerequisites of democratic transition, namely, the state's ability to monopolize the instruments of coercion. This problem could be exacerbated by a vicious circle in which the widespread use of illegal arms prompts continued demands for legal ones, despite the fact that easy access to weapons for whites since the 1980s has not prevented the growth of violent crime; it probably encouraged it.

These conditions create a dilemma for a new democratic government. On the one hand, confidence in the new order will decline if the authorities are seen to abandon any attempt to address crime in the (probably dubious) hope that citizens will adjust to it. On the other hand, promises of a concerted "war on crime" that exceed capability have destructive consequences—not only for the authorities but also for the democratic system—both by creating false expectations and by encouraging support for strategies inimical to civil liberties and prone to failure.

The longer the dilemma remains unresolved, the less likely the democratic authorities, and therefore the political process, will seem to be credible guarantors of personal safety; for those unable or unwilling to emigrate, self-policing and reliance on private security will become attractive options. Although the impact of these choices on democracy may be difficult to determine, at the very least they suggest a declining relationship between security on the one hand, and accountability and legality on the other. If the affluent, in particular, are forced to rely on their own responses to crime, their withdrawal from the rest of society will entrench, in a new form, the old divisions that the transition was meant to overcome.

Notes for Chapter Two

1. Quotation from *Business Day*, 4 Aug. 1994.

2. For a more detailed argument about the relationship between crime and political transition, see Shaw, *Partners in Crime? Crime, Political Transition and Changing Forms of Policing Control* (Johannesburg, 1995).

3. See Shaw and Lala Camerer, *Policing the Transformation? New Issues in South Africa's Crime Debate* (Johannesburg, 1996).

4. Unpub. crime statistics, January to June 1996, Crime Information Management Center, Pretoria.

5. See Shaw, "The Development of Organized Crime in South Africa," in Shaw and Camerer, *Policing the Transformation*.

6. Lorraine Glanz, "Crime in Gauteng," unpub. paper (Human Sciences Research Council, 1995).

7. For an overview of problems across the criminal justice system, see *Re-engineering the Criminal Justice System*, a joint project of the ministries of Safety and Security, Justice, Welfare, and Correctional Services, as well as Business Against Crime, June 1996.

8. The actual percentages are probably lower than the ones given. See Glanz, "The Not So Long Arm of the Law," *Indicator SA: Crime and Conflict*, 5 (Autumn 1996).

9. See Molefi Thinane, "End of the Line: South Africa's Overcrowded Prisons," *ibid.*, 7 (Spring 1996).

10. Departments of Correctional Services, Defense, Intelligence, Justice, Safety and Security, and Welfare, *National Crime Prevention Strategy* (Pretoria, 1996).

11. For a more detailed overview of the private security industry, see Shaw, "Privatizing Crime Control? South Africa's Private Security Industry," in *idem, Partners in Crime?*, 83–87.

12. This false-alarm figure is from *Re-engineering*. Figures for the other provinces, where statistics are available, are similar.

13. Shaw, "Buying Time? Vigilante Action, Crime Control and State Responses," *Indicator SA: Crime and Conflict*, 7 (Spring 1996).

14. Diana Ehlers, I. Hirshfield, and Charl Schutte, *Perceptions of Current Sociological Issues in South Africa* (Pretoria, 1996). This is a confirmation of previous survey data. A confidential government poll also drew similar conclusions.

15. *Ibid.*

16. *Ibid.*

3

Joan Wardrop

Soweto, Syndicates, and "Doing Business"

THIS PRELIMINARY exploration of the internal workings of organized crime in the province of Gauteng, South Africa, draws on the
experience of both the police of the Soweto Flying Squad and the criminals that they observe, chase, and arrest. The chapter does not deal with
random, spontaneous, or noneconomic crime (such as rape, which also
is often gang-based). Rather, its ambit is limited to organized crime, and
those who engage in it, namely the *ou manne*, the syndicate owners, and
the *tsotsis*, the young men who "do the work." The focus is on the day-
to-day realities of crime in Soweto, using the gaze of police "outside"
(on the streets) "in the area" (throughout Soweto) as the starting point.
As a result, the chapter inevitably reflects the bemusement of both
policemen and criminals regarding the pronouncements of parliamen-
tarians, academic researchers, and senior police (usually referred to
simply as "Pretoria," where the headquarters of the South African Police
Service [SAPS] is located) about organized crime and its structures.[1]

Organized Crime in Context

To many South Africans, the term "organized crime" conjures
images of Marlon Brando or Al Pacino, of Colombian drug lords, or of

45

passionate Sicilians defending medieval concepts of honor: images that are foreign, cinematic, and decidedly unconnected with life in the new South Africa. At least some white South Africans are aware that there have been gangs within the South African prison system since colonial times, as well as highly regimented and violent township gangs, at least since the establishment of the system of large-scale urban "locations," in the early years of this century. Yet, for the most part, the way of life for these gangs was hidden in the townships, seldom if ever impinging on the lives of nontownship residents. "Black" crime occurred primarily within the townships.

As late as the 1980s, such crime was not the most potent threat perceived by residents of the "white" suburbs; the worst fear was that the political disorder of the townships—the unrest increased by the call of the African National Congress (ANC) to make the country ungovernable— would spill into the suburbs. It provoked the building of ever-larger walls and the beginnings of the process of constructing fortress houses and suburbs. The suburbs little knew or understood that, for many residents and police in the townships, the political unrest was merely the surface of deep reservoirs of violent nonpolitical crime, from mugging and vehicle theft, to bank robbery, violent intimidation, rape, assault, and murder.[2]

Much of the crime committed against black residents was confined to the townships. Although it had devastating effects on the lives of many of those people, it was largely invisible, or at least ignored outside the townships, by the politically and economically dominant minority. On the Rand, it did not become relevant until the early 1990s when black crime exploded out of Johannesburg's townships, in particular Soweto and Alexandra, as the result of several otherwise unlinked factors:

• the effects of the repeal of the Influx Control Act (1986), which allowed black South Africans to move around the country freely, without having to carry the old *dompas*;

• the attempts of the Inkatha Freedom Party (IFP) leadership (based in KwaZulu/Natal) to expand the political base and influence of the organization through the concentration of Zulu labor migrants on the Rand, thereby creating, inadvertently or not, massive concentrations of illegal weaponry, routes for the movement of illegal commodities, and defensible strongholds for large numbers of foot soldiers, who could be mobilized for political purposes, or left to engage in criminal activities;

• the gradual breakdown of the "homeland" system, which sent many thousands of people to Egoli (the city of gold) looking for work, and stretched the resources of the townships, creating vast new shack settlements, such as Snake Park, and transforming the streetscapes of the townships proper through massive construction (sometimes flimsy *zozos* or *mkhukhus*, but more often clay or concrete brick "outside rooms");

• the cessation of wars in Mozambique and Namibia, which released large numbers of firearms and other weaponry onto the *skelm* market (literally "wicked" or "crooked"; black market), vastly increasing the supply in circulation;

• the new freedom of black South Africans to pass through white suburbs with less surveillance and control;

• rising unemployment rates from 1988 onward;

• the burgeoning minibus taxi industry (that sprang from the boycotts of the government-run bus and train systems), which provided both a large market for illegally acquired parts and/or vehicles and a means of laundering illegally gained cash;

• the revival of friendly political relations with other African countries and the consequent loosening of border restrictions;

• the influx of impoverished illegal aliens (*maputos, amagrikambas,* or *amakwerekwere*), who were often willing to work for negligible pay;

• the multitude of uneducated, unemployed/unemployable young men who emerged from the struggle of the 1980s with experience in vehicle or bank robbery and the use of violence.[3]

In response to changing political and economic realities, the transitional years of the early 1990s saw substantial changes in criminal practice and organization—for example, the rapid rise in vehicle robbery (as it is known in Soweto; it is called "hijack" in white South Africa) in the early part of the decade. This shift of method from simple theft of parked motor vehicles to armed robbery of vehicles stopped at robots (traffic lights), moving slowly in side streets, or entering/leaving driveways or carparks, is the direct result of the higher levels of vehicle-security technology introduced in the late 1980s. By then, almost all vehicles, commercial or private, had been fitted with immobilizers, which increased the time, from an average of fifteen to twenty seconds to as long as a minute and a half, that a thief had to work on the vehicle before getting it started. It was realistic and sensible, in an environment where firearms were becoming freely available, to adjust the means of stealing a vehicle.

By ripping open a driver's door or smashing the window with a firearm, and ordering the driver out of the vehicle—loudly, quickly, and competently—at a traffic light or on a side street, a robber can commandeer a fully operational vehicle, with keys in the ignition and engine running, and probably not get caught. Moreover, this new modus operandi also reduces uncertainty about the supply end of the equation, that is, the problem of where and when to look for a particular type or model of vehicle. Instead of working high-rise or shopping-center carparks, spotters can now operate freely on suburban streets and in the central business districts (CBDs), checking vehicle flow patterns over a period of weeks under the cover of selling flowers/strawbrooms/craftwork at robots, or acting as informal "parking attendants."

Despite the efforts of the Flying Squad and Vehicle Theft units, among others, to chase down the endless lists of "lookouts" of robbed and stolen vehicles—broadcast by the radio at the beginning of each twelve-hour shift and updated periodically—despite their skill in tracking the "spoor" of "wrong" vehicles, and in determining which vehicles, buildings, or scrapyards to investigate, despite their networks of informants and their numbers of recoveries and arrests, the widespread perception in 1995 was that the sheer volume of the numbers of robberies taking place was too much for them to handle.

Early in 1996, the effects of several initiatives began to impact on the epidemic of vehicle robberies in Johannesburg and Soweto. Although many police see the installation of concealed antihijack switches—whether on expensive vehicles such as BMWs or even on the now-ubiquitous Toyota Venture—as incapable of preventing robbery, often encouraging robbers to abduct the drivers so that they can bypass the antihijack switch, the introduction of concealed transmitters linked to a central control room—via satellite technology—and traceable by light planes or helicopters in the air and trained operatives (many former policemen) on the ground, shows promise. The operatives from the companies that manufacture them and police work together in the recovery of vehicles, often to great advantage.

Spotter flights by Flying Squad personnel in police air-wing or South African National Defense Force (SANDF) light aircraft or choppers, with the assistance of ground vehicles, have also been effective. Even though this technique is still in use and still productive, its days may be numbered; garages and zozos big enough to shelter stolen vehicles are springing up in backyards throughout Soweto.

Another initiative—the funding of 100 vehicles by BMW for a Highway Patrol—comprises 200 highly trained volunteers. Its headquarters is at Johannesburg Flying Squad, with sections based in the other regional Flying Squads, including Soweto (which has an allocation of eleven vehicles). The Highway Patrol attends to the same serious complaints as the Flying Squad, but it has to be even more mobile, handing over scenes to Tango India vehicles to secure. Its high recovery rate (in Soweto at least) is contributing to a reduction in this type of offense.

Structures

In most cases, the internal organization of gangs or syndicates is relatively simple. At the top, one or two men, sometimes brothers or cousins, work through a small inner circle of men who can be trusted to perform any task allocated to them. Most *makulu baas* (big bosses) live in Soweto, preferring direct and immediate control of their empires, though some have chosen to move away—to become what local residents refer to as "tourists." Such relocations can be prompted by a concern for security, although reputation is usually enough to preempt attack, and the fortresses within the township offer a substantial defense against house invasion by other gangs or, more likely, brash amateurs. Bosses also move to divert suspicion from themselves, to create the impression of a different status—upward social mobility, for example—to escape the pollution of the township, particularly in the winter months, or simply to acquire a larger plot of land. No matter where they live, however, they spend much time in the clubs and taverns of Soweto, conspicuously demonstrating their wealth and success.[4]

The picture is more complicated within the half-dozen massive labor-migrant hostels. The traditional political hierarchy of *indunas* (headmen), who, in many situations of hostel life, receive the total obedience of the block or section for which they are responsible, is not necessarily identical with the hierarchy of crime. Nonetheless, at its most basic, the criminal, as opposed to political, command structure within the larger hostels—such as Meadowlands, Diepkloof, or Nance-field—resembles the criminal leadership structures in the township. Whereas the indunas' principal interest lies in the maintenance of their own power, status, and influence, criminal leaders use these elements in the search for profit.

Beyond personal or gang power, complex relationships with other foci of township power often determine the shape of criminal action. Calls by local community policing forums for "no more guns on the streets," for example, sometimes are heeded by the bosses (although rarely by the young tsotsi for whom a firearm is an essential compo-nent of his identity and his notion of masculinity). Further, both the hostel hierarchies and the township's criminal structures function as what Blok has called "*mafiosi* as violent power brokers," playing an often barely visible role in the complex and continual negotiations that make up the politics of the township at the local level, concerning, for example, the delicate question of access to the stand-pipe water supply in a shack settlement, or the mundane but critical issue of rubbish removal in a township that has had rent-and-service-payment boycotts for more than a decade.[5]

Just as Hess, Gambetta, Arlacchi, and many others have shown with regard to the mafiosi, the Soweto criminal leaders often think of them-selves as "businessmen," keen to construct descriptions of their enter-prises in the language of business newspapers and magazines. For example, a "big taximan" in Chiawelo, owner of at least twenty taxis or more, described the brutal attack of one taxi association on another to me as "a negotiation," and I overheard another taximan refer to an out-break of the taxi wars in Meadowlands as "a takeover." Three passen-gers and a driver were killed.[6]

The trusted inner circle—henchmen, as they might be called in another context—rarely seem interested in succeeding or violently supplanting the bosses. Their most singular collective characteristic is their easy stereotyping, derived partly from "the old gangsters, the Americans and the Russians" (two famous, and still discussed Soweto gangs from the 1940s and 1950s) and partly from American films and videos—both the B-grade gangster movies of George Raft, Humphrey Bogart, and Jimmy Cagney and more contemporary images from "Miami Vice" or "Boyz n the Hood." Mobile clichés, they often wear mirrored wraparound sunglasses, even at midnight, multiple neck chains, gold rings, bracelets, and belt buckles, with black trousers and shirts, perhaps of leather or satin, and licensed firearms displayed ostentatiously in their well-worn shoulder or hip holsters. The intimidation is obvious, often reinforced by their size, their alertness, and their propensity to violence, which they display in the smallest of acts—pushing through a crowd or opening a door. Even in the relaxed atmosphere of clubs, taverns, or shebeens, if they are "working," they remain imposing and on guard. Much more than bodyguards, they seem to read the mind of their makulu baas, preparing deals, checking out propositions, and maintaining control over the "workforce" (as a club owner in central Soweto refers to both his legitimate employees and his staff of vehicle robbers and strippers; "they are all my people," he says).[7]

Depending on the nature of the criminal enterprise, the workforce functions as an integral part of the syndicate or as a subcontractor, recruiting individuals from local youth gangs, and training them for criminal activity: vehicle robbery and stripping, dagga (marijuana) selling, passing counterfeit money (generally R50 and R100 notes), and transporting gold, diamonds, vehicles or vehicle parts, stolen goods (increasingly from households), counterfeit notes, dagga, and illegal firearms (which travel in an endless chain between KwaZulu/Natal and the Rand, particularly weapons recently used in crimes). "Gangs" are tightly knit but comparatively disorganized groups of mainly young men, the tsotsis, aged thirteen to thirty, who constitute both the apprentices and the front-line troops of the criminal structures. They are often highly territorial, and their engagement in criminal activity is sometimes secondary to their battles for status and power. If they survive, they may graduate to the more powerful and centralized concerns, which are operated as businesses. Although the "big men" may engage in internecine warfare from time to time, doing so has purpose beyond simple status seeking or turf definition/maintenance.

Most syndicates (a word not often used in Soweto, where "gang" continues to be the term of choice even for large and sophisticated operations) depend on a small inner circle, and another slightly larger circle of men, who conduct the "business" of the syndicate and protect its leadership with their lives. The outer circle, the apprentices, do the most dangerous and visible work. Many clearly are exhilarated by the risks—the fast driving and the possibility of armed confrontation with the police—as well as the status of being "big men" who have graduated from carrying a *tipa,* or knife, to wearing a firearm, concealed between their shoulder blades, on the top of their heads underneath their knitted spotties, which are the trademarks of the tsotsi. They cruise the streets in late-model (legal) BMWs, complete with loud, expensive sound systems, perhaps a CD or an American-flag scarf hanging from their rear-view mirrors, and their seats laid nearly straight. Thus is their status demonstrable, not to be gainsaid by parents, church leaders, or rivals.

Many tsotsis fall into the category of the *comtsotsi,* or "comrade tsotsi" (although the expression is less common now than in the early 1990s). The term resonates with the mixed fear and forced respect that the young comrades who effectively ruled the townships in the 1980s demanded. Many of them were the shock troops of the struggle in the 1980s, and perhaps later in the Self-Defense Units (SDUs) established by local ANC structures in 1990/91 to defend residents against attack from the increasingly IFP-dominated hostels, only to transfer their few, and rather specific, skills to a new arena in the 1990s. They are not to be confused with Hobsbawm's "social" or "noble bandits." If they prefer to represent themselves in a way that resembles Goddard's rascals of Papua New Guinea, who use a "Robin Hood" rhetoric to justify themselves, they are abetted in this self-image (as both Morauta and Goddard suggest) by academics, journalists, politicians, and bureaucrats, who teach criminals that "poverty and unemployment [are] partly acceptable excuses for crime," and that they are "organic heroes of the lumpen-proletariat, or delinquent avengers battling sociopolitical injustice." [8]

Although a few still claim to rob the rich ("black" or "white") to give to the poor, or, in the language of the politically educated, to "redistribute," not many township residents seem to take their rationalization seriously. The "poor" in this case, as Morauta also found in Papua New Guinea, are not defined by class; the "criminal makes his gifts to particular individuals, strengthening and marking personal rather than class relationships." Whereas in Papua New Guinea these gifts might be just "radios, food, clothing and money," in Soweto they often include educational expenses for extended family members, house rebuilding and extending, new furniture and household utensils (particularly microwave ovens, refrigerators, freezers, etc.), as well as large-screen television sets, tools, and even vehicles. [9]

The explanation, still voiced in certain quarters, that crime is committed "for politics" (that is, to raise money for an ongoing "struggle" or to strike against "the system") attracts open derision from many residents, although even a year or two ago, most people would have been too frightened to contradict it in public. Politics as an explanation for violent crime was privately rejected by many politically engaged and active residents even during the 1980s. The complementary notion that many of the tsotsis in Soweto would benefit from retraining programs designed to replace the education that they lost during the struggle and to produce plumbers, carpenters, or bricklayers is predicated on the liberal assumption that no one actually wants to be a lawbreaker. Linked with that assumption is the idea that the threat of punishment alone is enough to rehabilitate a criminal. An equally common misconception is that placing an offender under arrest is sufficient to have him quietly and politely put out his wrists for handcuffs. Few "businessmen" operate on liberal middle-class conceptions of right and wrong. Fewer still will give away their freedom when they have any chance at all to escape, even if they have to injure or kill police, bystanders, or their own colleagues to do so. To be a "big man" in Soweto is to have power, status, and glamour, none of which are easy to attain in the formal economy. To be eighteen years old and the owner of a customized automobile is an impossible dream for most young men. There are not enough rich fathers to go round, but there are always recruiters from the syndicates looking for likely candidates to serve as spotters, drivers, and strippers.

The Commodities

If Mandrax and dagga are treated as separate commodities (as they should be, since they are bought, sold, and consumed by different groups of people), there are essentially nine categories of major illegal commodities circulating in Soweto and branching into the various routes that connect the township to other regions of the country and to foreign countries: vehicles and vehicle parts; Mandrax (a hypnotic drug, similar to Quaaludes, usually crushed and smoked), dagga, counterfeit notes, firearms (and other weaponry, such as grenades), gold, diamonds (closely linked with the gold trade), robbed/stolen goods (liquor, foodstuffs, electrical goods, furniture, etc.), and people—in particular, illegal aliens.

Although this chapter focuses principally on the illegal vehicle trade, police of the Flying Squad and Dog Unit deal with crimes involving all nine categories. Often an epidemic of particular crimes or events occurs, or a number of similar incidents or seizures will take place in a comparatively small area—for example, illegal firearm seizures in White City or Orlando East, vehicle stripping in Zola or Emdeni, or maputo (illegal alien) complaints in Diepkloof or Chiawelo. In some instances, police can trace connections and use them to advance particular investigations, but frequently they cannot. The silence of onlookers and witnesses, and the stigma of the *mpimpi,* the informer, though not as severe as it once was, continues to be a factor in the new South Africa, limiting the effectiveness of police investigations.

Another category of commodity, which is of monetary value and used as a means of exchange, is information. Information passed from a member of the public, a confirmed criminal, or a "turned" suspect is often the only lead that the police have that criminal activity is taking place, but information within the criminal world is just as important, if not more so. It is often the most prized component of a relationship between criminals, whether within the same gang or in a cooperative relationship between gangs. It is currency that can represent potential profit, or early warning and consequent security. Its reliability is constantly checked and rechecked, validated or discarded, and downplayed or magnified. The interconnectivity of the Soweto gang structure, which is embedded in the complex social structures of the township, is such that no man would be able to run his "business" without appropriate and timely information.

The tsotsis receive more than status and the rush of adrenaline: The monetary reward for bringing an ordered vehicle to Soweto is between R500 (for an old vehicle) and R2,000—as much as R5,000 in exceptional circumstances (say, for a rare vehicle, such as a BMW 7 series, required in a hurry). The robbery or theft of up-market or late model vehicles is surrounded by planning and operational precision. After vehicles that fit the order are spotted in Johannesburg's CBD or suburbs during a period of time, a team of tsotsis (often two or three) strike quickly to hijack it, driving down the highway or secondary roads toward Soweto in a convoy that includes two or three legal vehicles that "clear the way," checking for police or private security vehicles and calling the information back by cellular (mobile) phone, until the vehicle is safely delivered to the "stripping" location. If police spot a vehicle in transit, and circulate details as a new "lookout" or if they try to pull it over because "it doesn't look right," a chase may ensue. Few regular police cars (Golfs or Opels) will go faster than 230 kph on the highways, whereas their targets (BMWs or Mercedes) can manage 50 kph more.

The advent of the new Highway Patrol BMWs has alleviated the situation. However, the relatively small number of robbed or stolen vehicles apprehended by Highway Patrol in high-speed chases is an indication that this is not necessarily the arena on which police should be focusing. A higher number of vehicles is detected inside Soweto, where both Flying Squad and Dog Unit members pride themselves that they can "outdrive any tsotsi." Although "the stolens" can outrun or outmaneuver police vehicles on rare occasions, some police claim never to have lost a chase throughout careers spanning seven or eight years.

The term "chop-shop," as used by journalists and senior police, evokes the image of garages or factory units with every imaginable piece of equipment necessary to transform a vehicle. The image is totally incorrect for Soweto. Police estimate that although as many as 1,000 stripping locations might be operating at any one time, few will be operating a month later. Vehicles—even luxury model—can be "worked" almost anywhere, most often behind ordinary Soweto houses (the occupants of which are usually, and understandably, too frightened to call 10111 or even Crime Stop), but also in the veldt, in the *vlei,* in school or church grounds, and near hostels—wherever seclusion can be guaranteed for an hour or two. Some vehicles are stripped totally, for parts; others are chopped and changed—engine, window, and chassis numbers ground down, manufacturers' secret tags removed, false JCs and JEs or the new AAPVs (police or municipal numbers indicating that the vehicle has been stolen or robbed previously and has had clearance from the Vehicle Theft Unit at a 13, or holding, Camp) stamped onto the appropriate parts of the engine.[10]

Stripping is not an expensive business; the total outlay may be as little as R500 to R1,000. Grinding the numbers does not add much more to the cost either. Adding the false numbers and falsifying the appropriate paperwork (registration and 13 Camp clearance) is more expensive: One false set of numbers currently used in Soweto (easily recognizable by the wrong shape of one number) costs R2,000. Another set in use during the summer of 1995 was said to be substantially cheaper, R500, but because it was owned by residents of the IFP-dominated Diepkloof hostel, many Sowetans were wary about purchasing it.

The aim is to produce vehicles that cannot be traced to previous owners, reducing the potential for charges of possession of stolen property. In many cases, this strategy entails the elaborate, but common, construction of a "dup"—the duplicate of a vehicle that has been crashed or moved elsewhere (often to KwaZulu/Natal). Many vehicles are acquired for use within Soweto itself. Police are resigned that "every taxi is wrong; none of them is right"—perhaps a slight exaggeration but not too far from the mark. Many other private vehicles, particularly *bakkies,* pick-up or utility trucks, are "wrong," too. Police often show frustration with a system that seems to tie their hands, allowing most suspects out on bail and insisting on chains of evidence and proof that are impossible to produce in the case of many obviously stolen vehicles. Duplicates in particular are difficult to detect and to prove stolen. Although the popular media conception is that most stolen or robbed vehicles are moved out of the area quickly, it is not necessarily true. Efficient duping can be used to work a vehicle so that it can remain in the township, or appear in the regional trade, although vehicles' "worked" papers go to other areas, such as Durban or Capetown, to be legalized.

The third principal arm of the trade is export, mainly of luxury vehicles but also, traditionally, of bakkies, and, more recently, of off-road vehicles, such as the Venture. Although there are sometimes rumors that large trucks (such as furniture vans) are used to transport them, most Soweto police dismiss these stories as inventions of the journalistic imagination, insisting that vehicles taken out of the country continue largely to be driven across various borders. The police express as much bitterness about the laxity of checks at the border posts—and their underlying causes—as they do about the number of police and civilians from Vehicle Theft units and 13 Camps who are charged with corruption.

Syndicates?

In trying to work out what proportion of vehicle robberies and thefts are for "a ride"—either to get home, to joyride, or to go to a funeral—and what proportion are "for business," police rely on educated estimates of how many vehicles of a certain type are being robbed or stolen at any particular time. The quantities vary, but experienced Flying Squad members place the percentage of vehicles acquired "for business" in a range of 30 to 50 percent (depending on type of vehicles at any particular time) of the nearly 1,000 vehicles forcibly robbed in Johannesburg each month (the number of unoccupied stolen vehicles is proportionately higher).[11]

As one experienced inspector told me, "When people hear a figure like 412 organized crime syndicates in South Africa, they think that the police must know the identity of every criminal. There are more syndicates even in Soweto." Part of the problem in finding the correct figure lies in the definition of "syndicate"; police and criminals in Soweto both have their own understandings: Criminals say that "a gang is a gang," amused by all suggestions to the contrary. Police, however, argue that any organized group, no matter how small, that "does crime for business" is a syndicate. However, whether determined by police or criminals, the number of groups, gangs, or syndicates doing crime as a business in Soweto far exceeds 412. Police also express cynicism about the assumption, seemingly emanating from senior police but often repeated in the media, that gangs are located principally in what were once called "Coloured" areas, such as Westbury, Newclare, or Eldorado Park. The gangs in these areas are prominent, but the notion that they have more impact than gangs operating in areas such as Dobsonville or Meadowlands strikes police as another example of the media's lack of attention to the realities of life in Soweto: "They want the action; that's all. But when it happens, they want to run, anywhere, under the vehicle, dropping their cameras."[12]

The working premise of the police in Soweto is that regardless of whether outsiders classify the gangs or syndicates as local or international, much of the crime in the township is well planned and businesslike; in other words, it is instrumental and functional in nature rather than arbitrary or expressive. The thousands of small groups that handle comparatively small quantities of such commodities as stolen/robbed vehicles, drugs, or counterfeit currency do not operate in a vacuum. They are, without exception, integrated within the larger networks that call on them for additional labor and probably buy from or sell to them (usually firearms). Without the approval, tacit or otherwise, of the larger groups who use their services, the smaller ones would be crushed. The more developed organizations—those that handle orders for as many as thirty to sixty vehicles per month, or deal with 50 kilogram bags of dagga at a time—are established on a different scale, connected to similar gangs in other townships on the Rand, in other provinces, and in other countries of the region.[13]

Nonetheless, such connections, even when they involve links with criminal organizations in other countries, do not have any substantial resemblance to such global organizations as the mafia, the triads, the Colombian drug cartels, or the yakuza, all of which significantly transcend political boundaries. The gangs that populate Soweto have connections, but not branches and subordinate arms in other areas. Rather than mirroring transnational crime, the structures and inner meanings of the gangs of Soweto and Gauteng Province resemble earlier phases in the development of the mafia or the yakuza. The histories of those organizations may have more potential analytical utility for the South African situation than their contemporary sociologies do.

Connections

Many individuals and gangs "do business together," more or less formally, when it suits them. Their links are formed just as much by circumstances that lie outside criminal activity as by mutual "business" interests. They may derive from family or clan, involve initiation brothers, old school friends, drinking *chommies* (buddies) from the shebeens, or sparring partners from boxing training decades ago. Often the links are obscure—to police as well as to the population of Soweto—deliberately so, operating at a subterranean level and causing both police and residents to spend hours speculating about them.

On a dry Gauteng winter day, for example, men from two Flying Squad vehicles sifted laboriously through endless piles of greasy engine blocks, differentials, electrical systems, and body parts at a scrapyard in Meadowlands zone 4, discovering evidence of nearly a dozen stolen vehicles. Even before the manager and four employees could be taken to the local police station to be formally charged, men were arriving from scrapyards on the other side of Soweto, fifteen km away. No phone calls had been made from the yard; none of the police was aware of any link between this almost-forgotten scrapyard and the larger, more visible, yards in Dhlamini, but they clearly existed, brought to the surface by the investigation: "Everybody knows everybody; somebody always knows," as a policeman said at that scene.

The connections can also stem from involvement in a church or civic association. Many men whose fortunes rest on illegally acquired foundations are careful to associate themselves with liberation politics, as insurance for the future. They are also assiduous in their networking with police: "The best informants are the best criminals" is a commonplace of Flying Squad wisdom, repeated and reinforced by story after story. Police learn early and quickly to exercise caution in their use of informants, wary of each relationship and each piece of information, but aware, too, that without them, and their varied motives, the policing of the township would become much more difficult.

Relationships can be temporary or selectively long-lasting, depending on the context: The complementary interests of the vehicle-robbery syndicate and the group that moves firearms to and from KwaZulu/Natal are immediately apparent, as are those of the vehicle syndicate and particular taxi owners or associations. Less obvious are the more convoluted deals that result in the export of vehicles to neighboring countries—often to the far north, in exchange for Mandrax pills, which are cheaper on the other side of the border, the price rising at least twofold inside South Africa due to the cost of smuggling, as well as the law of supply and demand. Vehicle syndicates, however, are highly specialized and not equipped to deal with other commodities, such as drugs, on any scale. There is little cross-dealing in commodities outside the specialty (although some entrepreneurs dabble at times, and almost all are capable of moving such common items as robbed liquor or vehicle parts). In order for a vehicle syndicate to handle large quantities of Mandrax pills as payment for exported vehicles, it needs to have a bulk market for them in advance. As middlemen, however, syndicates might be compensated with discounted counterfeit notes, firearms, or an interest in a gold or diamond shipment. Often intangibles enter into the deals—favors, paybacks, goodwill, and so on—any or all of which might be redeemed at some point in the future, but which have definite value in the present.[14]

At some point in the chain of transactions, real cash changes hands. The formal banking system rarely comes into play, although not because the syndicates fear mandatory reporting or any of the other inconveniences that might bother offenders in other countries. The years of subversion and concealment practiced during the apartheid government by almost every township resident—active participant in the struggle or not—have instilled a deep and lasting distrust of any declaration of resources or assets, not just on the part of those whose sources of income might be suspect. The smallest, most unreconstructed matchbox house in Meadowlands, may well hide a jacuzzi and elaborate sound system, if not caches of banknotes, rolls of R50 or R100 notes, or even packets of R10,000.

Evidence of these hidden resources is manifest in the massive changes that have beset the streetscapes of Soweto since 1990. As people gained confidence that political change was coming, they began first to fortify with the ubiquitous "stop nonsense"—the wall or tall fence around a matchbox house—and then to rebuild the house itself, often by constructing a new building around and over it. When the new construction was at lock-up stage, they would demolish any original walls that were no longer needed. As a result, few streets bear any resemblance to how they looked in the late 1980s. Many residents freely acknowledge that financing for these projects came from money squirreled away, concealed in the ceiling or buried in the yard.

The conclusions about the nature of organized crime drawn by Flying Squad policemen may lack the theoretical sophistication of academic formulations, but they receive support from a June 1996 report to the United Nations Commission on Crime Prevention and Criminal Justice: "Organized crime could be described . . . as a form of economic commerce by illegal means, involving the threat and use of physical force and violence, extortion, intimidation or corruption and other methods, as well as the use of illicit goods and services." The report drew a crucial distinction, arguing that "when organized crime groups seek business across their national borders, or when they seek alliances with crime groups elsewhere, it becomes organized transnational crime."[15]

As the Flying Squad police see it, crime as "business" in Soweto fits these definitions: It is comprised of thousands of groups/gangs/syndicates, in complex, interlocking local networks, extending to other nearby townships and shack settlements, such as Orange Farm to the south, to other regions such as KwaZulu/Natal, and to other countries, especially such neighboring states such as Mozambique, Botswana, and Zimbabwe, but also more distant countries like Zambia, Angola, and Kenya. Even though Soweto has no single criminal organization—or even 412 of them for that matter—that could be said to resemble the mafia, the triads, or yakuza, and even though it is a world apart in many ways, it is subject to strong globalizing influences, and functions as a hub of both organized and transnational crime networks. As the apartheid-era constraints on international contact and movement dissolve, the distinctive world that is Soweto—the style setter for southern Africa—is acquiring a different edge. Local men talk knowingly about international market conditions, boasting of the prices that they have received for vehicles robbed in the northern suburbs of Johannesburg, worked in Soweto, and sold in Lusaka or Nairobi. The sinews of organized crime in Soweto, however, remain the small local gangs, an inexhaustible pool of young men convinced of their invulnerability. As long as criminal activity continues to fulfill their need for money, identity, status, and power, the crime rates cannot but remain high.

Notes to Chapter 3

1. I have been engaged in participant observation fieldwork with Soweto Flying Squad (also known as Tango India, from its radio call sign) and a closely associated group, the Soweto Dog Unit (Tango Tango), in a series of field trips since March 1994. The Flying Squad is the emergency major-crime response unit for all of Soweto, Eldorado Park, and Lenasia. It is composed of four reliefs and a small unit of Highway Patrol. At the time of this writing, I had worked nearly 180 twelve-hour shifts "outside" with members of the unit, and had conducted hundreds of hours of interviews. My thanks are due to all the members of both units for their wholehearted participation in, and enthusiasm for, my ethnographic project—the attempt to understand "how they work"—as well as to the many residents of Soweto who answered my questions and helped me to know Soweto better.

The Flying Squad, like the huge township that it covers, is a multilingual unit, relying heavily on English, Afrikaans, and Fanagalo for linguae francae, both internally and externally. There are many words, phrases, and pronunciations that are specific to the unit, or even to a particular relief. Following the usual conventions, words not commonly used in English have been introduced in italic type, and quotation marks without specific referencing indicate idioms and characteristic terms.

2. The levels of crime within the townships are reported in a wide range of sources, from the populist autobiography of Soweto's self-styled "godfather"— Godfrey Moloi, *My Life* (Johannesburg, 1991)—to the academic descriptive analysis of Gabriel Lindumusa Ndabandaba, *Crimes of Violence in Black Townships* (Durban, 1987).

3. *Maputo* is the most commonly used term for an illegal alien/immigrant. The township perception is that, since 1990/1991, the largest number of illegals has come from Mozambique, of which Maputo is the capital. Most Mozambicans speak at least one language that is understandable in the polyglot township. Because other illegals from further north (Chad, Zambia, Zaire, Nigeria and even Malawi and Zimbabwe) often speak languages that cannot be understood, they are termed *amagrikamba*—those who speak Greek—or *amakwerekwere*—those who speak nonsense.

4. Raimondo Catanzaro (trans. Raymond Rosenthal), *Men of Respect: A History of the Sicilian Mafia* (New York, 1992), 34-35, discusses the notion of social mobility, arguing that "far from being backward, the societies in which the Mafia developed were characterized by considerable mobility. In fact, there were many examples of extremely rapid upward mobility of mafiosi."

5. Anton Blok, *The Mafia of a Sicilian Village, 1860-1960: A Study of Violent Peasant Entrepreneurs* (Prospect Heights, Ill., 1988), 225.

6. Henner Hess (trans. Ewald Osers), *Mafia and Mafiosi: The Structure of Power* (Lexington, Mass., 1973), 159; Diego Gambetta, *The Sicilian Mafia: The Business of Private Protection* (Cambridge, Mass., 1993), *passim*; Pino Arlacchi (trans. Martin Ryle), *Mafia Business: The Mafia Ethic and the Spirit of Capitalism* (London, 1986). See also the more theoretically based Gianluca Fiorentini and Sam Peltzman, *The Economics of Organised Crime* (Cambridge, 1995).

7. Crime, at least "for business," is almost totally gender specific in Soweto. The one substantial exception is the phenomenon of the shebeen queens, the female owners/operators of local drinking houses, which, though not yet legal, have been tolerated under a containment policy for so long that there are few of the old-style shebeen queens left. Most have subsided into "boring" respectability, although some still tell stories of the days when they had to outwit both police and rivals in order to make any money. The term, *tsotsi*, is reserved only for young males.

8. Eric Hobsbawm, *Bandits* (London, 1969); Michael Goddard, "The Rascal Road: Crime, Prestige, and Development in Papua New Guinea," *The Contemporary Pacific*, VII (1995), 58, which refers briefly to Louise Morauta,

"Law and Order: A Tenth Anniversary Report," in idem (ed.), *Law and Order in a Changing Society* (Canberra, 1986), 10-12.

9. Marauta, "Law and Order," 11.

10. 10111 is the location-specific, central-emergency number for police radio control. The number of anonymous stripping calls to 10111 and Crime Stop began to increase in 1995 and 1996.

11. All big funerals, and many small ones, produce a rash of stolen vehicles— bakkies in particular—although I have been with police when they have recovered everything from a Public United Transport Company (PUTCO) bus (robbed by a young man in full Umkhonto we Sizwe [MK] uniform with loaded AK-47) to minibuses to Mercedes in connection with funerals. During the three days before a big political funeral at Avalon cemetery in January 1995, for example, police remarked a number of times about a phenomenon that I noticed myself, that the lists of "lookouts" were remarkably long.

12. The figure of 412 was widely publicized, given legitimacy by both the national police commissioner and the Gauteng Member of the Executive Council (MEC) for Safety and Security during the Sword and Shield operation, June through July 1996. The quotation at the end of the paragraph exemplifies much of the Flying Squad relationship with the media.

13. In May 1996, an agreement was signed between the SAPS, the National Intelligence Agency, the SA Secret Service, and the SA National Defense Force (SANDF) to cooperate in the Joint Management Forum, coordinating intelligence operations against crime and criminals. Implicitly, both George Fivaz, National SAPS Commissioner, and Joe Nhlanhla, Deputy Minister of Intelligence, seemed to indicate that international syndicates had not yet entered the country. Fivaz promised that the SAPS and the intelligence agencies would take joint responsibility for making it "virtually impossible for the syndicates to infiltrate the country." Nhlanha declared, "We want to save this country long before it has international, Mafia-style syndicates," and "Our analysis shows that, unless something radical is done, we need to speed up the process [of detection] so we don't have a Mafia in our country" (*The Saturday Star* [Johannesburg], 11 May 1996). See http://www.independent.co.za/news/hard/crime/crimeplan.html.

14. At this level of business, Mandrax pills are sold only in bags of 1,000, and most often in lots of 10,000, with 10 to 50 lots of 10,000 not uncommonly moved at one time.

15. Inter Press Third World News Agency (IPS), 3 June 1996.

4

Glenn Oosthuysen

Shooting the Golden Goose
Small-Arms Proliferation in Southern Africa

THIS CHAPTER aims to review the extent and consequences of small arms-proliferation in southern Africa. It examines present controls used in the region and raises possible alternative strategies. It does not deal with such small arms as land mines or weapons in official military or security-force hands, but, rather, with those in the legal and illegal possession of civilians. Countries of the region under discussion are Mozambique, Angola, Swaziland, Botswana, Namibia, Zimbabwe, Zambia, and South Africa.[1]

Small arms have come to play a significant part in the shaping of southern Africa. Their influence, however, has not come to an end simply because the major conflicts in the region have ended or are winding down. Rather, the failure to control small-arms possession and flows has resulted in both the creation and exacerbation of instability. In fact, small arms continue to be so important in shaping southern Africa that they could ultimately determine whether peace, stability, and development or crime, violence, and conflict reign in the region. The extraordinary influence of small arms in southern Africa is reflected by their level of proliferation and its consequences.[2]

The Extent of Proliferation in Southern Africa

Examination of the consequences of small-arms proliferation and the possible methods for controlling it requires a review of how extensive the problem is and what controls are currently in operation on a state-by-state basis.

In Mozambique, the legislative criteria for issuing a firearm license are generally unknown to the average citizen. Nevertheless, an applicant for a licensed weapon must apply to the police, who have sole discretion over the process. Without recourse to legislative criteria, no challenges can be made to police decisions, which, given the high level of official corruption, increase the opportunities for corrupt licensing practices. Once an application has been approved, a license to import a firearm must be obtained; there are no gun shops or gunsmiths permitted in Mozambique. Firearms must be bought in foreign currency (at a poor exchange rate) and import costs and customs duties paid. This becomes a very expensive proposition for most Mozambicans, whose average annual per capita income is about $100. The effect is inadvertently to make the legal acquisition of firearms financially prohibitive for ordinary Mozambicans. In contrast, illegal weapons are freely available, cheap and unlikely to be detected by the police. Thus legal firearm-control practices in Mozambique could be helping to sustain the weapons black market, since many potential firearm owners can afford to purchase a gun only from this illegal source.[3]

Estimates of the number of small-arms in Mozambique vary from 1.5 to 6 million. Small arms were given to soldiers of the Front for the Liberation of Mozambique (FRELIMO) government, Mozambique National Resistance (RENAMO) rebels, and "people's militia," and to village chiefs and community leaders. These weapons were distributed even further afield during the war and have been since the war ended. Since no register was kept of weapons issued or recipients, it is practically impossible to calculate the exact number to be found in Mozambique, which in itself presents a difficulty for any possible control policy or program, as the United Nations (UN) discovered.

The United Nations Operation in Mozambique (UNOMOZ) provided for the demobilization, disarmament, integration (into the new defense force), and reintegration (into society) of the FRELIMO and RENAMO troops. To achieve disarmament, combatants were required to hand in their weapons upon registration at assembly areas (AAs). This procedure yielded 167,758 weapons, of which 104,000 were small arms—far short of even the most conservative estimate of 1.5 million thought to be in Mozambique.[4]

The failure to implement effective disarmament was not the sole responsibility of the UN. UNOMOZ might have been slightly more successful had it not been forced to battle against the operational limitations imposed by the Mozambican Ceasefire Commission, the UN Security Council mandate, and finite resources; ultimately, the UN was present only to provide Mozambicans with a neutral framework within which to disarm. Nonetheless, the UN still stands accused of gross negligence in securing and maintaining control of those weapons that were collected; many of the weapons handed to UNOMOZ were subsequently lost or stolen from UN armories and storehouses. Upon leaving Mozambique, UNOMOZ troops allegedly abandoned weapons storehouses that were later to be broken open and robbed of their contents, thereby returning the arms to society (as with the weapons reputedly abandoned by a Paraguayan contingent at Inhambane).[5]

The small arms available in Mozambique are the remnants of the civil war effort: weapons distributed in the course of the civil war, discovered in caches, and stolen from UN storage depots and even state armories. Most small arms are in the possession of demobilized former combatants, criminals, and civilians—categories not necessarily distinct from one another.

In Angola, the proliferation of small arms is even more alarming. No credible statistics for licensed or registered weapons are available from the Angolan authorities, partly because record keeping is not a priority in a country at war with itself. Firearm licenses are issued under strict conditions and include provisions that forbid diplomats from bringing personal weapons with a caliber larger than 9mm into the country. License holders must renew all firearm licenses annually, and all licenses are subject to final police approval. Import permits and customs approval are mandatory before weapons can be imported by private companies.

The number of unregistered small arms in circulation is difficult to determine because of the very nature of illegal weapons. Attempts to discover how many were supplied to Angola are unlikely to be accurate, since much of what was supplied—for example to UNITA—was

TABLE 4-1. Firearms Registered in Swaziland

Type of firearm	Total registered 1990	Total registered 1995
Rifle	1,393	2,217
Single-barreled shotguns	3,499[a]	4,176
Double-barreled shotguns	—	880
Revolvers	471	667
Pistols	285	2,101
Combinations	27	41
Miscellaneous	9	53
Total	5,684	10,135

SOURCE. Figures provided by Royal Swaziland Police, Mbabane, November 24, 1995.
a. Includes both single- and double-barreled shotguns.

shipped covertly via third parties. The United Nations Angola Verification Mission III (UNAVEM III) was entrusted with the unenviable task of encouraging and verifying disarmament in Angola. According to a report in early 1996, a total of 12,571 UNITA soldiers had been registered and disarmed, from whom 12,144 weapons had been recovered—a drop in the ocean when compared with the 700,000 weapons that were freely distributed in Luanda by the Popular Movement for the Liberation of Angola (MPLA) government after the peace process collapsed in 1992. It is likely that the disarmament process in Angola will leave thousands of weapons in the hands of the population, as it did in Mozambique. What becomes of those weapons could affect not only Angola, but southern African as a whole.[6]

In Swaziland, proliferation is measured on three fronts—legal, licensed weapons; illegal weapons smuggled from Mozambique; and former guerrilla arms caches. As of late 1995, there were 8,549 registered firearm owners in Swaziland, possessing 10,135 licensed firearms (see table 4-1). The Royal Swaziland Police (RSP) are responsible for issuing firearm licenses, but applicants must first seek the approval of village elders and inform them of their reasons for wanting them. A panel appointed by the king reviews the application of those who do not have a traditional authority to consult.

Every year gun owners must report to a police station and present their licensed firearms to be verified and their addresses and details to be updated. Otherwise, the police can impose a small fine, that is, if

TABLE 4-2. Weapons Seized by the Royal Swaziland Police

Year	AK-47s	Handguns	Rifles	Shotguns
1991	61	40	8	17
1992	65	30	15	17
1993	50	38	8	15
1994	21	52	15	12
1995	10	46	5	11

SOURCE. Royal Swaziland Police.

they can still trace the individuals. This regulation is designed to assist with the counting of firearms and to detect any unreported losses or thefts. However, since the RSP rely on a manual filing and record-keeping system, they are unable to take effective and timely action against gun owners who do not comply.

Although the 1964 Act prohibits possession of unlicensed firearms in Swaziland, the RSP seize relatively few weapons (see table 4-2). In addition to the weapons listed in table 4-2, two rocket launchers, seven surface-to-air missiles, two land mines, and eighteen submachine guns were recovered in 1993; four grenades in 1994; and two rocket launchers and three land mines in 1995. Because the efficiency of the RSP is hampered by poor border inspection facilities, the number of weapons recovered constitutes only a fraction of the arms moving through the country. Most of the weapons seized by the RSP are remnants of guerrilla arms caches that were buried or hidden in Swaziland. Even though the trafficking route from Mozambique through Swaziland and into KwaZulu/Natal is one of the largest, the Swazis have seized only 206 pistols/revolvers and 207 AK-47s since 1991—an indication of their limited capacity to police illegal weapons.

Botswana has long prided itself on its strict weapons-control policies, which, in stark contrast to those of its regional neighbors, kept the level of armaments within its society low. By the end of 1994, there were 28,223 registered firearms in the hands of an estimated 10,000 to 15,000 people. Botswana has by far the most stringent legislation concerning firearm ownership and is one of the most unarmed societies in southern Africa. Firearm licenses are not issued for personal handguns, which are prohibited in Botswana. Although foreign diplomats can obtain temporary permits for them, they must take their handguns with them on departure, and they may not sell them in Botswana.[7]

The Arms Quota Board—a responsibility of the Commissioner of Police—supervises the issuing of firearm licenses in accordance with government policy. Only 400 licenses are issued every year—200 for rifles and 200 for shotguns. Approximately 5,000 to 6,000 applications for firearm licenses are submitted annually. If applicants meet such standards as sound mental health and no criminal records, their names are placed in a lottery, which is normally conducted every March. Applicants cannot request more than one heavy caliber rifle, one light caliber rifle, and one shotgun. If unsuccessful, they must resubmit their applications to qualify for the next draw.

Botswana, much like Swaziland, has limited institutional capacity for the maintenance of firearm statistics, also relying on a manual filing system. The number of illegal weapons in Botswana is comprised largely of weapons smuggled through the country and former liberation-movement arms caches. However, a growing supply of illegal weapons is stolen in South Africa and smuggled into Botswana. Despite the fact that policing of weapons should be made easier by the ban on handguns, the Botswana Police recover only fifty illegal weapons or so a year. The number of weapons forfeited or surrendered (such as those of legal South African firearm owners entering Botswana without them) is high in comparison. In 1992, a total of 1,632 firearms were forfeited or surrendered; in 1993, the number was 1,955 and, in 1994, 352. The potential for further small-arms proliferation in Botswana rests largely upon the ability of police to counter the inflow of illegal weapons.[8]

In Namibia, the problem of small-arms proliferation encompasses both legal and illegal weapons. In early 1996, Namibia finally produced its own draft legislation for the control of firearms. The most notable provisions of the draft included a one-off requirement that all firearm owners reapply for new licenses within a period of eighteen months, that all automatic weapons be declared illegal without an express permit from the Inspector-General of Police, and that no person may license more than four weapons of various calibers. In 1995, 2,957 firearms were licensed and registered in Namibia—consisting of 856 pistols, 483 revolvers, 567 shotguns, 25 combination shotguns, 893 rifles, 129 air rifles, 1 dart gun, 2 carbines, and 1 muzzle-loader. These figures make Namibia the second highest licenser of firearms in the region, after South Africa.[9]

The licensing procedure evokes much resentment from the Namibian authorities. In fact, Namibian policing, in general, is a politically sensitive issue, since South Africa still lends considerable assistance in (some would say, control of) such areas as training, forensics, processing of license applications, and maintenance of statistical data. This reliance on South Africa reflects the limited institutional capacity of the Namibian Police (NAMPOL).

This same incapacity is evident in the few illegal weapons confiscated in Namibia, despite the volume thought to be leaving Namibia for South Africa. From August 1993 to December 1995, only 62 arrests were made for illegal possession of weapons, and only 122 weapons and 896 rounds of ammunition were seized. According to NAMPOL officials, the unit that polices firearms and smuggling activities consists of only five to seven people. Namibia faces the dual challenge of dealing with proliferation and control of both legal and illegal weapons with extremely limited resources.[10]

Proliferation of small arms in Zimbabwe is not nearly as problematic as could be expected, given the country's "Rhodesian War" experience. Unlike post–civil war Angola and Mozambique, Zimbabwe had a relatively strong institutional Defense Force and police department to maintain control of small arms.

The Zimbabwe police are responsible for the licensing of weapons, and reportedly their system is rigorous. Apparently, not even a certain brigadier in the Zimbabwean Defense Force has been able to obtain a firearm license. The vast majority of licenses are issued to farmers and businessmen, and all must be renewed every six months.[11]

Authorities maintain that the scarcity of illegal weapons in Zimbabwe is largely due to the fact that the weapons used in the Rhodesian War were recovered through the demobilization process. Ex-combatants had to hand in their weapons or else be disqualified from receiving benefits, pensions, and employment in the new defense force. This conditionality was possibly the decisive requirement in the Rhodesian disarmament process; the UN could learn from it in negotiating its demobilization and disarmament operation mandates.

Historically, Zambia has been the operational base for the various liberation and guerrilla forces in southern Africa. The small-arms proliferation there owes as much to this role as to any other factor, such as licensed arms. Licenses for firearms are limited to a number that varies from year to year. The police take applications and run background checks before a police board can approve individual licenses. Everyone must produce a permit before buying a weapon. The Zambian Police also legitimately sell weapons that have been confiscated or cannot be returned to their owners. Farmers can obtain licenses more easily than most other people because of the exigencies particular to their way of life. However, military style weapons cannot be purchased.

Most of the illegal weapons in the country originate from former guerrilla arms caches. Many of these weapons were lost, abandoned, or stolen when the various cadres were moving within the community. Zambian officials identify the repatriation of the African National Congress (ANC) cadres, in particular, as responsible for the spread of arms to Zambian society. Allegedly, as a result of the uncertainty inherent in the repatriation process (poor funding and support), many guerrillas resorted to selling their weapons or became involved in criminal activities. Hence, the control of small-arms proliferation in Zambia is focused primarily on illegal weapons.[12]

By contrast, two major factors contribute to the proliferation of small arms in South Africa: first, the continued growth in legal, licensed firearms and, second, the great number of illegal weapons that are smuggled across the country's borders or stolen from licensed gun owners.

The Arms and Ammunition Act, No. 75 of 1969, which regulates the licensing procedure, does not set overly stringent requirements. The largest obstacle to acquiring a legal firearm is mainly the cost of purchasing the weapon, rather than the licensing procedure. Although the Act sets strict standards for storage and responsible use, its reliance on police enforcement that, for one reason or another, is not available to back it up reduces it to a mere "wish list" of control measures.

South African Police Service (SAPS) statistics report that nearly 2 million South Africans own more than 4 million firearms (see table 4-3). SAPS statistics also show that during 1993 and 1994, just prior to and in the wake of South Africa's first fully democratic elections of April 1994, applications for firearm licenses were granted at an average rate of 20,208 per month. In one month, South Africa licensed almost as many

TABLE 4-3. Licensed Firearms in South Africa

Year	Total	Gun owners
1986	2,492,633	1,061,281
1993	3,717,463	1,637,141
1994	3,954,083	—
1995	4,100,015	1,944,066

SOURCE. South African Police Services.

weapons as the total number of legal weapons in Botswana, or more than double the total number of licensed weapons in Swaziland. In 1995, the average fell to 12,000 licenses granted per month. However, in the first three months of 1996, the number of licenses increased again to an average of 18,164 per month. The renewed surge in licensed firearms appears to be a response to the increased levels of violent crime—including murder, vehicle hijackings, and armed robberies.

Ironically, the rise in armed crime has been fueled by the rise in licensed weapons; many of the weapons in criminal hands have been stolen from licensed gun owners. The incidence of licensed firearms reported stolen or lost continues its upward climb. In 1994, there were at least 16,110 of them, in 1995 at least 17,617, and in the first three months of 1996, 5,246, or a projected figure of nearly 21,000 for the year. Between April 1, 1990, and September 12, 1995, the SAPS itself "lost" 7,261 firearms, and the South African National Defense Force (SANDF) "lost" 1,324 weapons. The security forces of the former homeland and TBVC states (Transkei, Bophutatswana, Venda, and Ciskei) were also credited with considerable losses of weapons. For example, in a 1995 stock taking of the former Transkei Police, 2,120 (38 percent) of the 5,634 weapons meant to be under its control could not be located. Many gun owners, fearing prosecution under the Arms and Ammunition Act for negligence or failure to comply with safekeeping regulations, often choose not to report the theft or loss of their firearms. Thus, the official statistics should be seen as a conservative estimate of the actual number of registered weapons illegally in the hands of unlicensed individuals.[13]

The SAPS estimate that they recover approximately 10 percent of the weapons entering the country illegally—an overly generous propor-

TABLE 4-4a. Weapons Seized, 1993–1995

Weapons and type	1993	1994	1995
Rifles			
AK-47s	1,403	1,589	1,392
Others	1,170	1,297	892
Shotguns	593	691	632
Total	3,166	3,577	2,915
Pistols			
Stechkins	20	10	4
Scorpions	11	16	32
Makarovs	174	164	172
Tokarevs	77	56	58
Others	4,327	5,150	6,934
Total	4,609	5,396	7,200
Revolvers	1,894	2,364	2,842
Homemade firearms	1,991	3,123	2,624
Grand total	11,660	14,450	15,582

SOURCE. South African Police Services.

TABLE 4-4b. Ammunition Seized, 1993–1995

Type of ammunition	1993	1994	1995
7.62mm	119,610	103,424	40,717
Other	1,194,826	203,367	108,259

SOURCE. South African Police Services.

tion, according to some. Nonetheless, a rough calculation of the number of illegal small arms in circulation in South Africa, based on a 10 percent recovery rate, would find that it has increased by more than 417,000 since 1993 (see tables 4a and 4b). The supply of small arms in South Africa is fed by the weapons that enter from Mozambique and Angola and ongoing demand for licensed weapons, many of which become illegal through theft and robbery. Legal and illegal weapons are equally responsible for the small-arms problem in South Africa.

Border Control

Since the southern African region has moved to reestablish normal relations and foster regional trade, the greater flow of people, goods, and vehicles across state borders has facilitated the illicit traffic in weapons. The illegal export of weaponry, especially from Angola and Mozambique, is rampant, largely because border-control measures are almost nonexistent in most states of the region. A look at regional border-control conditions quickly shows why it is possible for weapons to be smuggled with relative impunity.

In Mozambique, the military was required to halt all border patrols in accordance with the terms of the Rome Peace Accord; these patrols had yet to be resumed by the end of 1995. Mozambique had planned to demobilize voluntarily or integrate FRELIMO and RENAMO soldiers (estimated to number from 90,000 to 150,000) into a new military force of 30,000. Most of the soldiers, however, chose not to continue their careers in the military. As a result, the Forças Armadas de Moçambique (FADM) is comprised of just 10,500 soldiers—far short of the 30,000 target to perform the extensive border duties effectively. There is a shortage of sufficient border inspection facilities and, in some cases, even border posts.

In Angola, a specialized border police force—Policia Fronteiriça (PF)—is responsible for both border control and customs control of the country's 4,000 km long borders. Though it is the only specialist force of its kind in the region, its impact is limited by the fact that the MPLA government has access to or control over only 20 percent of its border, most of which is coastline. The land borders, across which most illegal arms pass, are either under the control of UNITA or bandits (such as ex-combatants who have joined forces to protect their interests in diamonds and oil reserves), or they are inaccessible to the military due to the nature of the terrain. To provide effective border control, the PF claim to need 15,000 border guards. At present, they have fewer than 4,000. The other 80 percent of Angola's border area outside the MPLA's reach has no police presence at all.[14]

The institutional capacity of those entrusted with border control and weapons control within Angola and Mozambique—the main suppliers of illegal arms to the region—is seemingly too limited to impede the internal distribution or regional flow of illegal weapons, or even to recover weapons from potentially destabilizing elements. Ultimately, the prospects for alleviating the situation rest upon the border-control measures of the recipient states as the first line of defense.

Swaziland's Defense Force has the task of patrolling the borders, but the scarcity of basic inspection facilities, or even sniffer dogs, makes the Swazi authorities no match for the methods employed by smugglers. Swaziland has to rely on cooperation with its neighbors to raise its border-control levels. Reputedly, however, it receives little assistance from the Mozambican authorities, with unfortunate consequences for conditions at its border.

Botswana is a transit route for arms from Angola into South Africa. Botswana's largely peaceful relations within the region previously exempted it from concentrating its resources on bolstering its defense or its border-control capabilities. As a result, insufficient resources at its border posts prevent it from conducting effective inspections; there is no equipment to unload cargo or containers. Significantly, Botswana maintains good cooperation with all of its neighbors, except Angola, with whom cooperation has yet to be discussed. Since Angola is thought to be the source for most of the illegal weapons that enter Botswana, this situation represents a significant weakness in Botswana's border-control efforts.

The Namibian Police have plans to create a separate border-patrol force consisting of at least 2,000 men—an optimistic figure, given that the police force totaled only 2,700 men by the end of 1995, and is beset with internal problems. The Namibian Defense Force (NDF) performs border-control responsibilities in support of NAMPOL. It has not expanded its bases beyond those that it took over from the former South African Defense Force and South West African Territory Force, which were located in the country's north. As a result, the South Africa–Namibia boundary is neglected for lack of infrastructure on the ground. The NDF is already stretched beyond its capacity just to secure the 1,500 km northern border with Angola. The border in the Kavango and Caprivi areas was temporarily closed in 1995—UNITA controlling the Angolan side of this border—to prevent illegal cross-border activities and allegedly to cut off supplies (apparently as a gesture of political solidarity with Angola's MPLA government). Since most of the people living in these UNITA-held areas are impoverished, the NDF can expect a flood of weapons to be put up for sale by desperate Angolans when this border eventually reopens.[15]

Controls do not exist along the border from Ruacana westward to the coast; large parts do not have even the simplest of border fences. Moreover, the main political support base of the Southwest African People's Organization (SWAPO) who live in the area would resist any attempt to tighten controls along this Ovamboland border. In the first place, 50 percent of the Ovambo people live in Angola; border controls would prevent divided families and relatives from visiting each other as they normally do. The family that takes the most direct route to Angola by crossing the river would have to walk 10, 20, or even 50 km or more to the nearest border-crossing point and then double back to their relatives on the other side. Second, some of Namibia's wealthiest businessmen reside in Ovamboland, and they also happen to be among SWAPO's biggest financial supporters. If access across the border were restricted, they would lose a significant part of the Angolan market that relies on them for supplies. They would stand to lose as much as 50 percent of their business. Neither of these two effects of border control would endear SWAPO to their supporters in Ovamboland. Hence, SWAPO is unlikely to let them happen. President Sam Nujoma's government has already turned down an NDF request for an electric fence, on the grounds that it would be too expensive, which begs the question of whether it is politically or financially prohibitive. Either way, Namibia does not have the capacity to prevent the illegal shipment of arms out of Angola.[16]

Zimbabwe's eastern border is the main point of entry for weapons from Mozambique. It is all the more difficult to control because the cross-border movement of *people* is not well controlled. The influx of people, and weapons, is aided by the Zimbabwean government's view that the border is artificial. With that attitude as a starting point, little in the way of policy can be expected to ensure effective border control.

Zambia shares borders with Zimbabwe (640 km), Botswana (0.4 km), Namibia (185 km), Malawi (640 km), Mozambique (360 km), Angola (1,200 km), Tanzania (300 km), and Congo (1,650 km). Not surprisingly, Zambia is in an excellent position to support a multitude of guerrilla forces operating in the region. The most problematic borders are those with Angola, Congo, and Mozambique.

Angola has no established border posts on its side, since these areas are under the control of UNITA. UNITA troops regularly trade their weapons for food from Zambians; an AK-47 is often exchanged for maize meal. To prevent this trade, the Zambian Defense Force deploys one company of troops in the west and another in the northwest border areas. These 300 men alone patrol the busy 1,200 km Angolan border. Nor can the Zambians set up effective bilateral cooperation on this border, because the Zambian government does not recognize UNITA.

Zambia reputedly has problems along the Congo border with its neighbor's military, who are allegedly involved in smuggling weapons. Zambian officials recently seized a plane load of weapons destined for Zaire. The weapons were allegedly bought in Angola and shipped to Belgium, where they were sold to Zaire and returned via Zambia, where they were seized. Despite the existence of a Zambia–Congo Joint Permanent Commission, cooperation about border controls remains poor.[17]

Zambia's border with Mozambique is threatened by former soldiers who enter Zambia to rustle cattle and trade in arms. In response, the Zambian and Mozambican governments set up a Joint Permanent Commission that allows for joint hot-pursuit operations. The Botswanan, Tanzanian, and Namibian borders are relatively trouble free.

The Zambian authorities seem to lack the resources to tighten any of their borders should they so wish. Unfortunately for Zambia, its geographical location and the ease with which weapons are able to flow into it from both Angola and Mozambique, places it in the pincer grip of small arms trafficking.

South Africa's eastern border has been the major supply route for illegal arms entering from Mozambique since 1992. Typically, weapons are smuggled over the border and transported via the N4 highway from Nelspruit into Johannesburg's East Rand townships, where they are distributed to other parts of the country. However, the political violence in KwaZulu/Natal led to the development of more direct supply routes from Mozambique, through Swaziland and into KwaZulu/Natal.

The border from Komatipoort to Mbusini (on the border with both Mozambique and Swaziland) stretches a distance of 62.2 km and is known as the "Norex fence." Despite the impressive looking rolls of barbed wire and electrodes, which are monitored by eight high-tech control rooms or substations, the effectiveness of this fence, erected in 1986, is somewhat less awe inspiring. It takes an illegal immigrant or smuggler anywhere from 30 to 90 seconds to crawl under the fence.

Since the voltage on the electric fence was turned down to nonlethal levels in 1990, its major function has been reduced to that of an alarm.

The Kruger National Park (KNP), which shares a 320 km border with Mozambique, is a weak link. It has no electric fence or alarm system to detect illegal border crossings; the border fence is a simple wire animal fence, which is in disrepair in some places. The KNP authorities oppose the erection of an electric fence because of the potential damage to wildlife and the likelihood of soil erosion. The bottom line is that they do not believe it would be much of a deterrent, anyway.[18]

According to the 1995 annual report of the SANDF, border control deployed, on average, thirteen companies of 2,000 soldiers, at a cost of R47.1 million. During that year, SANDF personnel detected 28,763 unlawful border crossings, and apprehended 15,216 people, and confiscated 1,872 unlawful weapons, of which 235 were AK-47s. The traditional concentration of border-control personnel and facilities on the northern and eastern borders provides for limited policing of weapons flowing from Angola. This weakness, combined with the Namibians' inability to prevent the flow of weapons through their country, could mean that South Africa will receive a greater number of small arms from Angola than from Mozambique—an increase in proliferation that South Africa can ill afford.[19]

As this review of border controls shows, the ability of states to prevent the import or export of illegal small arms is constrained by a lack of resources. However, border controls are rendered ineffective for other reasons as well—for instance, the vested political interests in Namibia, or, for that matter, the misconception among policymakers in South Africa that effective border controls would run counter to regional aspirations for free trade. The assumption would appear to be that the two are mutually exclusive—much to the detriment of improved border control.

Consequences of Small-Arms Proliferation in Recipient States

Yesterday's weapons of war and political liberation in the region have become today's weapons of crime and violence throughout southern Africa. They pose a threat to regional stability and development, should their availability facilitate "gun-barrel politics"—armed settlement of the intrastate and ethnic tensions that characterize the region, in particular, and the post–Cold War world, in general.

In Mozambique, the incidence of armed crime is said to be increasing. Most sources accuse the large number of unemployed, but armed, demobilized soldiers for it. The discontent of ex-soldiers also manifested itself in strikes and riots in Maputo, during which they voiced their demands for greater government assistance. This objective could possibly form the basis of an armed campaign to pressure the government into acceding to their demands. In rural areas, roving groups of armed bandits have resorted to robbery and looting, exploiting the low levels of policing. The tensions that exist between RENAMO and FRELIMO, specifically in provinces dominated by RENAMO supporters but subject to the local authority of a FRELIMO-appointed provincial governor, could erupt at any time. There are sufficient levels of armaments in Mozambique to convert any such hostility into armed conflict.

In Angola, reports suggest that armed banditry and crime are on the rise. The failure of the police to keep statistics on crime makes it difficult to obtain confirmation of this apparent trend, but demobilized soldiers and civilians seem to have seized weapons as a means of self-protection and survival. The possession of diamond and oil reserves by armed bandits, such as those in Soyo and Cabinda, indicate how access to small arms can get individuals resources they would not normally have. The conflict for control of the Cabinda enclave exemplifies the use of small arms to pursue a political and economic agenda. Just as the ending of the Cold War exposed new, or previously dormant, ethnic, territorial conflicts elsewhere in the world, so too might it expose them in Angola. The vast wealth or class gap between the "dollar economy" elites and the majority of poor Angolans, the long-standing antagonism between "northerners" and "southerners," or the racial conflict between so-called "creole mestizos" (of Portuguese origin) and "black" Angolans, are examples of potential conflict previously submerged by the civil war.

The trafficking of small arms from Mozambique to South Africa has led to the establishment of Swaziland as a market for small arms in its own right, as the use of small arms in armed robberies, car hijackings, and even the 1996 political strikes for multiparty democracy amply demonstrates. In fact, small arms from Mozambique are so prevalent

TABLE 4-5. Firearm-Related Crime in
Namibia, 1995

Type of crime	Number of incidents
Illegal possession	232
Theft of Firearms	204
Murder	82
Attempted murder	264
Armed robbery	212
Victims of armed crime	607
Suicides	54

SOURCE. Namibia Police.

that the formation of an armed opposition to the monarchy is not beyond the bounds of possibility.

Traditionally unarmed Botswana, too, has experienced such an increase in armed crime that it has established a well-armed rapid response unit to deal with it. Moreover, the growing dissent that led to student riots in 1995 could evolve into an armed conflict, given the increased availability of small arms.[20]

As shown in table 4-5, armed crime is becoming so widespread in Namibia that many South Africans living there feel that they might well be safer in South Africa, despite that country's high crime levels. The poaching activities that beset Namibia allegedly are instigated mostly from the Angolan side of the border. The country's political tensions revolve around turmoil within SWAPO. In 1995, former soldiers from the People's Liberation Army of Namibia (PLAN)—SWAPO's armed wing—started taking hostages and inciting riots to force pensions and other benefits from the government. It may be just a matter of time until access to weapons from Angola enables them to press their demands more forcefully.

In 1994, poaching activity was serious enough in Zimbabwe that the minister for national parks called in the Defense Force. Criminals are using guns more and more, and forming into groups of armed bandits in rural areas. The danger also extends to the political sphere, where many opposition groups are becoming impatient with the Mugabe government.

The Chimwenjes—an armed movement reputedly opposed to the Mugabe government—are one such manifestation of this frustration and served as a warning to the region that unless small arms are placed under official control, other similar groups could emerge.

Zambia has experienced instability mainly along the borders with Angola, Zaire, and Mozambique, due to incursions by poachers and armed criminals. According to Zambian officials, groups from the Katangese (Shaba province) region in Zaire often raid mining towns near the borders, stealing everything in sight. The Zambian "copper belt" region is a particularly popular target; the situation has drastically curtailed new investment in the area. Furthermore, the political tensions created by President Frederick Chiluba's government's manipulation of the 1996 election could make the political opposition resort to arms.[21]

In South Africa, the effects of small-arms proliferation are immediately apparent in the high levels of violent crime and the ongoing political conflict in KwaZulu/Natal. The number of licensed weapons stolen/lost, in combination with the weapons smuggled into South Africa from such countries as Mozambique and Angola, has led to a rash of armed criminal activity.

According to SAPS statistics, of the 68,320 robberies reported in 1994, as many as 43,279 (63.3 percent) were committed with firearms. In the first six months of 1995, a total of 33,441 robberies were reported; 26,563 (79.4 percent) of them were committed with firearms. Similarly, firearms were responsible for 7,083 (38.6 percent) of the 18,312 murders documented during 1994. In the first six months of 1995, they accounted for 3,346 (39.8 percent) of the 8,407 murders (see table 4-6).

Contrary to public perceptions, encouraged by the media, the AK-47 is not the weapon of choice for South Africa's criminals. SAPS statistics show that pistols and revolvers far outstrip AK-47s. Of the 7,803 murders committed with firearms in 1994, as many as 5,872 (75 percent) were committed with pistols or revolvers, 753 (9.6 percent) with rifles or shotguns, and only 458 (5.9 percent) with high-caliber automatic weapons (such as AK-47s). Similarly, in 1995, 5.7 percent of the 7,169 murders committed with firearms were by assault rifles; 75 percent of them by pistols or revolvers (see table 4-7). Incidents of taxi violence in 1994 and 1995 involved AK-47s in 8.8 percent and 13.5

TABLE 4-6. Use of Firearms in Violent Crime

Year	Murders	Attempted murders	Robbery
1991	3,803	n.a.	17,871
1992	6,122	13,276	26,665
1993	7,764	16,023	33,198
1994	7,803	17,744	43,279
1995	7,169	7,245[a]	45,216

SOURCE. National Crime Investigation Service (NCIS), South African Police Services.
a. For the period from January 1 to June 30, 1995.

TABLE 4-7. Annual Murders Committed Using Various Caliber Weapons, 1994–1995

Percent

	1994		1995	
Weapons Used	Deaths	Weapons Used[a]	Deaths	Weapons Used[a]
Assault rifle	458	5.9	408	5.7
Pistol/revolver	5,872	75.3	5,377	75.0
Rifle/shotgun	753	9.7	763	10.6
Homemade/unknown	720	9.2	62	8.7
Total	7,803	100	7,169	100

SOURCE. National Crime Investigation Service (NCIS), South African Police Services.
a. Percent.

percent, respectively, whereas 9mm pistols were identified in 21.7 percent and 19.7 percent of the incidents, respectively (see table 4-8). Overall, small arms entered into more than 70 percent of the incidents of taxi violence in both 1994 and 1995.

The relatively few incidents involving AK-47s cause such inordinate concern in South Africa because large quantities of these weapons are thought to be entering the country. The reasons why they would be smuggled into South Africa but not used (as reflected by crime statistics) are not clear. Political factions may be stockpiling them for future use, or dealers may be buying them cheaply from desperate Angolans

TABLE 4-8. Weapons Used in Taxi Violence, 1994–April 26, 1996

Type of Weapon Used	1994	1995	1996 (until April 26)
AK–47 rifles	45	76	12
9mm pistols	111	111	46
7.65mm pistols	10	7	7
R–4 rifles	8	16	3
Stechkin pistols	1	0	0
Makarov pistols	1	0	0
Shotguns	2	0	0
Unidentified firearms	186	185	89
Hand grenades	2	1	1
Limpet mines	1	1	0
Cultural weapons	14	22	10
Petrol bombs	4	2	1
Revolvers	2	0	0
Commercial explosives	0	1	0
R–1 rifles	0	2	0
Skorpion pistols	0	0	1
Stone throwing	10	11	9
Total incidents	512	563	231
Deaths	199	222	84
Injuries	346	391	164
Arrests	256	299	73

SOURCE. National Crime Investigation Service (NCIS), South African Police Services.

or Mozambicans for eventual sale to meet the small-arms needs of the world's numerous intrastate conflicts.

In the wake of escalating armed crime, violence, and smuggling, other consequences can be anticipated: violent drug and gang wars, more poaching (already meat syndicates operating from Mozambique poach such game as impala from the Kruger National Park) and a growth in the number of private security forces. The use of small arms for political purposes in KwaZulu/Natal has been a distinct possibility, and other potential flare-ups—such as demands for a Volkstaat, right- and left-wing extremism, or even labor disputes—could all be exacerbated by recourse to small arms. The upward trend in weapons smuggling into South Africa, with its accompanying problems, is likely to continue, particularly since the peace process in Angola has freed, and probably will continue to free, vast quantities of arms. When the chickens—or in this case, small arms—come home to roost, they will not hatch doves.

Since many states of the region stumbled upon a fragile peace through attrition rather than negotiation, their experience of conflict resolution is limited to one mechanism only, war. That fact alone gives sufficient cause for alarm that those in the region with desperate objectives might pursue them along the only course that they know, namely, the barrel of a readily available gun. Similarly, demobilized soldiers may have been well trained for careers in crime and violence; the only difference between wartime atrocities and criminal atrocities may be the presence of official sanction. In fact, anyone with enough greed or anger in southern Africa who has a gun is a potential hazard. Unremitting crime, violence, and armed conflict are the most significant direct consequences of small-arms proliferation. Policymakers (as opposed to policy implementers, who know the connection firsthand) and other interest groups, must understand this direct link if they hope to deal with the problem successfully.

Controlling Small Arms

As with nuclear weapons, it is not the mere existence of small arms that creates problems, but their use and misuse. The success or failure of controls can be judged only by how well they manage to limit the actual and potential consequences outlined earlier. There is no quick and easy remedy. For the purposes of this chapter, the discussion of controls focuses on South Africa primarily within the regional context of cross-border trafficking, rather than on specific domestic controls either in South Africa or elsewhere in the region.

Effective policies must start with the premise that small-arms-control measures are crucial to the establishment of a stable developing region, and, more crucially, that they require a re-evaluation of current thinking. If the long-term goal for southern Africa is regional integration, economic development, security, and stability, what are the short- and medium-term goals? In the medium term, South Africa must provide the engine for growth and development in the region. In the short term, South Africa must seek to assist other southern African states to lay the tracks for this engine, as well as ensure that the engine itself is in good working order. But, as outlined earlier, South Africa's neighbors must do a better job than they have. Measures should be taken to protect South Africa's efforts, not just for South Africa's sake, but for the sake of the entire region's prospects. If South Africa fails to bring small-arms proliferation under control, eventually it may be unable to control the consequences, namely, crime, violence, and armed conflict, which will have grave consequences for other pressing concerns in the region.

The institutions of state beyond South Africa's borders—particularly military, police, and customs—are far weaker than those inside the country. Widespread corruption, lack of accountability on the part of officials, and limited manpower, training, and operational resources are just some of the factors that compromise effective legal, policing, or border controls. Most states of the region have far more urgent domestic priorities than the allocation of resources for a problem that may begin in their territory but ends up on South African soil. Although this might be a cynical short-term view, it should not be forgotten in the formulation of both security and foreign-policy goals. The long-term solution to weapons trafficking may lie in better economic and educational opportunities, as well as in more stable political institutions that allow for full democratic participation, which might well result in integrated policing and the maximization of regional resources. But what can South Africa do in the meantime, given that the region is far from achieving its long-term goals, or even its capacity for small arms control?

Since the capacity of South African state institutions is far greater than that of its neighbors, South Africa could play a role in training and supporting regional security measures. If southern African states lack the political will, resources, or capacity to implement effective regional border controls, South Africa, as the recipient of small-arms flows, may have to take unilateral security measures that do not conform with the proposed "open borders" policy of the South African Development Community (SADC).

In the long term, illegal weapons must be removed from the hands of the communities to prevent their criminal use and their trafficking to neighboring states. Creative strategies have to be devised; policing and enforcement measures alone will not suffice. In the short term,

South Africa could revert to boosting its first line of defense—border controls—though these are obviously not the ultimate solution. Border controls should be the workhorse that limits and harasses small-arms trafficking to buy time for internal policing or incentive-based recovery of weapons. In the regional environment of small-arms proliferation, failure to curb the inflow of small arms threatens to stretch domestic policing beyond its capacity to recover lost ground. The costs of improved border controls may help to offset the spiraling costs of domestic policing, crime, and loss of investment. But, as a complete solution, reliance on more border controls would drain the country's resources and deliver few guarantees. In the short term, however, border controls must and can be made more effective by ensuring that the requirements of inspection be met.

There are four immediately identifiable obstacles to achieving this goal: First, the 1996 Defense Review debate (about the future role and resources of the SANDF) has centered on identifying and rating South Africa's security threats on a socioeconomic and a military level, but not enough attention has gone to the role of small arms. In fact, the Ministry of Defense has indicated that it plans to withdraw entirely from the role of border policing and from operational support of the SAPS within three to five years. Given the limitations on the SAPS' capacity to deal effectively with both internal crime and border policing, such a move by the SANDF is likely to increase the illicit traffic. The question is, should the SANDF not be permanently assigned to border control? There is an urgent need to define clearly the responsibilities of both the SAPS and the SANDF in this area; duplication of scarce resources and failure to fulfill respective responsibilities is contributing to South Africa's decreasing ability to safeguard its borders.

Second, the increase in regional container traffic necessitates better inspection equipment at points of entry and tighter legislation to regulate the loading and transportation of container goods. At present, many containers and cargo trucks cross the region's borders without inspection because off-loading equipment is not available. The responsibility lies with the state institutions of the region to provide effective border control through collective regional cooperation and coordination, such as standardization of loading and carrier regulations and intelligence gathering.

Third, neighboring states need formal agreements to provide for the repatriation and extradition of those who are involved in illegal activities and to affix appropriate penalties. Otherwise, the sense of impunity with which criminals conduct illegal activities will continue.

Fourth, border control is a politically sensitive issue. Calls for improvement run counter to the spirit of regional economic integration. But the choice need not be a zero-sum equation. If South Africa is to be the region's goose that lays the golden eggs, the goose has to be preserved for the eggs to have a safe place to hatch. Southern Africa as a whole must recognize that each state has the primary responsibility of building and maintaining its institutions before it embarks on regional efforts. What the region needs is a plan that begins with curbing weapons trafficking and follows with the recovery of weapons within each state through regional resource sharing and capacity building. Only then will the region be able to take productive steps toward integration and open borders. Failure on the part of South Africa's neighbors to effect adequate measures will result only in relegating any serious moves toward integration to the back burner.

The objectives of consolidating democracy, promoting and sustaining economic development, and diminishing crime in South Africa will remain unrealized unless the issue of small-arms proliferation is recognized as a fundamental threat to them. This warning applies as much to the southern African region as elsewhere in the post–Cold War world. For the present, however, if South Africa's national interests are to be served, it may have to abandon the soft policy of border control that it currently favors in the interests of fostering regional relationships; it may no longer be able to accommodate its neighbors at the expense of its own population.

Notes to Chapter 4

1. For a more detailed study of small-arms proliferation and control in southern Africa, see Oosthuysen, *Small Arms Proliferation and Control in Southern Africa* (Johannesburg, 1996).

2. Small arms are those weapons that can be carried on the person without the need for a mechanized or other platform: rifles, revolvers, pistols, shotguns, and explosives.

3. Not even a senior FRELIMO official could say whether any legislation

governing the licensing of firearms existed. It does, but it is definitely not public knowledge. Personal Interview with FRELIMO official, Maputo, November 20, 1995.

4. United Nations Institute for Disarmament Research (UNIDIR), *Managing Arms in Peace Processes: Mozambique* (Geneva, 1996).

5. Personal interview with SANDF officer, Nelspruit, September 14, 1995.

6. Reuters, SADA report, *Citizen* (Johannesburg), 9 July 1996.

7. Personal interview with senior Botswana police official, Gaborone, January 30, 1996.

8. *Ibid.*

9. Personal interview with senior NAMPOL officials, Windhoek, February 1, 1996.

10. *Ibid.*

11. Personal interview with senior Zimbabwe Defense Force official, Harare, May 28, 1996.

12. Personal interview with Zambian Ministry of Defense officials, Lusaka, May 30, 1996.

13. SAPS, *Firearms in South Africa: An Escalating Problem* (Pretoria, 1995).

14. Personal interview with senior PF officials, Luanda, February 7, 1996.

15. Personal interview with NDF officials, Windhoek, February 2, 1996.

16. Personal nterview with foreign Windhoek-based diplomat, February 1, 1996.

17. Personal interview with Zambian Ministry of Defense official, Lusaka, May 30, 1996.

18. Personal interview with KNP official, Skukuza, September 15, 1995.

19. SANDF Annual Report, *The National Defense Force in Transition* (Pretoria, 1994/95).

20. Personal interview with senior Botswana Police official, Gaborone, January 30, 1996.

21. Personal interview with senior Zambian Police official, Lusaka, May 31, 1996.

5

Jacklyn Cock

The Legacy of War

The Proliferation of Light Weapons in Southern Africa

SOUTH AFRICA has been described as "the most important experiment in democracy since the end of the Second World War." The level of violent crime linked to the proliferation of light weapons, however, threatens the consolidation of this democracy. In Mozambique, northern Namibia and Angola the proliferation of light weapons—especially anti-personnel land mines, threatens to subvert social and economic reconstruction.[1]

The fulcrum around which this chapter turns is the assertion that the problem of light-weapon proliferation requires a holistic approach. Discussions framed in narrow legal or technical terms are analytically deficient; the issue encompasses social relationships, values, beliefs, practices, and identities. The demand for light weapons is socially constructed; the supply is socially organized. Ultimately the proliferation problem in the

The author wishes to thank the following individuals for information: Eddie Koch—journalist, Johannesburg; Jenni Irish—independent Monitor of political violence, Durban; Dennis Jett—diplomat, Maputo, Mozambique; Vernon Joynt—Divisional Manager, Mechem, a division of DENEL, Johannesburg; Adel Kirsten—coordinator of Gun-Free South Africa, Johannesburg; Janine Rauch—SAP Policy Unit, Johannesburg; Karen Hansen—anthropologist, United States; Peter Bachelor—defense economist, University of Capetown;

region requires a social solution: a demilitarization movement that includes the demand for a ban on the production, stockpiling, export, and use of land mines and on private gun ownership.

The issue of light weapons is framed by a broader set of concerns relating to changes in the nature of armed conflict in the post–Cold War world. War is now less likely to be waged by states using major weapon systems than by combatants using light weapons within individual states. Almost all the wars in the world during the 1990s were civil wars, and virtually all of the violent conflict currently taking place involves violence between internal groups, often ethnically defined, rather than states. Klare cites one estimate that "only four of the eighty two armed conflicts recorded in 1989-1992 were of a classic interstate character, while all of the remainder entailed some degree of internal warfare, usually along ethnic and religious lines." Increased intergroup violence is a major characteristic of the contemporary world, particularly in Bosnia, Burundi, Croatia, Kashmir, Nagorno-Karabakh, Georgia, Rwanda, Sri Lanka, Somalia, Sudan, Yemen, Zaire, and the Kurdish areas of Iraq and Turkey.[2]

Post–Cold War changes in the nature of armed conflict have not only led to shifts in the global flow of weapons but to dramatic changes in the social organization of violence. In intrastate conflicts involving light weapons, "it is members of the opposing group who are seen as the enemy, not the armed forces of a hostile state." The boundaries of these opposing group identities are socially constructed and defined. Whether in a global or regional context, the issue of light weaponry is

Laurie Nathan—Ministry of Defense adviser and Director of the Center for Conflict Resolution, University of Capetown; Krish Naidoo—ARMSCOR, Pretoria; Penny McKenzie—researcher and Ceasefire organizer; Johan van Dyk—ARMSCOR, Pretoria; Capt. George Botha—South African Police, Pretoria; Mike Murphry, International Union for the Conservation of Nature, Harare, Zimbabwe; Col. Piet Lategan, Endangered Species Unit of the SAP, Pretoria; Louis Liebenberg—conservationist, Johannesburg; Jonathan Rosenthal—journalist, Johannesburg; Roland Hunter—economist, Johannesburg; Col. Rocklyn Mark (Rocky) Williams, SANDF, Pretoria; Gavin Cawthra, University of the Witwatersrand, Johannesburg; Lt. Col. Lenford Dlamini, Swaziland.

The author also wishes to thank the following for critical comments: Alison Bernstein, Cawthra, Greg Mills, Robert Rotberg, Penny McKenzie, Peter Bachelor, Nathan, and Williams.

connected with the clash between diverse social interests, values, group loyalties, institutions, practices, and cultural meanings.[3]

The issue is also relevant to current debates about the transition from authoritarian rule to democracy and the restructuring of the military. Huntington points out that nearly all of the forty countries that have gone from authoritarian to democratic rule during the past twenty years have seen dramatic reductions in the size and scope of their military forces. "By and large, the new democracies have been reasonably successful in establishing civilian control, in orienting their militaries towards professionalism, in reducing military power, in constructing new military roles and in establishing patterns of civil–military relationships that resemble those in established democracies."[4]

These processes are evident in South Africa with the establishment of the defense secretariat, a powerful parliamentary committee on defense, reductions in defense spending, and a downsizing of the full-time South African National Defense Force (SANDF) from 130,000 to 70,000 and of the part-time units from 600,000 to about 200,000. However one of the consequences of this public demilitarization has been a privatized militarization. Light-weapon proliferation is an indicator of both a privatized militarization and a level of social disintegration. Similarly, an increasing emphasis on arms exports in South Africa is partly a response to the reduction in domestic defense procurement. Paradoxically, state demilitarization is contributing to global militarization. Demilitarization needs to go beyond a restructuring of state institutions to involve a recasting of social relations in a much broader project of transformation.

This chapter is divided into four parts. The first deals with demand factors, the second with past sources of supply, the third with contemporary sources, and the final part with possible solutions. The intention is to map the cultural meanings and social practices in southern Africa that are implicated in the use of light weapons. On the demand side, such categories include political groupings, criminal networks, hunters, poachers, mercenaries, Self Defense Units (SDUs), security forces, citizens, and private security firms. Weaponry is often the basis of a militarized identity with profound social ramifications.

The supply of light weapons through the illegal arms trade is associated with many other social and economic activities that tend to be underplayed in technical accounts—for example, trade in ivory, teak, rhino horn, diamonds, drugs, and even secondhand clothing. Because the indigenous arms industry is built on linkages with most of South Africa's major manufacturing companies, the supplies of light weaponry are deeply embedded in the South African social and economic order. In fact, the state is contributing to the erosion of its own authority through its support for the import and manufacture of light weapons, and through the leakage of weaponry from the security agencies and state armories.

In the southern African context, the problem of light-weapon proliferation is grounded in four social processes concerning violence. The first social process is the region's tendency toward armed conflict during the past thirty years, which has been followed by ineffective disarmament and demobilization. The second related social process is broader and more encompassing—the militarization from 1976 to 1990, as the apartheid state mobilized resources for war on the political, economic, and ideological fronts. A powerful indigenous arms industry and a widespread ideology of militarism that views violence as a legitimate solution to conflict are among its legacies.[5]

Since the 1980s, South Africa has evinced two other social processes implicated in the proliferation of light weaponry: One is what Klare has termed the "privatization of security." Increasing numbers of citizens have lost confidence in the capacity of the state to protect them, turning to gun ownership and private security arrangements instead. This trend leads to the fourth social process tied to the proliferation of light weaponry, namely, the commercialization of violence. Many South African citizens have come to rely on criminal violence for their livelihood. Hence, light weapons are a means of subsistence as well as profit. Small arms are also currency in black market transactions throughout the region. Another aspect of this commercialization of violence is the rise of South Africa's arms exports through the state's arms procurement agency, ARMSCOR.[6]

The proliferation of light weapons in southern Africa both reflects and reinforces social and international tensions and cleavages. It feeds a culture of fear and insecurity alongside a culture of brutality. The region is characterized by fragile democracies and unstable economies. Wars of liberation, as well as post-independence armed conflicts, have created a precarious environment. The election of a democratic government in South Africa may serve to erode the political unity of the former Front Line States, fostering understandable concern that South Africa, which has the most powerful, diversified, and industrialized economy in sub-Saharan Africa, could well dominate the region.

Regional cooperation is essential to achieve sustainable development and overcome the legacy of the past. In the current absence of any serious military threat, the region needs to cultivate a broader conception of "national security"—emphasizing social, economic, and ecological factors—in order to address the problems created by poverty, war, drought, disease, and social dislocation. The current proliferation of light weapons is a major threat to both citizens and states.

The main source of supply for weaponry is leakage from the various armed formations involved in past conflicts in the area. Many of these weapons are now returning to South Africa in a "boomerang effect." However, any attempt to deal with the problem must be cognizant of the factors that create a demand for light weapons.

Social Demand for Light Weapons

The demand for light weaponry can be understood only in the context of general cultural meanings, social practices, and economic motivations among the various social categories. Many (though by no means all) of those who possess such weapons rely on them for subsistence. In some cases, weaponry is a requirement of their formal occupational identity; in others, it is a reflection of how light weapons have become a form of currency throughout the region. In any event, the attachment will be difficult to dislodge.

Many young South Africans who own guns, regardless of their culture, define themselves as soldiers fighting a "war," often understanding weaponry as emblematic of manliness. They have had ample encouragement. Eugene TerreBlanche, the Afrikaner resistance leader, was once heard to say, "Buy weapons, collect weapons, and clean your weapons. The Boer and his gun are inseparable," and the king of the Zulus once addressed a rally with the protest, "The call to ban the bearing of weapons is an insult to my manhood. It is an insult to the manhood of every Zulu man."

The words of one South African Defense Force (SADF) conscript illustrate the SADF's influence on white South African men: "This is my rifle; this is my gun. This is for fighting; this is for fun." A number of SADF conscripts have emphasized that the core of military training was to inculcate aggression and equate it with masculinity, thereby encouraging insensitivity, aggressiveness, competitiveness, violence, and the censure of emotional expression. Thousands of white South African youths were exposed to these messages, which were frequently harnessed to an ethno-nationalism.[7]

For many South Africans, ethnic identities, antagonistically defined, are the strongest source of social cohesion. As Forrest has written of the Zulu emphasis on cultural weapons (rawhide shields, clubs, and spears), "Support for the carrying of weapons is often seen as a simple call to arms, but it is more than this. . . . [I]t is a deliberate attempt to mobilize politically around symbols of nationhood."[8]

This politicized ethnicity often goes hand in hand with dehumanization of the "enemy," contributing to an ideology of militarism that views violence as a legitimate solution to conflict, and a means to both obtain and defend power. This militaristic culture also finds expression in such leisure pursuits as hunting, war games, toy guns, and violent films, none of which is insignificant in light of Mann's definition of militarism as "a set of attitudes and social practices which regards war and the preparation for war as a normal and desirable social activity."[9]

Light weapons have also become important symbols of liberation. Whereas, as Ellis has argued, the machine gun was a crucial means of colonial conquest and European domination, the AK "is more than a weapon; it has become a symbol. The Maxim [gun] represented the power of the imperial armies, while the AK has become an icon for many of the anti-establishment insurgent, freedom fighter, and terrorist organizations that exist today.[10]

POLITICIZED ETHNIC GROUPS. There are two distinct groups within South Africa seeking greater political power, autonomy, and economic resources—the white right, which boasts an Afrikaner identity, and the Inkatha Freedom Party (IFP), which maintains a Zulu identity.

Inkatha has always pushed for the maximum federal devolution of power to KwaZulu/Natal; its proposals for a new provincial constitution include a provincial army and envisage virtually an independent state. Violent conflict between IFP supporters and the African National

Congress (ANC) peaked during the 1990-1994 period but still continues. The weapons involved are mainly AK-47s, but include G-3 assault rifles, R-5, R-4, and R-1 rifles.

Elements within the white right are demanding secession and territory for an independent Afrikaner homeland or "volkstaat." Between 1990 and 1994, white right-wing organizations began mobilizing armed commandos countrywide. TerreBlanche, the leader of the Afrikaner Resistance Movement, said on many occasions that his organization was getting Afrikaners combat-ready for the day when the ruling National Party handed over power to the ANC. Robert van Tonder, another Afrikaner leader, declared, "The Boer Volk would start shooting on the day the Volk's right to decision making for itself was removed."[11]

White right-wing groups obtained considerable quantities of light weapons in thefts from various military bases and state armories, largely between 1990 and 1994. They used some of the weaponry for political violence prior to the April 1994 elections. In June 1995, a right winger arrested as a suspect in the murder of a progressive church leader was linked to the discovery of an arms cache in a cave near Groblersdal the year before. Most of these weapons had been stolen from the Swartkops Airforce Base. This suspect was also linked to a makeshift explosives factory discovered on a farm near Bronkhorstspruit earlier in 1995. Bombings linked to the right wing occurred in 1996, but no one had been charged at the time of this writing.[12]

According to a number of informants, there are covert links between these white right-wing groups and elements of the IFP. One informant maintained that the predominant weapon in Natal until recently was the "kwasha"—a home-made gun constructed from metal tubing, which fires conventional ammunition. "From 1994 the pattern started to change . . . . IFP and ANC supporters now have serious fire power . . . . IFP supporters own G-3s, R-4s, as well as AKs." These new weapons obviously contribute to the current high levels of violent conflict in KwaZulu/Natal.

CRIMINALS. Political violence in South Africa has declined dramatically since 1994; the monthly average of deaths from political violence had dropped from 244 to 144. However, this decline has been accompanied by an increase in criminal violence involving light weapons. For many, this criminal activity is a means of survival, resulting in what we earlier termed the commercialization of violence. Recent economic strains in South Africa have deepened the vulnerability of marginalized social groups who have come to depend on banditry and criminal violence for a livelihood. Yet, the country also shows traces of an anomie, or normlessness, that is characteristic of a society in transition; the repressive controls of the apartheid system have not been replaced by legitimate forms of social control and cohesion.[13]

Violent, recorded crime in South Africa, such as murder, armed robbery, car hijacking, and sexual assault, has increased seriously since the political transition began in 1990. The World Health Organization points out that South Africa's murder rate of 53.5 murders for every 100,000 people is more than five times that of the United States.

According to a police spokesman, "The criminal element in this country is in possession of illegal firearms and their purpose is to stay in possession." In 1994, police confiscated 386 AK-47 rifles and 120 handmade firearms, 1,650 revolvers and pistols, 547 explosives, and 67,301 rounds of ammunition, and they arrested 1,214 suspects.[14]

In 1994, 7,000 people were murdered with firearms in South Africa—40 percent of the total murders committed—and 17,700 murders were attempted with firearms—representing an increase of almost 50 percent since 1991. In 1995, firearms were used in 79 percent of all robberies, 16 percent more than in 1994. As of 1996, South Africa has licensed 4.1 million firearms; private individuals have reported 17,600 of them lost or stolen. Reliable information concerning the numbers lost or stolen from the security forces is not available.[15]

The extent of violent crime is best illustrated by the closing of several satellite police stations in the Johannesburg area on account of their vulnerability to gang attacks. In June 1995, for example, four bandits surrounded a satellite police station in Alexandra township, disarmed a policeman, and shot him before making off with "five weapons—an R1, an R5 and three service pistols."[16]

The AK-47 is the symbol of criminal violence, but "less than three percent of all murders in 1992 were perpetrated with AK-47's." In 1994, only 7.63 percent, or 458, of the 15,999 murder cases reported involved automatic weapons—a category that includes R-1 rifles and submachine guns, as well as AK-47s. This statistic would suggest that the South African media's obsession with AK-47s is an ideological hangover from the demonization of ANC guerrillas that was widespread during the apartheid era.[17]

As Cochrane wrote, "About two-thirds of the firearms seized by the South African Police Service are of non-Eastern block origin, suggesting that the great majority of crimes committed with firearms are committed with firearms of domestic origin. These are either legally owned weapons used for an illicit purpose, or weapons that are stolen from their legal owners. Clearly, legally owned weapons are a large part of the problem." Police claimed that in 1990, a total of 10,305 firearms were stolen—3,088 from houses and 1,042 from vehicles. In 1992, 4,034 thefts of firearms were reported. In 1993, the number was 4,758—an increase of 18 percent. A total of 2,370 legally owned and licensed guns was stolen in Gauteng alone in 1994. That same year, police confiscated 6,614 illegal firearms in KwaZulu/Natal and 2,309 in Gauteng.[18]

Reports link former Mozambican soldiers, as well as their weaponry, to violence. They were reputedly hired, for example, to eliminate rivals in South Africa's taxi industry feud. According to Maj. Pieter Swanepoel, "We already know that former Mozambican soldiers have a thorough knowledge of terror weapons such as AK-47's, as well as Makarov and Tokarev pistols. The last killings in the province were carried out by skilled assassins using these weapons, as well as R4 and R5 rifles."[19]

As Shaw pointed out, the availability of weapons "erodes one of the key requisites of democratic transitions, the State's ability to monopolize the instruments of coercion." Criminal violence associated with the proliferation of light weaponry threatens to subvert South Africa's consolidation of democracy. Since many people in South Africa feel that the central authority is not strong enough to protect them, more and more black and white citizens have come to rely on their own firearms. Affluent citizens have the option of engaging security firms that advertise "Immediate Armed Response." The social equivalent of this "privatization of security" in impoverished black communities is the establishment of SDUs.[20]

SELF-DEFENSE UNITS. SDUs were established by the ANC as a response to the violence of the apartheid state. Both members of Umkhonto we Sizwe (MK)—the armed wing of the ANC—and SDU members tended to view themselves as soldiers fighting a war against the apartheid regime and its supporters. SDUs continue to exist in diverse fragmented forms, defining themselves as "defenders of the community." Until recently, difficulties in the licensing procedures forced black citizens to obtain firearms through the illegal arms market. At first, SDUs were armed with knobkieries, spears, and home-made weapons, but more recently they have been able to get a variety of firearms, including AK-47s and R-4 rifles. Rosenthal found that SDUs were not armed by MK, but by gunrunners with commercial rather than political interests.[21]

POACHERS. Poaching, which is involved in both the supply and demand ends of the illegal arms trade, is getting worse in southern Africa. According to two informants, poached ivory and rhino horn are frequently exchanged for weaponry, and according to one source from the International Union for the Conservation of Nature in Zimbabwe, "there has been over the last fifteen years a major impact on wildlife populations in the southern African region as a result of the proliferation of light automatic weapons." Allegedly, most of the poachers in Zimbabwe and Mozambique are ex-combatants. In South Africa the head of the SAP's Endangered Species Unit maintained that in 1995, all of the arrested poachers had been in the possession of AK-47s, "apart from one case in possession of an R-4 rifle stolen from the military base in the Kruger National Park."

The overlap between different social categories is evident in the numerous reports that the SADF was involved in poaching. An investigation by the United States concluded that members of the SADF in Angola and Namibia were "actively engaged in killing and smuggling of wildlife species—including rhinos and elephants—for personal gain and profit." The SADF was also poaching springbok, elephant, and black rhinoceros in Namibia on such a large scale that the populations of each species fell dramatically. Furthermore, payment to the SADF for its support to RENAMO in Mozambique came in the form of ivory, and "tens of thousands of elephants were slaughtered by UNITA forces in southern Angola to pay for military assistance provided by the SADF." Evidence submitted to the Kumleben Commission of Inquiry established that the SADF was involved in illicit ivory and rhino-horn poaching in Angola and Namibia until at least 1986.[22]

HUNTERS. The culture of brutality in which the SADF participated was not confined to poaching and hunting animals; an internal investigation by the SADF in 1991 discovered that a "group of officers" shot twelve Bushmen in Angola "when they failed to find game on a hunt near their base."[23]

Hunters create a significant demand for light weapons. Big game hunting is a growth industry in South Africa. "Tourists from America, Germany, France and Spain are drawn to the South African farms by the low value of the rand, by the selection of 31 species of big game trophies and . . . by the fact that (unlike in the rest of Africa where hunting is seasonal), hunting takes place all year round." Hunting is extremely profitable but (with the exception of the Campfire program in Zimbabwe) mainly benefits the white safari operators who dominate the industry.[24]

MERCENARIES. According to one source in South Africa, several highly organized mercenary operations are engaged in extensive subcontracting with smaller companies that deal in drugs, car thefts, ivory, rhino horn, and illicit diamond buying. At least two large private firms of mercenaries operate out of South Africa—Security Options and Executive Outcomes (EO).

PRIVATE SECURITY FIRMS. The number of private security firms providing armed guards to companies and residences has multiplied in recent years. Security is the fastest growing industry in South Africa after tourism, and the number of private security guards—estimated at 180,000—now outstrips the size of the police force. In 1994, 130,000 registered security guards were employed in 2,700 companies in South Africa, c. 40,000 of which were armed. Johannesburg alone has 120 security companies. Some of these companies operate throughout the southern African region. For example, Gray Security Services, the second-largest security company in South Africa, also has offices in Lesotho and Namibia.[25]

LICENSED FIREARM HOLDERS. White South Africans are rated among the most heavily armed groups in the world; 1.8 million of them own 3.8 million licensed firearms. Firearm sales began to rise in 1976, mirroring increasing black resistance to apartheid. In 1985, authorities received 135,382 applications for firearm licenses; in 1993, the number of applications jumped to 256,989, of which 248,976 licenses were successful.[26]

Since the transition to democracy started, many whites have cited security as their reason for owning a firearm, and they have been able to obtain licenses far more easily than blacks have. During the apartheid era, it was customary to demand that blacks, Coloureds, and Indians be trained before they were granted a firearm license. Whites were not required to undergo such training. Nonetheless, there is apparently a massive amount of forgery in firearm licenses.[27]

Many young white South African men subscribe to a "gun culture" and embrace such militaristic social practices as participating in war games, enrolling in rifle clubs, frequenting shooting ranges, and reading gun magazines. Most licensed firearm owners acquire their weapons from dealers who are supplied both by local manufacturers and importers. In 1993, 640 licenses to deal in arms and ammunition were issued. According to one source, handguns often come from Brazil, Spain, the United States, Germany, and Israel, because they are both cheaper and better than the locally manufactured ones. Evidently, some dealers also take part in the illegal arms trade. For example, in 1993, the owner of an arms and ammunition shop in Witbank was found to be in illegal possession of merchandise worth more than R100,000.[28]

THE SECURITY FORCES. The largest category of people in the region with light weapons are the security forces. The new Angolan army will number 70,000, the Namibian National Defense force numbers 7,000, the Mozambican army 10,000 (considerably less than the 30,000 planned), and Zimbabwe is reducing force levels from 51,000 to 40,000. The integration process that created the new South African National Defense Force (SANDF) resulted in hugely inflated force levels of 130,000 before "rationalization" and demobilization began. This organization inherited the weaponry of the SADF—the most powerful army in sub-Saharan Africa. Considerable amounts of weaponry were issued to security force personnel in KwaZulu/Natal, the Transkei, and Lebowa before the 1994 elections. The KwaZulu police also issued 3,000 G-3 rifles to such civilians as "headmen and self-protection units." The government is attempting to repossess these arms. However, the IFP has said that it would resist moves by the central government to strip traditional chiefs of such KwaZulu-issued firearms as shotguns and G-3s.[29]

Arms were also issued to commando units of the SADF's Area Defense System in rural areas. According to Col. Rocky Williams of the SANDF, weapons control was poor, and "it is doubtful whether the SANDF can provide an audit of the weapons it has provided the commandos in the past twenty years." On the assumption that each security-force member received seven weapons, Mills estimated that the South African security forces could account for 4.9 million small arms (including government issue to the police and the army, as well as confiscated arms), the Angolan army 1.1 million, the Zimbabwe army 600,000, and the Mozambican army 700,000, "making a total for the security forces of the region of around 8.7 million."[30]

Demand from the social organizations and individuals listed above means that there is a resilient market in both legal and illegal arms. Arms smugglers operate in secrecy but with relative ease. The market embodies an expansive social network and incorporates diverse social groups. Money is not the only means of exchange; ivory, rhino horn, diamonds, drugs, and even secondhand clothing can be traded for weapons. Light weaponry is a widespread source of currency in the region. Much of the available supply dates back to the period of armed conflict.

Past Suppliers of Light Weapons

Original Suppliers

Southern Africa has had three main sources of light weaponry for armed conflict since 1975. The former Warsaw Pact countries, as well as Cuba and China, supplied arms to the Popular Movement for the Liberation of Angola (MPLA), the People's Liberation Army of Namibia (PLAN), MK in South Africa, the Zimbabwe People's Revolutionary Army (ZIPRA), and the Front for the Liberation of Mozambique (FRELIMO)—rifles, carbines, AK-47s, land mines, limpet mines, mortars, hand grenades, pistols, and ammunition. In Williams' words, "Control over this material was uneven."[31]

Western countries, including the United States, West Germany, France, Great Britain, and Israel, provided the apartheid state with military hardware, and various Western arms manufacturers sent clandestine military aid to South Africa in defiance of the UN arms embargoes. For example, during the 1970s, two U.S. gun manufacturers shipped thousands of firearms and millions of rounds of ammunition to South Africa through front companies. Both apartheid South Africa and the United States were major sources of weaponry in Angola.[32]

From 1976 to 1990, the ideology of "total onslaught" provided the underpinning for the militarization of South African society, when the apartheid state mobilized resources for war on political, ideological, and economic levels. The SADF, which spearheaded this process, was at the center of an undeclared war of destabilization that was directed first against neighboring states—creating what has been described as a "holocaust"—and later against the ANC inside South Africa.[33]

As part of this process, the apartheid state supplied weapons to the SADF, SAP, and various "homeland" armies and surrogate forces inside the country, as well as to the National Union for the Total Independence of Angola (UNITA), the Mozambique National Resistance (RENAMO), and other rebel movements in the southern African region, via the former SADF Directorate of Special Tasks (operating under Military Intelligence). According to Roland Hunter's court evidence, at least during 1982/83, the apartheid state had four projects underway—Op Disa (support of UNITA in Angola), Op Drama (support of Zimbabwe dissidents), Op Latsa (support of the Lesotho Liberation Army), and Op Mila (support of Mozambican RENAMO dissidents).[34]

Weapons for these projects were procured through the South African arms procurement agency (ARMSCOR) or were captured by the SADF during their direct military action in Angola and Namibia. Many of these arms had Soviet and Eastern bloc origins, including AK-47s, LMGs, RPG-7s, hand grenades, mortar bombs, and mines. Almost 40,000 AK-47s were purchased from Poland, Romania, Bulgaria, Yugoslavia, Hungary, and China between 1976 and 1986, specifically for UNITA. AK-47s from Hungary and Bulgaria obtained through ARMSCOR were also supplied to RENAMO. Overall, the South African government amassed a large stockpile of captured light weapons.[35]

One of the most deadly light weapons produced and supplied by the SADF was the anti-personnel landmine. An estimated 10 to 20 million land mines currently lie undetected in Angola, Mozambique, Zimbabwe, and Namibia—the remains of the apartheid state's destabilization strategy. The SADF delivered anti-personnel land mines as well as other weapons, ammunition, propaganda literature, and such commodities as maize seed, sugar, and tobacco to RENAMO. According to an informant who was involved in Op Mila, the material supplied did not vary much from month to month. In August 1983, 500 AK rifles, as well as various other weapons and large quantities of ammunition, were shipped as well. Many reports identify the payment for this South African assistance as ivory and rhino horn.[36]

After 1990, the destabilization strategy of the apartheid regime was turned inward to weaken the ANC and block the democratization process. A crucial element in this strategy was the training and arming of a surrogate force of Inkatha vigilantes who operated largely under the direction and control of what came to be known as a "third force," which was made up of elements from the army and police. Evidence reveals that it organized much of the township violence between 1990 and 1994.

Deaths from violent conflict involving light weapons between supporters of the ANC and the IFP peaked between 1990 and 1993 when almost 10,000 people were killed. The apartheid regime was not the only source of weaponry. Several informants maintained that IFP members had been involved in buying arms directly from RENAMO. In 1991, an extensive and sophisticated arms network supplying members of Inkatha in the Johannesburg area with AK-47s, shotguns, Makarov pistols, and scorpion submachine guns was exposed. Ex-Mozambican soldiers were cited as the source of these weapons, and an Inkatha supporter, originally from Natal, with strong links to hostel residents coordinated their distribution.[37]

Hostels housing mainly Zulu, Inkatha-supporting migrants from Natal were crucial participants in the various forms of political violence on the Rand, including terrorist attacks on train and taxi commuters, and expulsion of non-Zulu migrants from the hostels. The hostels were used as launching pads to attack surrounding township residents and ANC supporters. These antagonisms were rooted in the social construction of different political, ethnic, and class identities.

Many migrant workers defined this "low-intensity conflict" as a war, and many hostels on the Rand became armories. In a recent study of the connection between hostels and political violence on the Rand, all thirty-one of the residents of Meadowlands hostel who were interviewed mentioned one or more of the following weapons as frequently used by hostel residents against township inhabitants: AK-47s, R-5, R-4, and R-1 rifles, pistols, shotguns, knives, axes, spears, knobkierries, sharpened iron poles, stocks, tomahawks, pangas, and machetes. In the same study, one-third of the residents interviewed from Merafe hostel maintained that many of the weapons used in the political violence were manufactured in the hostel by inmates themselves. These handmade guns fired such objects as nails, as well as conventional ammunition. Hostels were both armories and factories.[38]

Ineffective Disarmament in Post-Conflict Peace Building

Although the apartheid regime, the United States, the Eastern bloc countries, China, and Cuba were the major sources for light weapons throughout the region during the period of armed conflict, the lack of effective disarmament after these conflicts were settled resulted in much of the current proliferation of weaponry. The collection, audit, control, and disposal of weapons was an important feature in most of the comprehensive peace settlements in the region, but not even heavy UN involvement could guarantee success.

New national defense forces created in Mozambique, Namibia, Zimbabwe, and South Africa theoretically represented attempts to integrate previously antagonistic guerilla and conventional armed formations and round up the weapons and ammunition of rival armies. The situation in South Africa was particularly complicated. Seven different armed formations had to be combined to create a single, legitimate, and representative defense force—the most significant of the seven being the MK, the SADF, and the four homeland armies. The process was supposed to entail full disclosure of arms caches established in South Africa by MK. However, a leaking of these weapons, as well as those from homeland military arsenals, since 1990, has undoubtedly contributed to criminal activity. MK arms caches were not cleared by the new defense force until early 1995 because they served, among other things, as insurance against the failure of peace negotiations and as a material base for future political bargaining.

Several countries in southern Africa maintained only weak control over the former guerrilla armies and their weaponry in the run-up to the integration process. "Many armories and caches established prior to independence were not claimed during the post-election period and these either lay dormant (and were incrementally reclaimed for various uses) or 'leaked' into civil society for use in a range of criminal and political activities." In Mozambique, for example, a number of informants reported that the integration and demobilization process involved substantial leakage of weaponry. Hidden arms caches were of major concern to the Ceasefire Commission as Mozambique prepared for national elections. According to one source, many weapons were stored in the assembly areas and were not secure. A total of 186,000 of them, collected by the UN, were registered and handed over to the Mozambican government. The serial numbers of these weapons were supplied to the South African government. However, "many weapons were kept in unguarded buildings," with no independent verification of the storage. Sources have pointed out that the UN later located 200 undeclared arms caches and that 186,000 weapons were considerably more than the 10,000 or so required by the new national defense force. The lack of effective disarmament in the aftermath of negotiated conclusions to long-standing armed conflicts has been a major problem in the region generally.[39]

Inadequate Control over New Armed Formations

The problem of light-weapon proliferation is sometimes due to inadequate control over the armed forces. Only South Africa, Namibia, Botswana, and Zimbabwe possess well-organized, cohesive armies.

Leakages from various official armories not only occurred during the demobilization process, but continued after the formation of new national armies. The new Mozambican army is not strong or cohesive.

Low military salaries, inadequate discipline, low levels of morale, and a ready market for the weapons in South Africa has led to senior members of the Mozambican armed forces being implicated in illegal arms deals . . . . [T]he Mozambican armed forces have in the past, according to one source, "leaked like sieves." South African members of the joint task force . . . estimate that the rate of recovery of weapons is fractional and isolate Mozambique as the major and unaudited ongoing source of arms transactions in the region.

As one source put it, the new Mozambican army is deeply corrupt. "Every commodity the Mozambican army gets its hands on will eventually be for sale."[40]

The Failure of Demobilization to Provide for the
Social Integration of Ex-Combatants

This lack of control over new armed formations is related to the failure of demobilization policies, particularly in Zimbabwe, Mozambique, and Namibia. Rarely has demobilization given ex-combatants access to employment, supportive social networks, or a culture of peace and respect for human rights. Instead, many ex-combatants throughout the region experience social marginalization and dislocation.[41]

In Mozambique, the UN set up forty-nine assembly points for RENAMO and FRELIMO soldiers to be demobilized and disarmed. As many as 90,000 soldiers have been demobilized and supplied with transport to the district of their choice, as well as eighteen months' salary, "as a personal incentive to actively reintegrate into economic and social life." However, the general lack of economic opportunity in Mozambique has made this integration problematic. Evidently, demobilized soldiers have sold their weapons to support their families. As Rana observes, "The sale of weapons spells cash to buy transportation, food, shelter and medical equipment for those who have left war behind."[42]

The SANDF has begun reducing its present inflated force levels of 130,000 to 75,000. This process, which is expected to take four years, will involve cash payments based on years of military service, as well as low-level skills training in the Service Corps. Angola has begun the integration of its 150,000-strong government army and UNITA's 90,000-strong rebel army under UN supervision. The new Angolan army plans to have force levels of 70,000, leaving 170,000 soldiers to be demobilized; each is scheduled to receive $2,000 per year for two years.

Southern Africa clearly needs not only effective disarmament but also demobilization policies that provide for the social integration of ex-combatants. Such social integration involves a far more complicated process of recasting social relations than a single cash payment can achieve.

The tragic case of Angola, as described by Mathiak, illustrates how armed conflict, ineffective disarmament, inadequate control over the new armed forces, and ineffective demobilization all contribute to the creation of the various markets for light weapons. In South Africa, the arms market contains both "deep black" and "shades of gray," that is, both dead-of-night smuggling of undocumented weapons and covert shipment of arms licensed under false pretenses. Although it seems unlikely that the illegal-arms market in southern Africa is controlled by a coordinated cabal of "deep black" operators, both its scale and its links with a diverse range of economic activities, including the trades in ivory, diamonds, rhino horn, and second-hand clothing, are striking.[43]

Present Sources of Supply

Illegal Arms Market

No one has any idea how many illegal firearms are in circulation. What is known, according to a 1993 report, is that "whites are at the head of many of the illegal arms smuggling rackets in southern Africa." The state is using a combination of amnesty, reward, and heavy penalty to deal with the proliferation of illegal firearms.[44]

The AK-47 is especially popular; the 70 million Kalashnikov-style weapons estimated to have been produced to date carry powerful social meanings. "The Kalashnikov isn't just a gun; it's a legend, a currency, a symbol of liberation." According to a SAP source, however, "The AK-47 has become one of the greatest curses in [South Africa]." It is durable, robust, mechanically simple, light, easy to conceal and transport, capable of rapid fire, and relatively cheap. It is called the "Soweto blank cheque," since it enables its users to obtain whatever they want. In parts of Mozambique, one can be bought for a chicken, or a small quantity of maize. In northern Namibia, an AK-47 in good condition goes for R25 and in the Johannesburg area and KwaZulu/Natal, for as little as R500. According to a police source, an AK-47 in working condition can be swapped in Angola for an old pair of shoes. Other weapons that have been described as especially popular with township youth include Makarovs and small automatic pistols. At present there are three main sources of supply of illegal arms.[45]

Cross-Border Smuggling

Smuggling of light weapons across the porous borders of Swaziland, Namibia, and Mozambique into South Africa is common. According to the SAPS Center for the Analysis and Interpretation of Crime Information and numerous informants, the main source of illegal weapons is Mozambique. Arms are either bartered for basic commodities or carried across the border by illegal aliens and then sold. Ex-Mozambican soldiers are the primary dealers, but there are also reports of young women on the Namibian border with Angola exchanging AK-47s for second-hand clothes. The exchange of guns for food by Angolans and Mozambicans is also said to be contributing to the dramatic increase in armed criminal violence in Zambia.[46]

Weapons are smuggled into South Africa by air, railroad, and foot. Smugglers use many ingenious methods, including hiding weapons in specially adapted fuel tanks. One source has described smuggling into KwaZulu/Natal as a large-scale commercial operation involving ski boats and sugarcane trucks, as well as private aircraft, and also reported the delivery of weapons off the coast from Czech or Slovak arms factories.

In 1992, the police established a special task force to deal with cross-border arms trade, and, in January 1995 President Nelson Mandela and President Joaquim Chissano of Mozambique signed an agreement for cross-border police cooperation. Operation Rachel was launched in June 1995. Within three days, the combined Mozambican–South African task group had found ninety AK-247 assault rifles, fifty-four Soviet submachine guns, and twelve RPG-7 rocket launchers, as well as hand grenades, mines, and explosives. In the same operation at Pumba, near the Kruger National Park, dozens of hand grenades and rifles were recovered from a cellar under a derelict house. "Many of these dated back to the days of the 16 year war but, although many of the weapons had rusted, most could easily be restored to working order. Local people, eking out subsistence livings, are being given mealie meal [maize] and dried fish in return for information about hidden weapons." Within the first three months, Operation Rachel traced 1,164 weapons, 685 of them AK-47s.[47]

Illegal Imports

Illegal exports from various countries, including the United States, to South Africa in defiance of U.S. law and the 1977 to 1994 UN arms embargo against the apartheid regime provided another important line of supply. Media reports have told of an illegal trade in weapons from the United States to South Africa, including shotguns made by U.S. companies, which have been used in township political violence. In 1992, a sergeant in the KwaZulu police was arrested in connection with an arms cache that contained shotguns made by Mossberg and Sons of Connecticut. The Africa Fund stated that hundreds of semi-automatic pistols, revolvers, rifles, and magazines, as well as many thousands of rounds of ammunition, worth millions of dollars, left the United States but never arrived at their stated destination of Harare, Zimbabwe.[48]

In 1995, Robert Mahler, a former U.S. gun dealer, was sentenced to eighteen months in jail for illegally shipping more than 200 guns from Oregon to South Africa. SAP reports said that Mahler belonged to the right-wing Afrikaans extremist group, the Afrikaner Weerstandsbeweging (AWB). In 1993, South African authorities seized a container belonging to Mahler near Pretoria that held more than 220 rifles, pistols, and shotguns and 46,983 rounds of ammunition.[49]

Leaks from State Armories and Security-Force Personnel

The weapons issued to the SANDF and the state armories are inadequately controlled. One informant describes attacks on members of the security forces as common. The Annual Report of the Commissioner of the SAP in 1992 registered a 10 to 14 percent increase in the number of firearms stolen from the national- security armory.

Several informants maintain that security-force personnel were involved in the illegal arms trade, largely for profit. There are also reports that R-4s and R-5s have been sold by "high ranking former SADF officers" who had obtained them when the SADF left Namibia and Angola and that poorly paid black policemen frequently sold their semi-automatic rifles (R-5s), shotguns, and handguns on the black market to the highest bidder in South Africa and Mozambique.[50]

In 1993, two policemen were arrested in connection with a large illegal arms network. In 1995, five policemen were arrested in connection with the theft of 38 firearms, 203 magazines, and more than 2,000 rounds of ammunition from the police training college at Koeberg. A police spokesman maintained that the theft had been "for financial gain and not for any political reasons."[51]

In 1993, someone broke into a Ciskei state armory and stole R-4 rifles. Several informants maintained that large numbers of G-3s and ammunition issued to the KwaZulu police had made their way onto the black market. In 1994, an official investigation found that only 3,514 of the 5,634 firearms issued to police stations in the former homeland of Transkei could be located. The missing 2,000 firearms included R-4 rifles and various handguns.[52]

Legal Arms Marketing and Manufacture

Many light weapons are domestically manufactured small arms and available commercially, including semi-automatic rifles modeled on the R-4 in standard use within the South African army, and the small handguns manufactured by Lyttleton Engineering Works (LIW). They are an important part of South Africa's indigenous arms industry—the other crucial source of supply.

In the mid 1980s, South Africa's armaments industry was ranked as the tenth largest in the world and as one of the leading third-world arms producers. This distinction was due largely to ARMSCOR, the state production and procurement organization. ARMSCOR developed into one of the largest industrial organizations in the country, and its importance to the national economy was demonstrated by its export performance; arms became "the country's principal manufactured export, and the third largest export after gold and coal."[53]

In 1992, ARMSCOR underwent a commercialization and a reorganization into two parts: the DENEL group, which assumed all of ARMSCOR's manufacturing capabilities and facilities, and ARMSCOR, which remained the state procurement agency. According to Willet and Batchelor, ARMSCOR, DENEL, and the 700 private companies comprising the local arms industry contributed nearly 1 percent of GDP in 1994. Krish Naidoo of ARMSCOR lists a total of six major companies involved in the production of light weapons: Pretoria Metal Pressings, Musgrave, and LIW from the DENEL group, and three independent companies—Republic Arms in Pretoria, Tressitu Ammunition, and Aserma (part of the Reutech group).[54]

The total number of people employed in South Africa's arms industry is c. 50,000. The sector is dominated by white Afrikaners at senior management levels and includes highly skilled workers. In this regard, "the defense labor market distorts human capital formation by absorbing disproportionate numbers of science and technology graduates and skilled technicians.... It is estimated that almost 15,000 workers in the sector are technically highly trained and of the upper income group."[55]

According to an ARMSCOR informant, the agency has a deeply rooted covert organizational culture: "You deal with people who are used to secrecy and who have been there for ten to twenty years; they operate as a clique. They all live nearby; they socialize together and share the same politics. The top management is almost entirely white and Afrikaans [speaking]." Until this year, ARMSCOR's operations have been shrouded in this culture of secrecy, which was established by law. However, President Mandela's Cameron Commision recommended that ARMSCOR undergo a fundamental transformation in social relations and a reduction in power. It found ARMSCOR's values and organizational culture too concerned with marketing and profit, at the expense of ethical considerations. The Commision suggested that "ARMSCOR's organizational culture was ... steeped in the duplicity of the arms embargo and its consequent evasions and untruths," reflecting the militarization of the Total Strategy era between 1976 and 1990. Hence, ARMSCOR, for the first time, has become subject to public scrutiny and debate.[56]

South Africa is the largest but not the only source of arms production in the region. The Namib Arms and Ammunition at Keetsmanshoop, which is Namibia's first arms factory, is expected to supply weapons for the Namibian Defense Force and produce 30,000 rounds of ammunition a day. A small arms factory in Harare, Zimbabwe, employing 300 people, is producing up to 5 million bullets a month and exporting small-arms ammunition and explosives to at least six African countries. A new land-mines factory has been established there as well.[57]

South African Arms Exports

South Africa has become a key player in the world's small-arms market, having exported $187 million worth of arms in 1993 to more than fifty countries. During the apartheid era, legislation regulating arms exports was weak, susceptible to duplicity, and void of any ethical considerations. Arms sales were sanctioned to repressive governments as well as to countries involved in civil war. South Africa provided arms to both sides in the Iran/Iraq war, the Pinochet regime in Chile, the Khmer Rouge in Cambodia, as well as to Israel, Taiwan, UNITA, and RENAMO. The bulk of weapons have been going to the Middle East but there is evidence that South Africa supplied arms to Rwanda and Croatia in defiance of the UN arms embargoes. Despite the transition from apartheid to democracy, ARMSCOR has announced plans to expand arms exports by 300 percent during the next five years, increasing South Africa's share of the global arms market from its present level of 0.4 percent to 2 percent, and raising export earnings from $244 to $800 million annually.

South Africa's official arms trade policy is in limbo while new policy guidelines and legislation are being determined. The crucial events leading to the current situation are: (1) the discovery in September 1994 that two consignments of surplus SANDF weapons—8,500 AK-47s, 15,665 G-3 rifles, and 14 million rounds of ammunition—supposedly destined for Lebanon, had apparently been sold to Yemen, a prohibited destination for South African arms; (2) President Mandela's appointment of the Cameron Commission in 1994, in the wake of the public outcry that followed this discovery, and of the Cabinet Committee early in 1995 to devise a responsible arms trade policy. The Cameron Commission recommended that the arms trade should be guided by new social values, specifically "to promote democracy, human rights and international peace and security."[58]

The restructuring of ARMSCOR and the creation of a new arms-control body are largely due to the Cameron Commission report. The National Conventional Arms Control Commission (NCACC), created in August 1995, is a four-tier organization headed by the Defense Secretary and accountable to the Cabinet. It is responsible for decisions about arms sales on a case-by-case basis and not on the basis of country classifications. In theory,

> transfers and trade will be avoided which would be likely to be used for the violation or suppression of human rights and fundamental freedoms, contravene South Africa's international commitments . . . endanger peace by introducing destabilizing military capabilities into a region . . . , have a negative impact on South Africa's diplomatic and trade relations with other coun-

tries, support or encourage terrorism, be used for purposes other than the legitimate defense and security needs of the recipient countries and contribute to the escalation of regional conflicts.[59]

Solutions to the Problem of Light Weapons Proliferation

Besides the state-initiated Cameron Commission, a demilitarization movement is also challenging the proliferation of light weapons in the region, though it is at present extremely small, fragmented, and, in South Africa, mainly white and middle-class in social composition. This movement is demanding a shift of power and resources away from the military, rejecting militarist values and social practices. The South African leadership of this embryonic movement comprises significant numbers of women; elsewhere in the region, women's groups, such as the Roots of Peace organization in Angola, have been established.

One organization, Gun-Free South Africa, focuses on micro-disarmament. Its campaign, which was launched in September 1994, encouraged people to hand in their guns on December 16, 1994, in return for food vouchers, lottery tickets, and a certificate of thanks from President Mandela. Although only 270 firearms—mainly white owned and licensed—turned up, in an interview of 1995, the coordinator of Gun-Free South Africa said that the campaign "raised public awareness about the proliferation of firearms in our society and made it an issue for public debate. It also placed the issue on the political agenda; the ANC December [1994] national conference adopted a resolution supporting Gun-Free."

The campaign has continued, using such imaginative strategies as the melting down of collected firearms into window frames, and declaring public buildings gun-free zones. In June 1995, Gun-Free submitted to the Constitutional Assembly that neither private ownership of firearms nor the "bearing of arms" has ever been recognized as a fundamental right in South Africa, and that each is fundamentally at odds with attempts to control gun ownership through the licensing system.

Another significant group in the embryonic South African demilitarization movement is Ceasefire, which is now involved in a national campaign against land mines. Its objectives were endorsed at a meeting of nongovernmental organizations (NGOs) in June 1995: promotion of the international ban on land mines, stopping the production and distribution of land mines in South and southern Africa, the destruction of all existing land-mine stockpiles in South Africa, the disarming of mines wherever necessary, contributions from South Africa to an international fund for such demining, and financial compensation and provision of rehabilitation services to land-mine victims in southern Africa.

Gun-Free South Africa and Ceasefire concentrate on the two most lethal and plentiful categories of light weapons dispersed throughout the region at present—anti-personnel land mines and firearms. The two weapons are at opposite ends of the spectrum as social symbols: Land mines are stigmatized, but firearms—particularly the ubiquitous AK-47—are still linked to romantic images of revolutionary struggle and national liberation. Nonetheless, the establishment of Ceasefire and Gun-Free is a significant development, since the problem of light-weapon proliferation in the southern African region is ultimately a social one.

The proliferation of light weapons is a destabilizing force throughout the world. Controls will be difficult, however, since both the legal and illegal arms trade are embedded in intricate social relations, institutions, and material interests. On the supply side, governments, manufacturers, and individual dealers will want to continue making enormous profits. On the demand side, the strong economic interests, cultural meanings, and social practices attached to the possession of light weapons will not easily dissolve. Meaningful arms control must be part of a broad process that emphasizes demilitarization and a shift in social values toward political tolerance and human rights, as well as economic development and political legitimacy. In short, arms control has to be understood as part of the transformation of social relations in post-apartheid South Africa.

It is also crucial to establish the legitimacy and accountability of key institutions—especially ARMSCOR and Parliament. "Politically, the critical issue in dealing with the use of small arms in intra-state conflicts is to bring small arms back under the authority of the State functioning through a democratic government which enjoys broad public support." This point has particular pertinence given that one of the strategies of resistance to apartheid has been a decided lawlessness to make the country "ungovernable"; consequently, one of the legacies of the apartheid regime is a distrust of authority and minimal public respect for the legal system. By the same token, the inadequacies of an overreliance on law as the principal mechanism of restricting the circulation of firearms is well illustrated by the case of Nigeria, where laws are strict but ineffective.[60]

Military solutions are problematic as well. For example, the high incidence of illegal weapon smuggling across the Mozambican border impelled the recent appeal by the SANDF to switch the electric fence to lethal mode. The alarm was switched back to alarm mode in 1990, however, after public protest about the ninety-four people or more who were electrocuted by it between 1986 and 1989.[61]

Clearly, as Goldring has argued generally, South Africa needs "an integrated policy of transparency, oversight and control." The most helpful measures would be the establishment of a regional arms register; tighter border control of illegal weapons smuggled from Mozambique, Angola, and Namibia into South Africa—particularly to the Gauteng, Mpumalanga, and KwaZulu/Natal provinces; a stronger criminal justice system; greater legitimacy for the SAP (hampered by its reputation during the apartheid era) and increased police activity to locate and destroy illegal weapons; heavier penalties for illegal possession, and especially for the dealing and smuggling, of firearms, particularly across international borders; more effective control of ammunition; tighter controls over state armories; the institution of bilateral and multilateral commissions to investigate and handle jointly small-arms proliferation (perhaps as part of the regional Inter-State Defense and Security Committee [ISDSC] of the SADC, of which Joe Modise, the South African defense minister, was appointed chair in September 1995); more effective disarmament after armed conflict; demobilization policies that provide for social and economic integration of ex-combatants to minimize the risk of banditry, which is a problem throughout the region; education about conflict resolution; the formulation of a coherent foreign policy with a strong ethical commitment; and, finally, economic development. South Africa has an unemployment rate of at least 34 percent and one of the most unequal distributions of income in the world, and the region as a whole suffers from high levels of poverty and unemployment.[62]

None of these measures will suceed without an indigenous demilitarization movement mobilized on the kind of scale that marked the anti-apartheid struggle. Social organizations are necessary to work for a national consensus. The goal is more than institutional defense restructuring. It also involves new forms of social integration, solidarity, identity, and citizenship. It means creating alternative values and meanings and eroding the ideology that views violence as a legitimate solution to conflict and an effective means of obtaining and defending power. But this kind of social mobilization will not come easily in South Africa. During the process of "elite-pacting," which marked South Africa's transition from authoritarian rule, an alliance of militarists from the various armed formations—the SADF and MK, in particular—was firmly established. No strong grassroots antimilitarist movement emerged during the 1990–1994 period to challenge it.

One reason for the strong entrenchment of militarist sentiment is that resistance to apartheid had been militarized since 1961 and "peace" widely interpreted as acquiescence to the apartheid regime. The apartheid state often depicted MK as a "phantom army," but what MK lacked in resources and personnel was offset by its powerful ideological presence. During the thirty-three years of MK's existence, its soldiers were much glorified, perhaps because of an even older historical linkage between military service and citizenship in South Africa. In 1986, on the twenty-fifth anniversary of MK, Oliver Tambo lamented, "our people have been deliberately deprived of the skills of modern warfare and denied access to weaponry." This same sense of deprivation had appeared during World War II. The 74,000 Africans who volunteered for duty were deployed in noncombatant roles and prohibited from carrying arms. Matthews wrote at the time, "It is argued that the taking up of arms is not the only way in which a citizen may serve his country, but the African looks upon that as the highest symbol of citizenship, and consequently as long as they are refused that privilege, they feel that it is sufficient announcement to them regarding their future place in the body politic of South Africa." This denial of arms was understood as a slight to African manhood as well as citizenship.[63]

The link between military service and citizenship deepened from 1976 to 1990, when conscription was extended to all white male South Africans, at a length of service that was one of the longest among the seventy-six countries in the world that practiced this form of defense procurement. Because conscription was framed in race- and gender-specific terms—that is, it applied only to white males—the organization formed to oppose it—the End Conscription Campaign— had little impact.

Subversion of South Africa's heritage of militaristic nationalism, in which prestige in international relations equates with military power, entails the eradication of current antagonistic ethnic identities and the creation of a common society characterized by peace and justice, democratic participation, tolerance, economic opportunity, and respect for cultural diversity. The control of light weaponry alone, without these values, will not eliminate violence; the use of the "necklace" in South Africa's liberation struggle illustrates what people whose only weapons are petrol and matches can accomplish.

The process of mobilizing collective action to shift values and identities away from the mentality that makes weaponry appealing requires courageous thinking about alternative social arrangements. Weaponry and war are not fixed topographical features of the social landscape; armies are not essential to the existence of a nation-state, as developments in Costa Rica and Panama have demonstrated; and private gun ownership is not essential to citizenship.

Gun-free societies do exist. In Japan, another society with a strong military tradition, no one may keep a gun at home, not even police officers. Punishment can be up to fifteen years for infringement. Not surprisingly, Japan had only thirty-two gun murders in 1994, compared with 15,456 in the United States. However, according to Mutsuro Donowaki, the Chair of the UN Commission on Small Arms, Japan owes much of its success in this area to a long process of education.

In a case closer to home, Botswana is also relatively gun-free. Only 400 licenses are issued every year through a raffle of applicants—200 for rifles and 200 for shotguns. None is issued for handguns.

In response to the Dunblane massacre, in which sixteen young children and their teacher were shot, Britain introduced some of the strictest gun laws in the world, banning all handguns, except .22 calibre target pistols, amounting to at least 80 percent of the 200,000 that were once legal. The exempted single-shot .22 calibre pistols, widely used in shooting competitions, now have to be held under lock and key at gun clubs. Australia has also introduced tighter control after the massacre at Port Arthur (Tasmania) in 1996 that killed thirty-five people.

The diverse examples of Japan, Botswana, Britain, and Australia suggest that a gun-free society is possible. Stricter licensing—in addition to the policy innovations mentioned above—could help to bring it about, but policy must be anchored in a holistic approach that recognizes social, as well as economic and political, factors.

Attempts to control the proliferation of light weapons in southern Africa are fixated on curbing the *supply* by means of such legal and technical measures as more effective border patrols or arms-transfer monitoring mechanisms. These are necessary but not sufficient measures. Policymakers need to address the underlying social factors that create the *demand* for these weapons. Once demand declines, it may be possible to dismantle the social organization responsible for weapons production and distribution. The challenge is to stimulate a movement to restructure institutions and ideas so that we can achieve nothing less than a new social order.

Notes to Chapter 5

1. Chris Smith, "Light Weapons and the International Arms Trade," in United Nations Institute for Disarmament Research (UNIDIR), *Small Arms Management and Peacekeeping in Southern Africa* (Geneva, 1996), 31. Michael Klare points out that "there is no precise, formal definition for light weapons. In general, light arms can be defined as all those conventional weapons that can be carried by an individual combatant, or by a light vehicle. . . . This category includes small arms, grenades, machine guns, light anti-tank weapons, bazookas, shoulder-fired anti-aircraft missiles, light mortars, light anti-aircraft guns, and anti-personnel landmines. Excluded is anything heavier." ("Light Weapons Arms Trafficking and the World Security Environment of the 1990s," paper presented at the UNIDIR Conference [Berlin, 1995], 3).

2. Klare, "The Global Trade in Light Weapons and International System in the Post-Cold War Era," in Jeffrey Boutwell, *idem*, and Laura Reed (eds.), *Lethal Commerce: The Global Trade in Small Arms and Light Weapons* (Cambridge, Mass.,1994), 38.

3. Klare, "Light Weapons," A1.

4. Samuel Huntington, "The Ungovernability of Democracy," *The American Enterprise* (November/December,1993), 36

5. Cock, "Introduction," in *idem* and Laurie Nathan (eds.), *Society at War: The Militarisation of South Africa* (New York, 1989), 1-13.

6. Klare, "Light Weapons," 40.

7. Cock, *Women and War in South Africa* (Cleveland, 1991), 81.

8. Drew Forrest, *Weekly Mail*, 5 May 1991.

9. Michael Mann, "The Roots and Contradictions of Modern Militarism," *New Left Review*, 162 (1987), 116.

10. Frederick Ezell, foreword to James Ellis, *The Social History of the Machine Gun* (Baltimore, 1975), 2.

11. van Tonder, quoted in Ronald Lessick, "Guns in South Africa," unpub. B.A. thesis (Univ. of the Witwatersrand, 1990), 12.

12. *The Star*, 17 June 1995.

13. Human Rights Committee, *Human Rights Report* (Pretoria,1995), 2.

14. *Weekend Star*, 6 Aug. 1994; *The Star,* 20 July, 1995.

15. Information provided by the South African Police (SAP).

16. *The Star*, 21 June, 1995.

17. Terence Cochrane, "A Hole in Our Heads," *The Weekend Star*, 6 Aug. 1994; personal communication with Capt. George Botha, SAP, Sept.1995.

18. Cochrane, "Hole in Our Heads," 11; *The Star*, 21 Aug. 1991; SAP, *Annual Report*, 111; *The Star*, 31 May 1995.

19. *Ibid.*, 1 Aug. 1995.

20. Mark Shaw quoted in *ibid.*, 26 June 1995.

21. Jonathan Rosenthal, "Self Defence Units and Their Relations to the Communities in Which They Are Found," Sociology 111 research project (Univ. of the Witwatersrand, 1994), 16.

22. South African Research and Documentation Center (SARDC), *State of the Environment in South Africa* (Harare, 1994), 258.

23. *The Sunday Times*, 28 July 1991.

24. Mike Cameron, cited in *The Star*, 21 May 1988.

25. Greg Mills, "Small Arms Control—Some Early Thoughts," *African Defence Review*, XV (1994), 44.

26. SAP, *Annual Report*, 119.

27. Cochrane, "Hole in Our Heads," 11; *Saturday Star*, 12 May 1990.

28. Lessick, "Guns" (1990), 50; SAP, *Annual Report*, 119; *The Star*, 30 Sept. 1993.

29. *The Sunday Times*, 20 Aug. 1995.

30. Mills, "Small Arms Control," 45.

31. Rocklyn Mark (Rocky) Williams, "Small Arms Proliferation in Southern Africa," paper delivered at the conference, "The Proliferation of Light Weapons in the Post-Cold War World: A Global Problem," UNIDR (Berlin, 1995), 13.

32. Klare, "Secret Operatives, Clandestine Trades: The Thriving Black Market for Weapons," *Bulletin of the Atomic Scientists*, XLIV (April, 1988), 23

33. Phyllis Johnson and David Martin, *Apartheid Terrorism: The Destabilisation Report* (London, 1989), 11.

34. Roland Hunter was a conscript in the SADF who was sentenced to five years imprisonment for passing information about destabilization activities to the ANC.

35. Personal communication with Hunter, 1995; Cameron Commission Inquiry into Alleged Arms Transactions between ARMSCOR and one Eli Wazan and Other Related Matters, *First Report* (Johannesburg, 1995).

36. *Ibid.*; SARDC, *State of the Environment*, 258.

37. *Weekly Mail*, VII (15), 1991.

38. Babyon Xeketwane, "The Relation between Hostels and the Political Violence on the Reef from 1990-1993: A Case Study of Merafe and Meadowlands Hostels in Soweto," unpub. M.A. thesis (Univ. of the Witwatersrand, 1995), 45.

39. Williams, "Small Arms Proliferation," 2

40. *Ibid.*, 5

41. Cock, "Towards a Common Society: The Integration of Soldiers and Armies in a Future South Africa," Human Sciences Research Council Report (1993); Charles Alao, "The Defence and Security Implications of the Liberation War on Zimbabwe, 1880-1987," unpub. Ph.D. diss. (Univ. of London, 1991).

42. Republic of Mozambique, *A Demobilization and Reintegration Programme for Mozambican Military Personnel: First Phase 1991-1992* (Maputo, 1992); Swana Rana, "Small Arms and Intra-State Conflicts," paper presented at the conference, "The Proliferation of Light Weapons in the Post-Cold War World: A Global Problem" (Berlin, 1995).

43. Lucy Mathiak, "Light Weapons and Internal Conflict in Angola," in Jeffrey Boutwell, Klare, and Laura Reed (eds.), *Lethal Commerce: The Global Trade in Small Arms and Light Weapons* (Cambridge, Mass., 1994), 81-97.

44. *The Citizen*, 21 Apr. 1993.

45. *New York Times*, 29 May 1994; Gen. Lionel Mellet, cited in *The Citizen*, 16 July 1993; *Ibid.*, 21 Apr. 1993.

46. Russian News Service (TASS), 9 Nov. 1993; *The Sunday Mail, Zambia*, 20 Aug. 1995.

47. *The Sunday Times*, 25 June 1995; *The Argus*, 22 Aug. 1995.

48. *Weekly Mail*, 18 Sept. 1992.

49. *The Star*, 15 June 1995.

50. *The Sunday Times*, 27 Aug. 1995.

51. *The Star*, 20 July 1995.

52. *Business Day*, 13 Oct. 1993; *The Sunday Times*, 10 Sept. 1995.

53. Peter Bachelor, "South Africa's Armaments Industry," paper prepared for Economic Trends Research Group meeting (Univ. of Capetown, 1992), 18.

54. Sue Willet and Bachelor, *To Trade or Not to Trade* (1994), 8.

55. Bachelor, "Dirty Secrets: South Africa's Arms Trade Legacy," *Budget Watch*, I (1995), 3.

56. Cameron Commission, *First Report*, 59. For more information about the Total Strategy, see the chapter in this volume by Steven Metz, "The Conceptual Transformation of the South African Military: Changing Strategy, Ethos, and Civil-Military Relations."

57. *Engineering News*, 20 Sept. 1991; *The Star*, 17 Feb. 1995.

58. Cameron Commission, *First Report*, 39.

59. Press release from the NCACC, 4 Sept. 1995.

60. Rana, "Small Arms," 18.

61. *The Star*, 29 June 1995.

62. Natalie Goldring, "Towards Restraint: Controlling the International Arms Trade," *Harvard International Review*, XVII (1994), 34. Although the relationship between police resources and crime levels is contested, resources have shifted significantly away from the military to the police. The size of the police force has more than doubled since 1984, now numbering 141,535 men and women of all ranks as well as 37 generals. Cock, "Towards a Common Society."

63. ANC, *Dawn, Souvenir Issue* (Lusaka, 1986); Z. K. Matthews, cited in Mark Roth, "If You Give Us Rights We Will Fight: Black Involvement in the Second World War," *South African Historical Journal*, XV (1983), 85; Ellen Hellman, "Non-Europeans in the Army," *Race Relations*, X (1943), 48.

6

Hussein Solomon

From Accommodation and Control to Control and Intervention
Illegal Population Flows into South Africa

ONE IN EVERY 114 people is displaced worldwide today. Almost every world capital—in both the first and third worlds—views these population flows with alarm. The purpose of this chapter is to seek to understand one aspect of the global migration crisis in a particular context, namely, that of illegal immigration into South Africa. It explores the various causes that lead to population displacement, as well as the effects on the host states, eventually reaching policy-relevant conclusions. It strongly emphasizes the comparative dimensions of the problem. A comparative study not only enriches the field of migration research but also enables South Africa to learn from the experiences of other states facing similar problems.[1]

Typology of Migrants

It is imperative to identify the various types of migrants and understand the relationship between the different categories: Contract labor

The author wishes to acknowledge the intellectual debt that he owes to Myron Weiner and Goran Melander, whose works greatly shaped his thinking in the preparation of this chapter.

122

migrants are similar to Germany's *gastarbeiters*, or guest workers. As the name suggests, they are the results of contracts drawn up between an employer—for example, the South African Chamber of Mines—and prospective foreign laborers. According to the contract, the employer undertakes to pay the foreign workers a certain remuneration for work during a fixed period (usually between twelve and eighteen months), after which the contract laborers are supposed to return to their countries of origin.

Gomel draws a distinction between *migration*—the permanent relocation of individuals from one place of residence to another—and *temporary emigration*, which largely consists of contract migrant laborers and students. Hence, the application of Gomel's view of the situation to southern Africa would mean denying the presence of 165,825 of the region's people toiling in South African mines and 100,000 more employed in the Republic's agricultural sector. Such an assessment, however, would do justice neither to Europe nor to southern Africa, where a strong relationship exists between contract labor migrants and illegal immigrants. In both Europe and South Africa, foreigners enter the country legally as contract migrant labor and then overstay their contract period. In South Africa, for example, 750,000 people classified as illegal immigrants or illegal aliens originally entered the country legally via temporary residence permits.[2]

Another category of migrant is the *asylum-seeker*, which refers to a quasi-legal process in which one state grants protection to nationals of another state. International law, however, allows this process to be challenged by a request for extradition, although the absence of a relevant treaty between two states nullifies any legal duty to extradite. The primary difference between refugees and asylum-seekers is that rights of asylum belong to states, not to individuals, in spite of the fact that Article 14 of the Universal Declaration of Human Rights of 1948 gives individuals a right to asylum. But, since the Declaration took the form of a *resolution* of the General Assembly, it is not legally (though it may be morally) binding on states. At the time of writing, the number of asylum-seekers residing in South Africa could not be determined. Given the stringent procedures that the government has instituted to discourage them from entering the Republic, the figure is probably negligible.[3]

Legal migrants divide into two categories: first, the brain drain of South African professionals and business people emigrating to Europe,

North America, Australia, and New Zealand—10,235 citizens in 1994; second, the brain drain of African professionals and business people from the rest of the continent into South Africa—25.4 percent of all immigrants in South Africa in 1994. The quality of these legal immigrants is evinced by the fact that, in 1991 alone, 200 medical doctors left Zimbabwe to settle in South Africa and Botswana. This kind of migration holds serious long-term consequences for neighboring economies.[4]

Since other categories of migrants, such as illegal immigrants and refugees, are contested, analysis of the controversy is unavoidable if a clear policy is to emerge. Conceptual fudge can only lead to policy fudge. Who is an illegal immigrant? It seems self-evident that an illegal immigrant is someone residing within a country illegally. Such a view would be strengthened by a perusal of South Africa's Aliens Control Act of 1991, which stipulates that "undocumented immigrants" or "illegal aliens" are those who enter South Africa at a place other than a port of entry; who remain in South Africa without a valid residence permit; who act in contravention of their residence permits; who remain in South Africa after the expiration of their residence permits; who are prohibited from entering South Africa; or who become prohibited persons while in South Africa.

The idea of a distinction between illegal immigrants and refugees is evident in the current international definition of the term "refugee." The 1951 *United Nations Convention Related to the Status of Refugees*, Article 1.2, as amended by the 1967 *Protocol,* defines refugees as "persons who are living outside their country because of a well-founded fear of persecution for reasons of race, religion, nationality, membership in a particular social group or political opinion." Using this definition, Weiner classifies 18.9 million of the world's migrants as refugees.[5]

Several scholars have criticized this United Nations (UN) definition as too restrictive. Woehlcke, for instance, notes that since the *Convention* originally intended to regulate the European refugee problem after World War II, it is no longer applicable today, when "economic refugees" (that is, those fleeing poverty and economic hardship) and "environmental refugees" (those fleeing ecological catastrophe) comprise the bulk of the numbers. Loescher further elaborates: "[I]n many developing countries which have few resources and weak government structures, economic hardship is generally exacerbated by political violence. Thus it has become increasingly difficult to make hard and fast distinctions between refugees (as defined by the 1951 UN Convention with its political bias) and economic migrants."[6]

In the same vein, Astri Surhke notes that the key criterion determining refugee status is persecution, usually an act of government against an individual. This criterion, she asserts, excludes those fleeing from generalized conditions of violence, insecurity, and oppression—as in the case of, say, Zaire—as well as the inhabitants of states where the violence is externally induced. South Africa's destabilization of the Front Line States (FLS), during much of the 1980s—through its support of such proxy groups as The Mozambican National Resistance Movement (RENAMO) in Mozambique, the Union for the Total Independence of Angola (UNITA) in Angola, the Lesotho Liberation Army, and the Mashala Gang in Zambia—is an example of externally induced unrest.[7]

In South Africa, scholars like Dolan argue that since the conventional distinction between illegal immigrants and refugees does not adequately reflect empirical reality, it is bound to produce ineffective policy. Many critics argue for a more inclusive definition of *refugee* and point to the Organization of African Unity's (OAU) *Convention Governing the Specific Aspects of Refugee Problems in Africa*, adopted in Addis Ababa in 1969 as providing one. According to the OAU *Convention*, a refugee is a person who, "owing to external aggression, occupation, foreign domination or events seriously disturbing public order in either part of or the whole of his country of origin or nationality, is compelled to seek refuge in another place outside his country of origin or nationality."[8]

Is this argument true? Is the 1951 UN *Convention* irrelevant to today's global migration crisis? On both counts, the answer appears to be "no." The 1951 definition is relevant to the contemporary world for several reasons. More important, various flaws are discernible in the arguments of its critics.

What are the likely consequences of broadening this definition? Arguably, it could adversely affect domestic stability by opening borders and letting large numbers of people from impoverished and authoritarian states stream through national boundaries to relatively more prosperous and stable polities. The complications in the receiving states would become serious, since only a minority of the world's people live in societies that respect human rights, or can meet the material needs of its members. As Weiner puts it,

> There are, however, several legitimate objections to broadening the definition of refugees. If acts of discrimination short of persecution are the basis of claiming asylum, a large part of the world's population could do so. Asylum on the basis of discrimination could plausibly be claimed, for example, by over a hundred million Indian Muslims whose mosque at Ayodhya was destroyed and who were fearful after many Muslims in Bombay and elsewhere were killed by Hindus. Millions of women around the world could similarly point to discriminatory restrictions imposed by their state or society as justification for seeking asylum. Moreover, a country that does not want its minorities could engage in systematic discrimination and impel countries that embrace a liberal conception of refugees to admit all whose human rights have been violated. The more liberal democratic states and international agencies become in granting asylum to persecuted minorities, the greater the inducement for a nationalist regime to engage in some form of ethnic cleansing.[9]

This situation is illustrated graphically in the relations between the United States and Cuba. For years, the United States automatically granted refugee status to everyone who fled from the Communist regime in Havana. President Fidel Castro took advantage of this policy by opening up the jails and mental asylums and encouraging the inmates to migrate to the United States. Horrified at the surge of criminals and psychopaths arriving on its shores, the United States ceased the liberal granting of refugee status to Cubans. Building on this theme, Martin notes that refugee status has become a "scarce resource." Governments must decide to whom this entitlement should be given and how generous it should be. The broader the definition, and the less restricted the privilege, the more refugees will change locations. The cost of such refugees' support will have to be assumed by the host governments.[10]

But critics of the 1951 UN *Convention* will not be stilled. They argue that, although the interests of a potential host state call for a narrow definition, the interests of the potential illegal immigrants/refugees thereby suffer and that the UN *Convention* is too state-centric and not sufficiently sympathetic of the plights driving people away from their homes. Melander, however, disagrees, noting that, in practice, the 1951 definition is far more flexible than its critics would have us believe. For example, the immediate aftermath of the Soviet suppression of the 1956 Hungarian uprising saw all Western governments following the lead of the United Nations High Commissioner for Refugees (UNHCR) in declaring that all of the Hungarians fleeing from their native land were refugees. More recently, the UNHCR's broad interpretation of the 1951 UN *Convention* allowed the UN to get involved in the early stages of the Yugoslav crisis. The UNHCR set up "safety zones" within Iraq to provide protection for displaced Kurds under UN Security Council Resolution 688 of 1991. On a strict interpretation of the 1951 refugee definition (which clearly excludes internally displaced people from refugee status), the UNHCR was overstepping its mark. But a UNHCR representative explained that the UN held a wider interpretation of the 1951 *Convention*'s definition of *refugee*, and she upheld a clear linkage between the internally displaced and refugees generally.[11]

Why not simply broaden the formal definition of *refugee*, if the practical definition is so broad? To protect against an even broader interpretation that would invite more abuse is one answer. The broader the definition, the looser become borders, producing more refugees and more chances for domestic instability.

One of the most fundamental criticisms of the 1951 *Refugee Convention* is its lack of precision about what constitutes persecution; critics assert—unfairly—that emphasis on individuals negates the concept of "group persecution." Although the UNHCR acknowledges that there is no universal definition of *persecution*, there may well be internationally acceptable criteria for determining what qualifies as a "well-founded fear of persecution."[12]

Melander observes a growing tendency to refer to basic human rights as a set of criteria for defining persecution; that is, applicants have begun to complain explicitly about the violation of basic human rights. These human-rights violations include not only civil and political rights but also economic, social, and cultural rights. According to Melander, the UNHCR can use the existing human-rights instruments to help determine the meaning of *persecution*. The *Universal Declaration on Human Rights* of 1948 and the *International Covenant on Civil and*

Political Rights of 1976 provide good guidelines in that regard. Anyone who fears arbitrary detention, contrary to Article 9 of the *Universal Declaration*, may be under persecution. The same applies to anyone who fears punishment contrary to Article 19 of the *Universal Declaration*. Melander notes that all substantive articles of the *Declaration* are useful precedents for the meaning of *persecution*.[13]

In order to guard against swelling the ranks of refugees too much, Melander stipulates the international community cannot afford to consider all persons faced with human-rights violations in their countries of origins as refugees. An important prerequisite is that the violation reach a certain degree of severity before it can be classified as persecution. An arbitrary arrest must last a certain length of time to fulfill the criterion. Hence, the continued incarceration of Moshood Abiola in Lagos—now in its fourth year—would warrant preferential treatment under the refugee rubric; the overnight imprisonment of a Nigerian journalist critical of the Abacha regime would not. In addition, each complaint of a human-rights violation must be motivated by one or more of the five causes of persecution mentioned in the 1951 *Convention*, namely, race, religion, nationality, membership in a particular social group, or political opinion.[14]

Finally, according to the 1951 UN *Refugee Convention*, the fear of persecution must be individualized; that is, each applicant must express the fear of human-rights violation personally. This fact, however, does not preclude group persecution or group violations of human rights, when based, say, on race. For example, the policy of apartheid was directed against every single person in South Africa who did not belong to the white minority. As such, black South Africans were accorded the status of refugees in such host states such as Zambia and Tanzania.

Nobel, too, argues strongly for the retention of the 1951 *Convention*, noting that any confusion relating to the status of refugees is harmful to their protection. Moreover, he attacks scholars like Woehlcke and Loescher who wish to extend refugee status to economic and environmental migrants, because such terms as "economic refugee" and "environmental refugee" do not exist in international law. The underlying rationale for this legal stance is that a distinction can be made between illegal immigrants and refugees, based on the causes prompting them to leave their countries and settle in another. As Toolo and Bethlehem put it,

It is possible to argue that there is a difference between refugees who have been driven from their own countries in large numbers as a result of a national crisis and illegal immigrants who make a primarily individual decision to come to South Africa. While such an individual decision may reflect the conditions faced by people in the home country, this would be different from the crisis-driven nature of refugees. Refugees are only in a position to return home when the crisis in their own country has been resolved, whereas illegal immigrants would not be dependent on a political/military solution.[15]

Contrary to the claims of those who reject the 1951 *Convention*, the 1969 OAU *Convention* does not extend the same protection to illegal immigrants as to refugees. Weiner detects more similarities than differences between the two conventions, however. Both view refugees specifically as victims of persecution and violence at the hands of their governments, not individuals otherwise discomfited by the authorities or those fleeing from natural disasters (floods, droughts, or earthquakes). Neither definition includes individuals who flee from tyrannical regimes, unless they are personally persecuted or their societies torn by life-threatening violence. The preamble to the 1969 OAU *Convention* categorically states that it is meant to complement, not oppose, the 1951 *Convention*.[16]

Thus, the 1951 *Convention* seems to steer a middle path between the rights of the individual and those of the state. Undue emphasis on the rights of individuals can lead only to anarchy (open borders with their attendant domestic instability); undue emphasis on the rights of states can lead only to regimes unconcerned with moral obligation outside their own boundaries. Any attempt to widen the definition of the term *refugee* would be a mistake. From the South African perspective, anyone falling outside the parameters of the 1951 *Convention* and inside the Aliens Control Act of 1991 must be termed an illegal alien or an undocumented migrant.

The Magnitude of the Problem

How many illegal immigrants are there in South Africa? Answers range from 2 million to 8 million. The wide discrepancy in the estimates exposes the central problem that any study of illegal immigration faces: The clandestine nature of the phenomenon does not lend itself easily to quantification.

How then does the South African Police Services (SAPS) or the Department of Home Affairs arrive at their estimates? George Orr, director of admissions in the Department of Home Affairs, attributes his department's estimates to a complicated formula based on the number of migrants who have entered the country legally and temporarily, but have left no record of their departure. Reitzes finds that calculation and the formula largely speculative.[17]

Another method used to arrive at these "guestimates" is extrapolation from repatriation figures. Once again, however, the reliability of the formula is open to question. For one thing, the repatriation figures do not indicate cases in which individuals have been deported several times. One illegal immigrant was arrested and deported twenty-eight times in the space of six months![18]

Whether they number 2 million or 8 million, illegal immigrants arguably have a largely negative impact on the South African state and on the lives of ordinary South Africans. The pressing issue that needs to be addressed is why this large population influx into South Africa occurs in the first place.

The Causes of Migration into South Africa

Broadly, eight components are involved in migration: sociocultural factors; communications and technology; geographical proximity; precedent; demographic influences, including population growth; environmental conditions; economic opportunities, which, although originally local, have become increasingly global; and political issues.

Sociocultural Factors

These may not only act as a push in the area of origin but also as a pull from the destination. Take, for example, the early Indians who came to the colony of Natal as indentured laborers in the 1860s to work on the sugarcane plantations. Most of them were Harijans—the lowest caste in India's rigid caste system—who had suffered political, economic, and social discrimination in their homeland. Recognizing that they could not improve their lot significantly there, they chose to relocate to Natal. More contemporaneous examples of cultural identities pushing people to leave their homelands can be found in Bosnia, Rwanda, and Burundi.

That sociocultural factors can also pull populations to new places is, in large part, the legacy of history. Southern Africa has been marked by constant population movements for 125,000 years, but the arrival of Dutch colonists in 1652 introduced a new context for them. The next major event was the early nineteenth-century rise of a militarist Zulu kingdom under Shaka, which inaugurated a period of tremendous upheaval, known as *mfecane*—a word in the Zulu language signifying forced removal—during which other tribes in the area fled Shaka's militarist hegemony: Xhosa, Rolong, Pedi, Kora, Ndebele, Tlokwa, Hlubi, Mpondo, Swazi, Ngoni, Griqua, Sotho, and Tswana were all part of this great population movement. These centrifugal pressures were strengthened further by the "Great Trek" of the 1830s, when thousands of Afrikaner families left their British colonial masters in the Cape Colony to establish their own Afrikaner homelands in the interior.[19]

The significance of this legacy of ethnic diaspora for present-day southern Africa cannot be overstated. Consider the number of Swazis inside South Africa relative to those in Swaziland; the number of Tswana inside South Africa relative to those in Botswana; and the number of Basotho inside South Africa relative to those in Lesotho. Evidence suggests that, in Africa, ties of clan, lineage, or tribe take precedence over those of state citizenship, thereby encouraging illegal immigration. For instance, part of the reason for the large concentrations of undocumented Mozambicans in Northern Province is that, being Shangaan speakers, they share a certain cultural similarity with the indigenous population, as well as the belief that they can expect assistance from their kin on the South African side of the border. These sociocultural factors have helped to pull them away from their rightful state.[20]

Communications and Technology

The revolution in communications and technology that began with the microchip has been a tremendous spur for the mobility of populations. The advances in information technology—witnessed by, among other things, live CNN broadcasts via satellite—have helped people to make more informed decisions regarding the feasibility of migration. Some scholars, such as Loescher, believe that television programs, in particular, show people in the third world and the former Eastern bloc how economically and politically deprived they are, further strengthening the impulse to migrate. Television is undoubtedly one of the contributing factors to east–west, south–north and, more recently, south–south migration in Africa.[21]

The communications revolution has not influenced population movement so much in southern Africa as it has the flow from east to west. Traditional word of mouth is still the most active medium in the south, especially as it relates to the contract migrant labor system, which underscores the interconnectedness of the region. For example, in both Lesotho and Mozambique, people in rural villages sing about how wealthy South Africa is.

Geographical Proximity

Gomel maintained that foreign populations originate primarily from the same geographical area, illustrating his theory with the waves of migration into France from Algeria, Morocco, and Tunisia. His point receives further confirmation in southern Africa by the 1.7 million people who left Mozambique during the early 1990s: 1.1 million of them ended up in Malawi, 230,000 in Zimbabwe, 240,000 in Zambia, 25,000 in Swaziland, 72,000 in Tanzania, and 250,000 in South Africa.[22]

One reason for this phenomenon is that migrants tend to retain a certain loyalty to their home countries, as represented by loved ones left behind or the desire to return there someday. For example, a survey of Mozambican refugees residing in South Africa found that 83.7 percent of them intended to return to their former homes if circumstances stabilized there. Refugees also can have more mundane reasons not to stray far from their original homes; they may simply know more about neighboring countries than about those further away.[23]

It stands to reason that professionals and skilled laborers are less confined to a single geographical area than unskilled or semiskilled laborers are. As a case in point, the Economic Commission for Africa estimated that, in 1987, an astonishing 30 percent of the skilled manpower in Africa was living in Europe. Further confirmation comes from the fact that the overwhelming majority of Mozambican migrants in South Africa are unskilled.[24]

Precedent

A successful pioneer group can act as a magnet for further migration. In Korner's words, "Once migration has been routine, as it has been in most of the countries concerned [that is, traditionally receiving countries], relevant information is more or less common knowledge. The fact that migration paths and procedures have been 'run-in' also makes the risk less-daunting. Migration may then become a mass phenomenon."[25]

Gomel elaborates further by noting the tendency of migration to flow toward an area with an initial nucleus of immigrants from a given country, which makes the relocation of subsequent arrivals less costly. For example, most foreigners in Germany are from Turkey (34 percent) and the former Yugoslavia (13 percent). In South Africa, George, a Mozambican residing there illegally, admitted that his cousin's successful negotiation of the obstacles to emigration—including an electric fence and South African military patrols—gave him the necessary incentive to emigrate. He also knew that his cousin and friends would provide him with food and shelter while he sought employment.[26]

Demographic Influences/Population Growth

Population growth in itself does not necessarily urge people to cross international borders, unless it is coupled with economic decline— fewer employment opportunities and greater stress on the social and welfare services of the state, which ultimately lead to social and political discontent. This seems to be the case in the Maghreb. Each year more than 1 million youths join the Maghrebi workforce; the population is increasing at an annual rate of 3 percent. Faced with a declining economic performance and less work, many choose to emigrate to Western Europe. Similar population pressure is responsible for much of the emigration from Mexico to the United States.[27]

In southern Africa, the population is growing at a rate between 2.5 percent and 3.5 percent per annum, although living standards throughout the region are on the decline. For example, Angola's real GDP has fallen to only 70 percent of its 1973 level, and Mozambique's real GDP declined by 15 percent between 1982 and 1987. An added complication, as Baynham notes, is the youthful profile of southern Africa's population—what amounts to a built-in demographic momentum. As employment opportunities decrease, or even remain constant, and the labor force continues to expand at an alarming rate, unemployment will rise and with it the motivation to migrate.[28]

Environmental Conditions

Policymakers are more aware than ever that ecological damage can foster major population movements. Environmental migrants result from two categories of catastrophe, those without an anthropogenic cause—volcanic eruptions, earthquakes, whirlwinds, hurricanes, droughts, landslides, avalanches, floods, and forest fires—and those with an anthropogenic cause—the destruction of arable and grazing land, sustained heavy flooding, and even damage from hurricanes, whirlwinds, hailstorms, landslides, avalanches, and forest fires that occur as the direct, or indirect, result of human activity. Woehlcke states that most environmental migrations stem from "direct anthropogenic destruction," especially the degradation of soils. Various studies have demonstrated the causal link between environmental decline and mass migration. Heisbourg, for example, argues that "environmental prospects in Eastern Europe will play a key role in provoking population movements to the prosperous West," and the poverty caused by, among other things, soil erosion and deforestation has caused 1 million people to flee Haiti.[29]

In southern Africa, natural disasters with an anthropogenic component also provide a stimulus for human movement. For example, Alfredo, another Mozambican informant, explained that because the peasants in his village did not engage in crop rotation, crop yields were low and the soil degraded. The civil war in Mozambique, RENAMO's devastation of the countryside, and the decimation of the local population, which forced massive evacuations, all further conspired to leave potentially productive fields dormant.[30]

Southern Africa's population movements have also been sparked by natural disasters without an anthropogenic stimulus, such as the drought of 1992, often regarded as the worst to affect the region in eighty years. Moreover, the erratic rainfall in the central and southern provinces of Angola, coupled with a civil war, left 1.9 million people starving in 1991. Not surprisingly, many Angolans moved from the provinces hardest hit toward the country's borders and then to neighboring states. The drought of 1992 intensified these population movements.[31]

Until 1990, the countries of the Southern African Development Community (SADC) were producing enough food to feed their populations of more than 85 million people. But in 1991/92, the region experienced a food deficit of 2.8 million tons. Those living in the worst areas of the drought, who faced starvation, first relocated within their own countries but ultimately crossed borders to escape the famine.[32]

Economic Opportunities

Larrabee claims that most migrants in the 1990s are motivated by economic considerations—including the westward movement of people from the former Eastern bloc countries, the movement of Haitians, Mexicans, and El Salvadorans to the United States, and the movement of North Africans to Western Europe. This desire for a better life also seems to be a prime motivation for migration in Africa. For instance, between 1986 and 1990, countries in central Africa lost between 2 percent and 5 percent of their populations to eastern and southern Africa. This shift coincided with differential GDP growth rates—higher in eastern and southern Africa, by an average of 3.2 percent, and lower in central Africa by 0.5 percent.[33]

Economic variables also play a role in the migration of people within southern Africa, from, say, Mozambique, Lesotho, Angola, and Zimbabwe to more inviting places like South Africa, Botswana, and Namibia. South Africa, particularly, serves as a magnet to those seeking employment, a higher living standard, and brighter economic prospects. The size of the South African economy makes the allure of the country almost overwhelming to many in the region. But the allure also relates to another of southern Africa's historical legacies.

The discovery of diamonds in the Orange Free State in the 1860s and the subsequent discovery of gold on the Witwatersrand in 1886 created a massive stir in nineteenth-century southern Africa. The demands of the mining industry created the contract migrant labor system that crisscrossed the whole of southern Africa. Neighboring states became labor reservoirs of cheap, unskilled black labor for South African mining magnates. Eventually, the economies of South Africa's neighbors became dependent on the contract labor migrant system for foreign exchange. A survey in 1991 revealed that almost 40 percent of rural households in Lesotho were dependent on the remittances of migrants working on the mines of the Rand.[34]

The latter half of the twentieth century saw significant changes in the South African economy—an emphasis on the recruitment of skilled labor and the expulsion and reduced employment of unskilled labor. In 1991, nearly 200 Zimbabwean doctors settled in South Africa. Conversely, the number of foreign workers employed in South Africa's mines fell from 606,000 in 1951, to 587,000 in 1960, to 490,000 in 1970. This downward spiral continued through much of the 1980s and 1990s. In 1986, the number of foreign workers on South African mines stood at 211,247; by 1995 this figure was 165,825 (with another 100,000 employed in the Republic's agricultural sector). This downward trend shows every indication of continuing—especially in light of Pretoria's intention to employ more of its own citizens. It holds serious consequences for states like Lesotho, which rely heavily on the remittances of its migrant labor force.[35]

Yet, this slant on the matter begs an important question. Has closing, or restricting, the legal channels of immigration for unskilled labor resulted in an increase in the illegal migration of unskilled labor? In other words, does a functional relationship exist between contract labor migration and illegal immigrants? The literary evidence suggests so, but uneven economic development, skewed patterns of growth, or economic disparities do not themselves induce population movements. The affected populations must have a knowledge thereof first, which is the province of the communications technology discussed earlier. The linkage between advances in communication and mass migrations is vividly illustrated in Europe, where television programs beamed from the former West Germany to East Germany, from Finland to Estonia, from Italy to Albania, and from France to Algeria told of superior living standards in the West, thereby planting the seeds of migration.[36]

In southern Africa, the consciousness of economic disparity has been reinforced by the contract migrant labor system, a century-old structure of transnational migration that criss-crosses the subcontinent and carries word of better prospects. The incentive to migrate is also sharpened by the effects of economic structural adjustment programs (ESAPs). In an attempt to confront economic crises, most countries in southern Africa have resorted to ESAPs brokered by the International Monetary Fund (IMF) and the World Bank, which have adversely affected the local populations wherever they have been implemented. In Zambia, for instance, the price of maizemeal, the country's staple food, increased by 500 percent since subsidies were cut. The aim of such restructuring under the auspices of ESAPs was to curb production costs by the retrenchment of thousands of workers. In the public sector, 20,000 civil servants lost their jobs, and, in the private sector, an estimated 70,000 more. The actual effect (some argue that it is a short-term effect) of the ESAPs was to increase poverty, not relieve it, and, thus, encourage migration, legal or otherwise.[37]

Political Issues

The organic link between political instability and mass movement has been evident from time immemorial. More recently, the 2 to 3 million Iraqi Kurds who escaped persecution and repression by taking shelter in neighboring Iran and Turkey are testimony to this phenomenon. An even more poignant recent case is in the former Yugoslavia, where disintegration, civil war, and the redrawing of boundaries are creating internal hemorrhaging and the release of large numbers of refugees into both Hungary and Germany.[38]

In Africa, turmoil resulting from political rivalry, ethnic strife, socioeconomic inequities, or regional imbalances tends to promote south to south migration. Its roots take various forms: persecution of minorities, denial of political rights, mass expulsions, coups, and civil war. In 1992, a United Nations' report revealed that, besides those killed in the civil war, an additional 1.4 million Angolans (out of a population of 10 million) suffered material loss—primarily the destruction of crops and homesteads—the loss of employment opportunities, and personal loss—the deaths of family and friends. The report also stated that 4.7 million Mozambicans (out of a total population of 15.7 million) have suffered the effects of civil war, all of them potential emigrants. In 1990 alone, an estimated 600,000 to 1 million people died, and three million were uprooted. A graphic illustration of the link between political turmoil and mass displacement occurred in Mozambique, in 1991, when RENAMO attacked the border town of Ressano Garcia, driving 3,000 residents into South Africa.[39]

The Effects of Hosting an Illegal Immigrant Population

Proper analysis of what effect the large population of illegal aliens has on South Africa requires an understanding of the illegal aliens themselves. As noted earlier, one of the primary reasons for the lack of statistical information about them is the clandestine nature of their migration. In 1993, however, the Southern African Catholic Bishops Conference's (SACBC) Masungulu Project did a survey of 6,348 Mozambican households in South Africa. Although bold generalizations about the whole illegal alien population in the Republic based on this limited source might seem ill-advised, there are three reasons why the survey can speak to issues that touch the entire illegal immigrant population residing within the country. First of all, Mozambicans make up the bulk of that population in South Africa. Second, research findings by individual researchers and the Department of Home Affairs have arrived at similar conclusions regarding illegal aliens from countries other than Mozambique. Finally, the push factors operating in the various countries of the region are roughly similar, producing a similar type of emigrant.[40]

What the Masungulo survey revealed was that Mozambican migrants in South Africa are a young and growing population; that the dependency ratio (that is, the number of people under the age of fifteen and over the age of sixty-four, relative to all others in the population) is high; that a greater percentage of them are women of child-bearing age; that most do not have more than three years of formal education; and that most do not have the skills to work outside of subsistence agriculture. The costs of hosting an illegal population with such a demographic profile are prohibitively high. Col. Brian van Niekerk, national coordinator of border control and policing of the South African Police Services, stated that it cost the country R1,985 million to house an alien population in 1994.[41]

Clearly, the large concentration of illegal immigrants in South Africa places an inordinate burden on the state, decreasing the capacity of its

Reconstruction and Development Program (RDP) to improve the lot of ordinary South Africans. Consider the strain that illegal immigrants place on health services. Clinics in the former KaNgwane and Gazankulu that were established to meet the needs of South African citizens are overstretched because of the thousands of illegal Mozambicans residing in both areas. Since aliens are generally destitute, or come from strife-ravaged areas, they usually need much more attention than the locals—all of it at the expense of South African citizens.[42]

Also disturbing are the diseases of epidemic potential that poverty-stricken, malnourished illegal immigrants bring with them. Aliens are susceptible to, for example, yellow fever, cholera, tuberculosis, and AIDS. Malaria and other cases of chloroquine resistance have been associated with migrants from Mozambique in the Northern Transvaal. The relationship between illegal immigration and epidemics is borne out in the Nsanje district of Malawi—15 km from the Mozambican border—where migration resulted in roughly the same percentages of AIDS, malaria, cholera, and tuberculosis cases on both sides of the border. Schutte traces a causal link between illegal immigrants and the spread of the HIV virus in South Africa.[43]

A functional relationship also exists between illegal aliens and the crime rate. During 1993, 4,969 illegal aliens were arrested in South Africa for serious crimes (rape, murder, theft, burglary, etc.). In 1994, however, 12,403 illegal aliens were arrested for serious crimes. Police associate 14 percent of the crime within South Africa with illegal aliens—mainly gun-running, drug trafficking, prostitution, and money laundering. Crime and violence affect the economy in two ways: Rising crime and violence reduce investor confidence, and they allocate resources that would have gone into RDP programs into the security apparatus. The present national budget has witnessed a significant increase in expenses for the South African Police Services.[44]

The influx of illegal immigrants also contributes to squatting in South Africa. Many aliens arrive in South Africa destitute, jobless, and homeless. The vast majority of them find their way to squatter areas. It is estimated that 80 percent reside in informal housing settlements and squatter camps. PLANACT (a service organization that undertakes, among other things, social studies) found that 20 percent of the inhabitants of these informal settlements and hostels in Gauteng are Zimbabwean and Mozambican. This figure not only indicates the extent of migration into South Africa; it also reveals an additional burden on the RDP. The government is not only attempting to provide services and upgrade facilities in squatter areas but also trying to provide houses for all South Africans. However, as Schutte notes, because it is extremely difficult to distinguish between aliens and citizens in squatter communities, illegal immigrants come to benefit from the facilities and houses provided under the RDP, at the cost of the South African taxpayer.[45]

Toolo and Bethlehem reveal that many citizens blame illegal foreign workers for low wages, which, according to union officials reflects that local people have decreased access to employment. They report that illegal immigrants are active in the following sectors of the economy: agriculture, hotel and restaurant staff, construction, domestic service, and informal trading.[46]

In the food and agriculture sector, Food and Allied Workers Union (FAWU) organizers have noticed large numbers of aliens working on farms in Mpumalanga and on the sugar plantations of northern KwaZulu-Natal. They claim that farmers employ them because they work for less—many for just shelter and a plate of food a day—because fear of exposure makes them resistant to union activities.

South African Commercial, Catering and Allied Workers Union (SACCAWU) officials have detected increasing numbers of illegal aliens in the hotel and restaurant sector. Officials of the Tea-Room and Restaurant Industrial Council believe the majority of them to be Mozambican and Zimbabwean. The SACCAWU organizers report that these workers, like their counterparts in agriculture, are prepared to work for extremely low wages and that their vulnerability makes them wary of union activism. The results again are depressed wage levels and decreased employment opportunities for South Africans. A popular example of the problem is the Cafe Zurich in Hillbrow, where the owner dismissed twenty South African waiters and replaced them with twenty Zairese waiters who received no pay, only tips.[47]

Both the Construction and Allied Workers Union (CAWU) and the Construction Industrial Council confirm that illegal aliens have entered their industry—the majority of them employed by subcontractors. Since subcontracting has grown in recent years, accounting for 80 percent of employment in housing construction, it is likely that foreign workers occupy a large portion of this labor market. The CAWU points out that subcontractors are difficult to regulate and that their hiring of aliens allows them to pay wages as low as R80 ($19) per week.

The South African Domestic Workers Union (SADWU) has observed a similar rise in illegals—most of them from Malawi and Zimbabwe. Since they too are willing to work for subsistence wages and are unable to join the union, employers prefer them to South Africans. They appear not only in the suburbs, but also in the townships and rural areas.

Illegal aliens in the informal sector have elicited much concern from the African Chamber of Hawkers and Informal Business (ACHIB). Aliens engaged in hawking come from Taiwan, China, India, and Pakistan, as well as southern Africa. Because they sell their goods cheaply, local hawkers are losing their only source of livelihood.[48]

The extent to which illegal immigration can contribute to domestic instability is evident in an incident that occurred in August 1994. ACHIB members marched through the center of Johannesburg, physically abusing all of the foreign hawkers that they could find. They also marched to the Hillbrow police station and demanded the immediate removal of all foreign hawkers.

The rising tide of xenophobia is not confined to ACHIB members. A survey by the Human Sciences Research Council (HSRC) in October 1994 found that 56 percent of South Africans wanted tighter government control of illegal immigrants. By February 1995, the figure was up to 72 percent.[49]

Xenophobia has serious implications for domestic and regional politics. There already exists a marked degree of dissension between political parties about how to approach the issue of illegal immigrants. The HSRC survey revealed that the Inkatha Freedom Party (IFP), National Party (NP), and the parties of the white right-wing are far more xenophobic than their African National Congress (ANC) counterparts. In September 1994, the Inkatha Youth Brigade threatened strong action against illegal aliens if the government failed to do so. The illegal-immigration issue may occupy a central platform for political parties for the 1999 elections. Moreover, should any political party manage to gain political office on a tough anti-immigrant stance, the consequences for regional relations will be serious. The Republic of South Africa will be living once more against its neighbors rather than with its neighbors. The tensions between Pretoria, Harare, and Maputo concerning South Africa's enforced repatriation of Mozambican and Zimbabwean nationals are already palpable.[50]

Managing Mass Migrations: Toward Strategic Perspectives

The tremendous burden that illegal immigration places on the South African government and people is undeniable. The South African government realizes that the influx of illegal aliens into the country must be curbed, but Pretoria's responses have generally been reactive and ad hoc, ranging from such control measures as enforced repatriation and more police and army personnel on the borders to outright accommodation. Witness, for instance, the recent cabinet decision to legalize illegal immigrants who have resided in the country for longer than five years, who have been gainfully employed, who have no criminal record, or who are married to a South African spouse. These measures, however, have failed to deter illegal immigrants; they may be entering the Republic at a rate as high as one every ten minutes. Penuel Maduna, the former deputy minister of home affairs, was recently quoted as saying, "History has shown us time and time again that hunger and fear are driving forces which are much stronger than even the most sophisticated aliens control measures. South Africa has become the country of survival for many."[51]

South Africa needs to adopt a "strategic perspective," modeled after the relatively successful European one that, unlike control and accommodation, addresses the root causes of population movements. The objective of this long-term interventionist approach would be to provide incentives for prospective emigrants to stay within the borders of their own country by improving the political and economic conditions that give rise to mass migrations.[52]

One line of the strategy argues for the encouragement of political pluralism in the third world—mainly in the form of liberal democracies, multiparty systems, and free, fair and frequent elections—to curtail political conflict and civil war and reduce refugee flows. Notwithstanding the importance of pluralism, it is important to recognize, however, that transition from a single-party state to political pluralism is delicate. As the resumption of fighting after the 1992 elections in Angola showed, it can have the opposite results to those desired. The point holds special relevance to southern Africa where "the difficulties which transitions pose are exacerbated by the overall weakness of the polities within which change is taking place."[53]

Since poverty—or, rather, the lack of economic opportunities—is often at the root of population movements, the interventionist approach may be able to promote economic development within the sending states by forging special trade agreements, investment programs, and educational schemes. Italy and Spain have proposed a program of this kind with regard to North Africa, in an attempt to create enough economic stability to reduce population movements into southern Europe. As a third-world state with development needs of its own, however, South Africa may not be able to become such a donor country in the foreseeable future.[54]

Another possible weakness of this tactic is that it tackles the global nature of the problem on a piecemeal basis. Globalists argue that only a restructuring of the international economy will reduce south to north and south to south flows. South Africa is facing not only an influx of illegal immigrants from its neighbors, but also from places as far afield as Nigeria and Algeria, and even from Asia and Eastern Europe. Moreover, even if the donor strategy is to prove successful in the long run, it may have contradictory results in the short to medium term. As Hamilton and Holder put it, "The development process itself tends to stimulate migration in the short to medium term by raising expectations and enhancing people's ability to migrate. Thus the development solution to the problem of unauthorized migration is measured in decades—or even generations. . . . Any co-operative effort to reduce migratory pressures must stay the course in the face of shorter term contradictory results."[55]

A more sophisticated strategy is to encourage regional integration, which proponents see as the key to stem migration flows, pointing to the European Community (EC) as a successful example. Gomel states that countries of southern Europe in the 1970s (Italy, Greece, Spain, and Portugal) ceased exporting their "surplus labor" to the more affluent countries in northern Europe as a direct result of EC regional integration, which decreased wage differentials and increased economic and social homogeneity. On the surface, this strategy seems to have been effective. However, closer inspection reveals its flaws. For example, the decrease in population flows from southern to northern Europe was not only the result of economic factors; demographics also played a role. A drop in birth rates decreased the pressure on social and economic infrastructure, thus increasing the overall living standards of the population.[56]

Meissner has contested whether wage differentials between southern and northern Europe were that far apart in the first place. She also points out that Turkey's application for membership in the EC was turned down for fear that economic integration might lead to substantial emigration from Turkey to Western Europe, the wage differential being ten to one. The example of possible migration acting as a deterrent to economic integration holds an important lesson for the states of southern Africa that are currently considering it; for they show large wage disparities—for example, between South Africa, Botswana, and Namibia on the one hand, and Angola, Lesotho, and Mozambique on the other.[57]

Could such wage disparities serve as a spoke in the wheel of regional integration in southern Africa? The case of the EC suggests the possibility. However, doubts regarding the future of the regional project are further reinforced by the weakness of the SADC and the lack of an integrated vision, as evinced by the plethora of regional organizations in southern Africa—in addition to SADC, the Southern African Customs Union (SACU), and the Common Market for Eastern and southern Africa (COMESA).

Would the failure of southern Africa's current regional project necessarily mean the failure of the interventionist approach to the problem of mass migration? Emphatically not. The interventionist approach is still useful. Instead of a multilateral forum, South Africa and its neighbors could establish a number of bilateral relationships. Africa has a long history of bilateral treaties between countries connected by population movements—for instance, the agreement between Nigeria and Equatorial Guinea and that between Burkina Faso and Cote d' Ivoire. Bilaterals also exist between Burkina Faso and Gabon, between Gabon and Cameroon, and between Ghana and Libya, all of them concentrating on issues of entry and departure. More comprehensive bilaterals covering not only issues of entry, residence, and departure, but also occupational and social rights, participation in trade unions, and social security rights exist between France and its former colonies of Senegal, Mali, and Mauritania.[58]

Building on this long African tradition, South Africa also seems headed in a bilateral direction. Consider the bilaterals that the minister of home affairs has had with his Zimbabwean and Mozambican counterparts. The objective of such bilaterals need not only be control and regulation of population flows, but also proactive intervention to address the root causes of population movements. Pretoria's success in raising concerns about the lack of democracy in Swaziland with King Mswati III is particularly relevant in this regard. Subsequently, the Swazi monarch decided to undertake constitutional reforms.

The merit of this approach lies in its ability to bridge the concerns of illegal aliens and the state. An effective policy would treat the root causes that push illegal immigrants out of their homeland, as well as relieve the burden on the socioeconomic infrastructure that illegal immigrants inevitably cause in the host country.

Notes to Chapter 6

1. Solomon, "Population Movements into South Africa: Trends, Outlooks, Policies," *Foundation for Global Dialogue (FGD) Occasional Paper Series*, 2 (1995), 3; Myron Weiner, *The Global Migration Crisis: Challenge to States and to Human Rights* (New York, 1995), 1.

2. Giorgio Gomel, "Migration Toward Western Europe: Trends, Outlook, Policies," *International Spectator*, XXVII (1992), 67; Solomon, "In Search of Canaan: A Critical Evaluation of the Causes and Effects of Migrations within Southern Africa and Strategies to Cope with Them," *Southern African Perspective*, 24 (1993), 15; George Orr, "Migration Management," paper presented at the "Seminar on Migration Management in South Africa," hosted by the International Organization for Migration (IOM) and the UN Population Fund (UNPF) (Pretoria, 1995), 1.

3. Graham Evans and Jeffrey Newnham, *The Dictionary of World Politics: A Reference Guide to Concepts, Ideas, and Institutions* (New York, 1992), 22; Southern African Catholic Bishops Conference (SACBC), *Report on Immigrants, Refugees and Displaced People* (Pretoria, 1995), 2–5.

4. G. S. Labuschagne and Marie Eloise Muller, "Population and Migration in Southern Africa in the 1990s," *Politikon*, XX (1993), 48–49; I. B. Logan, "The Brain-Drain of Professional, Technical and Kindred Workers from Developing Countries: Some Lessons from the Africa–United States Flow of Professionals (1980-1989)," *International Migration Quarterly Review*, XXX (1992), 289–312; Alida Casteleijn, "Migration Trends in South Africa," paper presented at the conference, "Managing Mass Migrations," hosted by the IOM and the UNPF (Pretoria, 1995), 4-6; K. Makombe, "Brain-Drain: Cause for Concern," *Southern African Research and Documentation Center* (SARDC) (1992), 1.

5. Weiner, *Global Migration Crisis*, 2.

6. M. Woehlcke, "Environmental Refugees," *Aussenpolitik*, XLIII (1992), 287–288; Gil Loescher, "Refugee Movements and International Security," *Adelphi Papers*, 268 (1992), 7.

7. Quoted in Solomon, "In Search of Canaan," 3–4; *idem*, "Change and Continuity in South Africa's Foreign Policy, 1978-1991," unpub. M.A. thesis (Univ. of Durban-Westville, 1994), 169.

8. Chris Dolan, "Policy Challenges for the New South Africa," *Southern African Migration: Domestic and Regional Policy Implications*, Workshop Proceedings 14, Center for Policy Studies (Johannesburg, 1995), 53–54; Article 1.2, *Organization of African Unity Convention Governing the Specific Aspects of Refugee Problems in Africa* (Addis Ababa, 1969), 2.

9. Weiner, *Global Migration Crisis*, 189

10. David Martin, "The Refugee Concept: On Definitions, Politics and the Careful Use of a Scarce Resource," in Howard Adelman (ed.), *Refugee Policy* (Toronto, 1991); Weiner, *Global Migration Crisis*, 190.

11. For critics of the UN *Convention*, see Andrew Shacknove, "Who Is a Refugee?" *Ethics* (January 1985), 274-284; Goran Melander, "The Two Refugee Definitions," *Report 4*, Raoul Institute of Human Rights and Humanitarian Law (Lund, Sweden, 1987). Weiner, *Global Migration Crisis*, 190. Personal communication with Pia Prutz Phiri, senior protection officer, UNHCR Southern African Office, Halfway House, July 3, 1996.

12. UNHCR, *Handbook on Procedures and Criteria for Determining Refugee Status* (Geneva, 1979), 14.

13. Chris Humana, *World Human Rights Guide* (London, 1983), 13–23.

14. UNHCR, *Handbook*, 14; Melander, "Two Refugee Definitions," 13–14.

15. P. Nobel, "Protection of Refugees in Europe as Seen in 1987," *Report 4*, 26–28; Hilton Toolo and Lael Bethlehem, "Labour Migration to South Africa," paper presented at the National Labour and Economic Development Institute (NALEDI) "Workshop on Labour Migration to South Africa" (Johannesburg, 1994), 5.

16. Weiner, *Global Migration Crisis*, 188–189.

17. *The Economist*, 4 March 1995; Maxine Reitzes, "Alien Issues," *Indicator South Africa*, XII (1994), 7; Toolo and Bethlehem, "Labour Migration," 5; Reitzes, "Divided on the 'Demon': Immigration Policy Since the Election," *Policy and Review Series*, VIII (1995), 4.

18. Anthony Minnaar and Mike Hough, "Illegal in South Africa: Scope, Extent, and Impact," paper presented at the IOM and UNPF conference, "Managing Mass Migrations" (Pretoria, 1995), 4.

19. T. Rodney H. Davenport, *South Africa: A Modern History* (Hong Kong, 1991), 5, 12-15.

20. See Solomon, "In Search of Canaan."

21. Loescher, "Refugee Movements and International Security," *Adelphi Papers*, 268 (1992).

22. Gomel, "Migration," 74. See also François Heisbourg, "Population Movements in post-Cold War Europe," *Survival*, XXXIII (1991), 35; R. Chidoware, "Refugees and Exiles in South Africa," *Southern African Research and Documentation Center* (May 1991), 2; *Christian Science Monitor*, 19 Feb. 1991, 42.

23. SACBC, *Mozambican Refugees in South Africa* (Pretoria, 1993), 36.

24. *New York Times*, 12 Feb. 1993; *Washington Post*, 26 Nov. 1990.

25. H. Korner, "Future Trends in International Migration," *Intereconomics* (January/February, 1991), 42.

26. Gomel, "Migrations," 74; Solomon, "In Search of Canaan," 9.

27. Aderanti Adepoju, "Preliminary Analysis of Emigration Dynamics in Sub-Saharan Africa," *International Migration Quarterly Review*, XXXIII (1995), 315–390; Reginald T. Appleyard, *International Migration: Challenge for the Nineties* (Geneva, 1992); Heisbourg, "Population Movements," 35; K. A. Hamilton and K. Holder, "International Migration and Foreign Policy: A Survey of the Literature," *Washington Quarterly*, XXVI (1991), 197.

28. Robert Davies, "A Statistical Profile of the SADCC Countries in the 1980s," *Southern African Perspectives*, 3 (1990), 4; Solomon, "Migration in Southern Africa: A Comparative Perspective," *Indian Journal for African Studies*, V (1992), 13–39; S. Baynham, "South Africa and the World in the 1990s," *South Africa International*, XXIII (January, 1993), 14.

29. Woehlcke, "Environmental Refugees," 289, 290; Heisbourg, "Population Movements," 35; Hamilton and Holder, "International Migration," 197.

30. Personal interview with Joao and Roberto, Mozambican immigrants, March 15, 1993.

31. M. Tafirenyika, "SADCC's Food Security—What Went Wrong?" *Southern African Research and Documentation Center* (February 18, 1992), 1; *Christian Science Monitor*, 7 Jan. 1991.

32. S. Kuwali, "The Food Situation in Southern Africa," *Southern African Political and Economic Monthly*, VI (1992), 3; United Nations Program of Action for African Economic Recovery and Development (UNPAAERD), "Extracts from Economic Crises in Africa: Final Review of the UN-PAAERD," *Backgrounder*, V (1991), 3, 5.

33. F. S. Larrabee, "Down and Out in Warsaw and Budapest—Eastern Europe and East-West Migration," *International Security*, XVI (1992), 6–7; Hamilton and Holder, "International Migration," 197; Loescher, "Refugee Movements," 7–10; Heisbourg, "Population Movements," 34-35; UNPAAERD, "Extracts," 3.

34. Solomon, "Beyond Refugee Crisis Management," paper presented at the Salzburg Seminar on Involuntary Migration (Salzburg, 1995), 6.

35. Erich Leistner, "Migration of High-Level Manpower to South Africa," *Africa Insight*, XXIII (1993), 218; J. O. Oucho, "International Migration and Sustainable Human Development in Eastern and Southern Africa," *International Migration*, XXXIII (1995), 35; Solomon, "Population Movements," 6.

36. Loescher, "Refugee Movements," 10.

37. Chidoware, "The Effects of ESAPs on Workers," *Southern African Research and Documentation Center* (May 18, 1993), 1–2.

38. Loescher, "Refugee Movements," 3, 28.

39. H. Arnold, "South-North Migration and North-South Conflict," *Viertaljahresberichte*, 127 (March, 1992), 1; Heisbourg, "Population Movements," 39; Loescher, "Refugee Movements," 28; *Washington Post*, 26 Nov. 1990; UN Spotlight on Humanitarian Issues, *Enlarging the UN's Humanitarian Mandate* (New York, 1992), 1; *Christian Science Monitor*, 2 May 1991.

40. Orr, "Migration to South Africa," paper presented at the seminar, "Migration: Sources, Patterns, Implications," hosted by Witwatersrand Branch of the South African Institute of International Affairs (Johannesburg, 1993); Danie Schutte, "Migration: The Status Quo and Prospect for Southern Africa," *Institute for Security Studies, University of Pretoria (ISSUP) Bulletin*, VII (1993), 2–5; Peter Vale and Solomon, "Migration and Global Change: Understanding the Tsunami Effect," paper presented at the seminar, "Migration, Sources, Patterns, Implications."

41. SACBC, *Mozambican Refugees*, 36; Brian van Niekerk, "The Impact of Illegal Aliens on Safety and Security in South Africa," *ISSUP Bulletin*, 7 (1995), 5.

42. Schutte, "Migration," 7.

43. Solomon, "Changing Patterns of Migration in Southern Africa," in Minnie Venter (ed.), *Migrancy and AIDS* (Capetown, 1994), 22; Schutte, "Migration," 8.

44. Personal correspondence with Minnaar, Human Sciences Research Council, January 17, 1996; Reitzes, "Alien Issues," 8.

45. Schutte, "Migration," 9.

46. Toolo and Bethlehem, "Labour Migration," 6–8.

47. This last point was related to the author by a researcher at the National Labour and Economic Development Institute (NALEDI), Johannesburg, August 31, 1994.

48. Reitzes, "Alien Issues," 9.

49. Chris de Kock, Charl Schutte, and Diane Ehlers, *Perceptions of Current Socio-Political Issues in South Africa* (Pretoria, 1995), 22–23.

50. Minnaar, personal correspondence, January 17, 1996.

51. Reitzes, "Alien Issues," 9; *idem*, "Divided on the 'Demon,'" 15.

52. Larrabee, "Down and Out," 31–32; Sarah Collinson, *Europe and International Migration* (London, 1994); Astri Suhrke, *Towards a Comprehensive Refugee Policy: Conflict and Refugees in the Post–Cold War World* (Bergen, 1992), 1–3.

53. Heisbourg, "Population Movements," 39; Vale, "Southern Africa's Security: Some Old Issues, Many New Questions," paper presented at the "Seminar on Confidence and Security-Building Measures in Southern Africa," organized by the UN Office for Disarmament Affairs (Windhoek, Namibia, 1993), 5.

54. Hamilton and Holder, "International Migration," 201; S. Bearman, *Strategic Survey 1990–1991* (London, 1991), 45.

55. Hamilton and Holder, "International Migration," 201.

56. Gomel, "Migration," 70.

57. Doris Meissner, "Managing Migrations," *Foreign Policy*, LXXXVI (1992), 82.

58. Sharon Stanton Russel, Karen Jacobsen, and William Dean Stanley, *International Migration and Development in Sub-Saharan Africa* (Washington, D.C., 1990), 106-107.

7

Katherine Marshall

Regional Development Strategies and Challenges
Some Economic and Social Underpinnings

THIS CHAPTER sketches some of the key economic and social issues confronting southern Africa. Many of these issues have critical importance in and of themselves but they also show the specific linkages between peace and prosperity, inequality and poverty, and stability and peace. Although some of these linkages may seem intuitively apparent, hinted at by history and experience elsewhere, they are both complex and uncertain. At a fundamental level, peace and prosperity should go hand in hand, and deep social divisions and inequalities must be seen as profoundly destabilizing.

The underlying hypothesis is that long-term prospects have never been better for this part of Africa, and that prosperity is an attainable dream, but the rapids ahead are fast moving, strewn with rocks and white water at every turn. The key questions, which are tightly bound, are, How fast can and will economic growth come, and What effect will it have, or not have, on the extraordinary levels of inequality and poverty in the region? "Lessons" from other regions of the world, as well as specific reflections on how the "Africa development drama" appears, are worth bearing in mind, as they relate to the central issues of war and peace, and particularly the policy approaches and instruments that might best help in the conquest of poverty that remains the central problem for southern Africa.

Regional Portraits and Issues

Southern Africa has taken on an entirely new face, with the dramatic shift in South Africa's position and the near end of the major armed conflicts in the region. For the first time, this vital region can look to a coherent development strategy, building on the overall, sizable market and the comparative advantages and significant resources of its countries. (For present purposes, the southern African region includes Angola, Botswana, Lesotho, Malawi, Mozambique, Namibia, South Africa, Swaziland, Tanzania, Zambia, and Zimbabwe— the SADC countries minus Mauritius.)

One clear lesson that has emerged from the regions that now see extraordinary success in development is the importance of a "neighborhood effect" for growth and prosperity. Significant benefits that spill across national boundaries can come simply from the proximity of successful neighbors. All too often, however, failure also seems to spread across boundaries. If South Africa achieves success, and if Mozambique or Zimbabwe or Namibia takes off, then the whole group of countries is likely to benefit. Since the neighborhood effect until now has been extremely negative, this possibility is a clear source of hope. At this juncture, the neighborhood's promise is bright, with many assets, foremost among them the powerhouse that the new South Africa represents.

Nonetheless, in looking to this potential for synergy and regional development, it is important to focus on the region's many disparities and differences. Two facts stand out sharply: the enormous economic weight of South Africa, and the extraordinary levels of inequality, both within countries and between countries. Figures 7-1 and 7-2 illustrate the large gaps between the relative sizes of the populations and the economies within the region. South Africa is the largest in terms of population, but these disparities are dwarfed by the picture that emerges regarding relative economic strength. Table 7-1 provides additional data.

The wide variations in both GDP and GDP growth present a central challenge for the future. This picture is clear to both economic actors and outside partners, but not so the solutions. Many questions about direction and policy prescriptions remain.

FIGURE 7-1. Southern Africa: Relative Size of Population

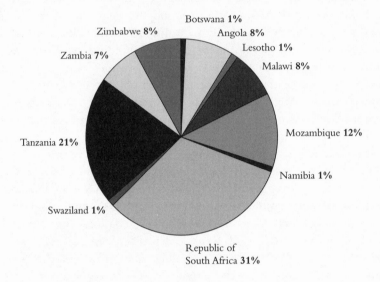

FIGURE 7-2. Southern Africa, Relative Size of Economies

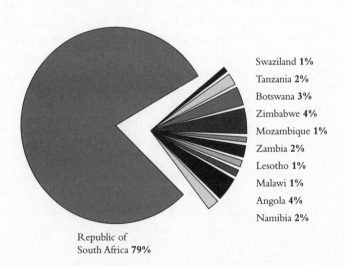

TABLE 7-1. Population and Economy, Southern Africa

	Population mid-1994 (millions)	Average annual percentage population growth			Average annual percentage growth (GDP, real, in millions of U.S. dollars, constant 1987 prices)				Average annual percentage growth (GDP per capita)
		1975-84	1985-89	1990-MR	1994	1975-84	1985-89	1990-MR	1985-89
Angola	10.7	2.7	2.9	3.7	7,238	—	4.7	-4.7	-7.0
Botswana	1.4	3.6	3.5	3.2	2,574	11.3	10.5	5.0	6.6
Lesotho	2.0	2.7	2.8	2.7	637	4.8	6.9	5.3	0.5
Malawi	10.8	3.3	5.0	4.0	1,290	3.3	2.6	0.6	-2.0
Mozambique	16.6	2.8	0.5	3.4	2,060	—	6.0	6.0	3.5
Namibia	1.5	2.7	2.7	2.7	2,375	—	2.8	3.8	3.4
South Africa	41.6	2.7	2.5	2.3	86,775	2.7	1.7	-0.4	-1.4
Swaziland	0.9	3.2	3.5	3.5	695	3.5	5.8	1.8	-1.0
Tanzania	28.8	3.2	3.3	3.1	4,412	—	4.0	3.3	0.8
Zambia	9.2	3.5	3.5	3.1	2,330	0.2	2.1	0.0	-1.3
Zimbabwe	11.0	3.1	3.4	2.8	6,778	2.7	4.1	1.1	-0.6
Total	134.6				117,164.2				
Sub-Saharan Africa	573.9	2.9	2.9	2.9	275,472	2.4	2.4	0.9	-1.2
excluding South Africa	532.3	2.9	2.9	3.0	188,713	2.2	2.8	1.5	-1.0
excluding South Africa and Nigeria	424.4	2.9	2.9	3.0	150,741	2.9	2.6	1.1	-1.5

SOURCE. World Bank.

Regional Development Issues

Regional development is widely preached and advocated as a high priority for southern Africa, and a plethora of regional institutions exists. The Southern African Development Community (SADC) is an institution with a rich history of achievement, now grappling with its role in the new South Africa. The leaders and governments of the region, with South Africa in the lead, repeatedly stress their determination to forge stronger links among nations. Likewise, countries and their partners invest time and other resources in meetings and other collaborative initiatives. Nonetheless, beyond the rhetoric and a few significant examples of successful regional ventures, the establishment of a long-lived reality behind the principles and ideals seems one of the more frustrating goals facing southern Africa's leaders and many of its partners. Many basic questions persist.

Some important examples of successful regional collaboration in the "new southern Africa" are the various peace-making initiatives, the Maputo Corridor initiative, common responses to drought, electric-power cooperation, and the Lesotho Highlands Water Scheme. These successes notwithstanding, the regional institutional picture is, to say the least, complex; many differing currents are involved in the process of changing objectives and structures. The Southern African Customs Union (SACU), SADC, and the Common Market for Eastern and Southern Africa (COMESA) still overlap, complicating efforts to work with the individual institutions and the issues at hand.

Beside southern Africa's many shared interests lie important areas of conflict and tension, real and potential. Some are readily discernible now—for example, trade tensions and the conflict between South Africa's need to address its extraordinary unemployment levels and the strong pressures for migration from poorer and less stable neighboring countries. Other issues are likely to emerge in the future—water resource allocation and land, to name but two. In the first instance, the basic aridity of the region and water courses that cross boundaries suggest the need for cooperation, and compromise. Concerning land, the disparities between high-density cultivation in Malawi and large unexploited land resources in Mozambique symbolize what could fuel international as well as national tensions. It is worth recalling that these two issues have fueled international conflict as well as social unrest from time immemorial. The aim is to avert such explosive tendencies in southern Africa, the more so given its high population growth and pressure on natural resources. If these issues enter more directly into the policy and media forums, the quest for avenues of solution and effective institutional mechanisms can begin before tensions fester and grow.

Transport, power, telecommunications, and research are among the areas that stand out as priorities for more active collaboration. The region-wide impact of droughts in recent years is another example of the pitfalls of the shared environment. Likewise, the spread of AIDS across boundaries calls for sharing of information and action. Again, initiatives in all areas have begun but stronger integration measures, ranging from the very specific (like cross-border roads and common training institutions) to efforts built on the broader notions of community, are possible.

Trade within the region is still limited. The major part of imports into the region originate from outside Africa, and most exports from the region leave the region. Nevertheless, the SACU is more important to the rest of the region than vice versa, and the imbalance is getting worse. Southern African countries depend more on the SACU for imports than the SACU depends on its neighbors for exports (see figures 7-3 and 7-4). To some extent, these countries depend on the same type of goods for export revenues. Hence, not only are they competitors in the same markets; their economies are likely to suffer specific market crises more or less simultaneously. The region needs to work out trade policies that will benefit individual countries as well as the region overall. The trade-policy initiatives by several countries and common approaches through SADC and the Cross Border Initiative of the European Community, the International Monetary Fund (IMF), and the World Bank have contributed to significant improvements in competitiveness and export growth, but many unresolved problems lie ahead.

Labor issues will also figure in regional policies and politics. The wide disparities in skills, salary levels, and economic prospects are already playing out in new migration patterns and are likely to do so more intensively in the future. Bridging gaps between the formal economy and the informal economies of the region, within countries and across boundaries, presents the classic challenge of building on

FIGURE 7-3. Destination of SACU Exports, 1993

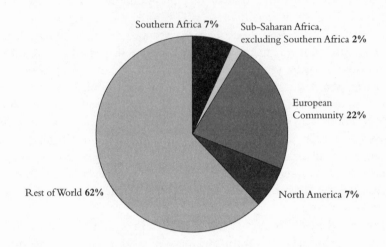

Southern Africa **7%**

Sub-Saharan Africa, excluding Southern Africa **2%**

European Community **22%**

North America **7%**

Rest of World **62%**

FIGURE 7-4. Origin of Imports, 1992

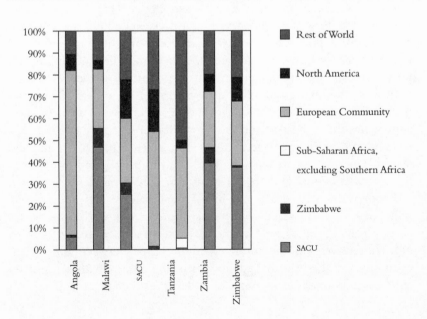

Rest of World

North America

European Community

Sub-Saharan Africa, excluding Southern Africa

Zimbabwe

SACU

potential strengths of informal sector dynamism and creativity while avoiding the perils of illegality and insecurity.

Inequality and Poverty

A core issue, and a striking feature of southern Africa, is the extraordinary levels of inequality. Among the nations of the region, the disparities in social welfare are wide and, in some instances, widening. South Africa, the region's and Africa's richest and most powerful country, has a per capita income approaching $3,000; the region's and Africa's poorest, Mozambique, has a per capita income of $100.

Inequality is dramatic within virtually all of the countries. The southern African countries display some of the highest, if not the highest, Gini coefficients—an indicator of income disparities—in the world. The gap between rich and poor in Malawi, Zambia, Zimbabwe, and South Africa is extraordinarily wide. The "Canada Congo" pattern of South Africa is indeed replicated in far more countries of the region than may be fully recognized: Rich South Africa, in this case still largely white, has incomes approaching those in Canada, whereas black, poor South Africa is comparable to the Congo. It bears note that the patterns of landholding in this part of the world reflect this sharp inequality and differ markedly from other countries and regions of Africa. The gap between large, visibly prosperous modern farms and poor subsistence farms is so stark that faith in smallholder agriculture—the hope of Malaysia, China, Kenya, and other countries—seems weak among policymakers in the region. Land reform stands as one of the central and most troublesome challenges. Since it has few successful precedents, the path ahead is far from clear.

The plain fact is that southern Africa has large pockets of great poverty, massive human suffering, and wasted potential. A rough estimate based on international norms is that half of the population of the region is poor. An international norm of poverty sets a frontier at c. $1 per day. Human-welfare indicators of health, literacy, water, shelter, and food are extremely low. The portrait of this poverty shows major concentrations in rural areas—affecting women and children even more than men—rising urban poverty, inadequate social services, far from

adequate basic education and health services, and escalating unemployment. The sheer numbers of new formal sector jobs created versus
young people coming onto the job market is a dramatic illustration of
the problem at hand.

Dynamism and Change

Southern Africa is engaged in a process of rapid and fundamental
change. This observation is so common as to appear trite in the late
1990s, but the pace and depth of change in southern Africa stands out
globally; the countries in the region are emerging, individually and
collectively, from a period of relative isolation and economic stagnation. Despite numerous conferences and scholarly writings on the
globalization issues, full recognition of the force of global change and
its likely import for southern Africa sometimes seems to elude policymakers in southern Africa. A striking example is the frequently
expressed desire to reverse the trend toward urbanization and restore
traditional patterns of life. Another is the murky debate about protec-
tionism and the desire to calibrate carefully the rate of change in the
trade-regime area.

A clear understanding of the socioeconomic factors at work seems
an essential ingredient in the effort to move ahead. It would seem wise
to accept, even to embrace, the dynamic of change and to develop
strategic and institutional initiatives in its light. Southern Africa
belongs at the vanguard of world economic forces, seizing opportunities and shaping policies, not in the rear, resisting growth and looking
inward.

Forces of change are not easy to define and to control. In southern
Africa, the challenge is even more profound, seen against the rapid
social change that has characterized the region in its troubled, insulated
recent past. The social revolution was not always perceived as positive,
since it originated from the historical, insidious processes that affected
virtually all countries, though in different ways: apartheid, migration,
war, changes in family structure, and the growth of cities. The new
landscape has brought new opportunities and new relationships, to
which the extraordinary population movements in the region bear
witness. The region also faces the extraordinary perils accompanying

the AIDS epidemic. Changes in relationships between women and men are apparent in many fields, as is the impact of a radically different age pyramid resulting from the rapid birth rates of the past decades. With this turbulent social backdrop, the need for fast economic growth becomes even more pressing, to fuel new opportunities throughout the region and open up new areas for enterprise and jobs.

Many leaders of the southern African countries see a common destiny, and look forward to forging it together. Prospects for mutual benefit, both economic and social, are great, and the size of markets and promise of stability across boundaries offer unprecedented hope. However, there are important destabilizing factors that tend to impede regional cooperation—among them the wide disparities in wealth and resources, the economic competition between countries with similar resources, and the social upheaval across increasingly porous boundaries. The central problems in this region may well be its extraordinary income disparity and social inequality.

Economic Policy Challenges and Issues

In the past two years, at least, two central objectives have been echoed by virtually every government in the region: More rapid economic growth is essential to bring improved welfare to the people of the region; and basic macroeconomic stability—"sensible economic policy"—is a prerequisite for rapid growth. Neither of these two objectives are as self-evident as they appear, but the emergence of a consensus around several key elements is encouraging.

The goal of rapid economic growth is both an objective and a promise. Africa has suffered from an affliction of lowering expectations, and many partners, pressed to realism by successive disappointments, came to see 3 to 4 percent economic growth as an impressive achievement. Emerging from the dismal picture of "economic free-fall," in which economic collapse wiped out decades of hard-won gains (Zambia stands out), positive economic growth was indeed an encouraging achievement. However, the grim "rules of doubling" (the time it takes at a 4 percent growth rate with close to 3 percent population growth to double per capita income—close to seventy-two years) drive home that, by decent human-welfare measures, as well as political realities, 3 to 4 percent growth is simply not good enough to bring widespread improvements in welfare, whether by redistribution or "trickle down," nor to achieve real inroads against the more complex matter of poverty. Lower growth with some redistribution would imply reducing living standards for the wealthier segment of the population, which, in turn, presents the drawback of destabilization—hurting the goose that has laid and sits on the golden eggs. The challenge is to create policies that can spur sustainable 5 to 6 percent growth, at least.

The promise for the future lies in the conviction of many observers that such growth rates are attainable, and most of the key ingredients for success are evident. This faith comes from both international experience and the glimpses of successful policy in many African countries. The export spurt of Lesotho and Zimbabwe, investments of South Africans in Zambia and Mozambique, smallholder responses to the opening of burley tobacco in Malawi, and the surge in production in Mozambique with the restoration of peace are all clear examples of what can work. They fuel hope that much more rapid growth is feasible. More and more leaders are setting higher growth objectives and are working to identify the means necessary to achieve them.

A heartening consensus is taking shape around the concept of "sensible economic policies." National budget speeches, media analyses, official leadership statements to the public, and Consultative Group meetings (the central international aid coordination forums) are all using a new vocabulary, calling for certain key ingredients to underpin and fuel economic growth: low budget deficits, a market-driven exchange rate, low inflation, a stable and healthy financial system, efficient use of resources, and sufficient revenues to meet needs as part of a tax system that offers proper incentives for growth and investment. Investment is rightly fingered as the key to growth. The need for sound government—meaning sound institutions, fair and honest public service, and rule of law—are also common objectives echoed in many policy statements. The close linkages among all these elements have become manifest to a widening group of policymakers.

Beyond this consensus (which contrasts sharply with the ideologically driven debates of a decade ago), there seems to lie a new understanding about the respective roles of the public and private sectors. The agreement that better and smaller government intervention in economic affairs is needed may be more fragile than that around the essential macro tools, but it is also reflected in many policy statements. The difficulty is to translate theory into practice—for example, to eliminate the heavy controls inimical to private-sector operations, yet still intrinsic to the "culture of government." The move from a neutral, nonhostile investment climate to an encouraging, even seductive, climate is necessary if the potential for private investment and growth is to be realized. Clearly the legacy of past policies, and some of the social divisions in the countries, still play a role. The consensus about what the state can and should do is still thin and fragile.

To tread on more delicate ground, I identify these elements of reform and change as the core of what governments and their partners were trying to achieve with their "structural adjustment programs." Now, however, it is widely recognized that "sensible economic policies" and macroeconomic balance do not signify an "adjustment" per se, but a vital, continuing need and prerequisite for other policies, whether policies of dynamic change or of stability. The recognition of the macroeconomic basics requires a new thinking about the role of the state and the laws of economics, and the lessons are heightened by global developments and the pace of change. Aid institutions, constituencies, and the markets have hardened, demanding clarity and discipline on macroeconomic fundamentals. The prevailing idea is that without macroeconomic fundamentals in place, there is little prospect for prosperity and hence little basis for investment beyond minimal humanitarian aid.

The Consensus

The consensus is wide but not wide enough, showing the need for public debate and education about macroeconomic issues. As recently as five or six years ago, an aura of mystery surrounded many issues of economic policy. Happily, the days are long gone when budgets, parastatal accounts, Policy Framework papers, and structural adjustment loan documents were classified as top secret, and were seen, much less understood, by only a tiny, beleaguered group of economic policymakers. However, the comprehension of macroeconomic policy is still often limited. Many in government (noneconomic ministries, parliaments), the media, non-government organizations (NGOs), and civil society have heard confusing messages about how economies work and the forces that have contributed to the declines that they have witnessed. My hypothesis is that basic economics needs to be explained in terms that any intelligent citizen can grasp. The potential benefit of public-information campaigns is great; they are essential in southern Africa, not to mention elsewhere in the world.

Bolstering the consensus about "sensible policies"—which, in my view, is largely the result of pragmatic empirical factors—are the growing products of worldwide analysis, like the studies of the "East Asian Miracle," and the experience of Latin America, which demonstrate persuasively that the policy package, or the "policy frontier," is much less debatable than it appeared to be even five years ago. Certain policy ingredients work; others do not. Increasing globalization and interdependence accentuate the linkages between states and policies, and the central importance of investment illustrates the competitive nature of the world economy and the critical role, for any lasting development, of international investment and the international investment climate. A key barometer for southern Africa will be foreign investment. The region has enjoyed a promising flurry of interest and investment, but it has a long way to go before reaching the levels that are seen in other emerging market countries.

Trade

The international community, at least the economics profession, includes another ingredient in "sensible economic policy," though it would be disingenuous to claim the same level of consensus and public understanding for it—namely, the call for open economies, with low tariff barriers, based on the underlying conviction that a competitive environment is indispensable for growth. The objective is to promote exports and to create opportunities for exporters, rather than penalizing them, as has often occurred in the past. Indeed, the trade-policy element seems to emerge from the literature as a crucial element in the high-growth formula. Official policies in virtually all of the region's countries call for opening up and lowering trade barriers. However,

TABLE 7-2. Exports of Goods and Nonfactor Services

Millions of U.S. dollars, current prices

	1980	1985	1986	1987	1988	1989	1990	1991
Sub-Saharan Africa	89,472	58,685	55,775	62,220	65,505	69,345	79,939	77,076
excluding South Africa	61,248	40,940	35,866	38,391	40,095	44,253	52,732	50,287
excluding South Africa and Nigeria	32,915	27,794	28,751	30,675	32,764	34,299	38,625	38,132
Angola	—	2,431	1,462	2,688	2,553	2,656	3,546	3,146
Botswana	516	668	909	1,010	1,848	1,862	2,228	2,605
Lesotho	74	31	35	60	81	62	58	73
Malawi	307	274	271	301	322	299	447	513
Mozambique	399	143	148	175	189	200	229	310
Namibia	1,661	851	1,036	1,086	1,177	1,269	1,202	1,344
South Africa	28,267	17,812	19,916	23,883	25,463	25,173	27,326	26,871
Swaziland	404	204	309	474	523	578	665	694
Tanzania	—	428	586	386	458	529	525	525
Zambia	1,608	821	702	894	1,242	1,071	1,227	1,160
Zimbabwe	1,623	1,302	1,535	1,679	1,902	1,960	1,994	2,173
Total	34,860	24,964	26,910	32,637	35,758	35,659	39,447	39,412

SOURCE. World Bank.

TABLE 7-3. Micro-Level Evidence of Supply Response:
Swarp Spinning, Zambia

Company profile	Before liberalization	After liberalization
Product line	Garments	Spun yarn
Market	Domestic	Export (95%)
Spun-yarn production	4,000 tons (1993)	10,000 (1995)
Employees	480 (1992)	725 (1995)

SOURCE. Tyler Biggs, Margaret Miller, Caroline Otto, and Gerald Tyler, "Africa Can Compete! Export Opportunities and Challenges for Garments and Home Products in the European Market," World Bank Discussion Papers, 300 (Washington, D.C., 1996).

TABLE 7-4. Micro-Level Evidence of Supply Response: Zimtex, Zimbabwe

Company profile	Before liberalization	After liberalization
Product line	Garments	Garments
Product range	Very broad	Sharply reduced
Market	Domestic (100%)	America 100%
Sales	n.a.	U.S.$20 million (1995)
Employees	95 (1993)	1,600 (1995)

SOURCE. Tyler Biggs, Margaret Miller, Caroline Otto, and Gerald Tyler, "Africa Can Compete! Export Opportunities and Challenges for Garments and Home Products in the European Market," World Bank Discussion Papers, 300 (Washington, D.C., 1996).

the issue is generally framed in terms of time, with the argument often advanced that disruptions caused by rapid change can outweigh the benefits of competition. Table 7-2 provides data on recent export and import performances.

Debate continues on this topic. We need to beware that the apparent consensus is not false or too shallow to support real action. The weight of experience seems to suggest that a wide range of economies has adjusted faster than expected to open trade policies, that exports can pick up extraordinarily quickly, and that markets can develop and function, even where they seem moribund. Some commentators,

TABLE 7-5. Comparison of Factor Costs between Select African and Non-African Countries, 1994

	Zimbabwe	Kenya	Ghana	Mauritius	India
Monthly wage[a]	$70.00	$55.00	$40.00	$120.00	$60.00
Electricity[b]	$0.0178	$0.0970	$0.0570	$0.0900	$0.0480
Water[c]	$0.38	$0.52	$0.32	$0.46	$0.32
Diesel fuel[d]	$0.26	$0.47	$0.37	$0.27	$0.28

SOURCE. Tyler Biggs, Margaret Miller, Caroline Otto, and Gerald Tyler, "Africa Can Compete! Export Opportunities and Challenges for Garments and Home Products in the European Market," World Bank Discussion Papers, 300 (Washington, D.C., 1996).
a. Wage for a semi-skilled machine operator in the garments industry.
b. Industrial electricity rates per KwH during peak load period.
c. Industrial water rates per cubic meter.
d. Diesel fuel cost per liter.

TABLE 7-6. Productivity and Unit Labor Costs in Standardized Garment Production in Selected Countries, 1994

	Zimbabwe	Kenya	Ghana	India	EPZ China
Number of men's shirts produced per machine operator in 8-hour shift	12-14	12-15	12	16	18-22
Index of unit labor cost	0.22	0.14	0.14	0.14	0.23

SOURCE. Tyler Biggs, Margaret Miller, Caroline Otto, and Gerald Tyler, "Africa Can Compete! Export Opportunities and Challenges for Garments and Home Products in the European Market," World Bank Discussion Papers, 300 (Washington, D.C., 1996).

however, cite evidence and experience that suggest alternative routes (that is, temporary or partial protection). Plainly, every situation is unique and needs to be treated as such. Tables 7-3, 7-4, 7-5, and 7-6 provide data about positive responses to trade reforms in Zambia and Zimbabwe.

This issue of trade within southern Africa, but, above all, with the outside, is the fulcrum of current policy debate. The diagnosis of the economies still suggests difficulties concerning competitiveness; high labor costs in some economies (above all South Africa) are limiting opportunities. But political and social realities are also influential; the pains of transition, witnessed recently in Zambia, are not to be ignored. Tuning and clarifying the terms of this debate merit a high priority.

The connection between trade policy and prosperity are well established, turning around the economics of markets and competitiveness. The linkages with peace and stability are more complex, working their way through the social dimensions of development. In southern Africa, increasing trade is tied to labor mobility and to the various sources of migration. Ideas come with trade, and many of the old information barriers are coming down. Less positive forces, like the movement of arms and criminal activity, have accompanied the trend toward lower trade barriers and freer intraregional economic movement. The development of informal markets, already an important force, will have significant implications for both economic and social development and, above all, jobs. More proactive and creative policies for informal sector development are needed throughout the region.

The shrinking world that comes with globalization could make inequalities even more visible and engender more impatience for both economic progress and reductions in income disparities. The melting of national barriers could also allow poles of economic prosperity to move rapidly and accentuate the poverty of less-favored regions—say, in Zambia where dryland agriculture is, and probably always has been, marginal. Moreover, the declining mining areas of South Africa, for example, in a regional economy with fewer barriers, could provide labor and skills for other, more promising areas.

Land and Smallholders

Another "macroeconomic fundamental" that is involved in the economic policy thrust of the past decade is the effort to alter the bias against agriculture, particularly smallholder agriculture. The concern is whether the "real" policy emphasis is as strong as the "stated" policy focus; for policy statements in Africa as a whole almost universally recognize the importance of small farmers. Major steps have been taken to reverse some of the insidious practices and institutions that severely penalized farmers—for example, confiscatory pricing policies, marketing controls, and unworkable purchase schemes—but the question remains as to how deeply governments are committed to smallholder agriculture, as opposed to the large-scale, commercial farming that represents the image of agriculture in much of southern Africa. The statistics on population (the preponderance of poor people and growing population in rural areas) and job prospects (slow, formal-sector job creation) offer a compelling case for strong reliance on smallholder agriculture, and the examples of Kenya, Uganda, Malaysia, and China offer hope for its feasibility. Contacts between southern African policymakers and these countries have sparked interest and more confidence, but the region still lacks a forceful push toward agricultural policies where they might do the most good in alleviating rural poverty.

Inequality Issues

Another important question for southern Africa concerns the role that the extraordinary inequality in incomes will play in formulating and managing economic policy. Three points must be kept in mind:

First, stability is a key to growth; markets today are notoriously jittery and responsive to signals, real and imagined. Stable financial markets backed by predictable policies take on increasing importance. Even with the "new" regimes and the different political character of southern Africa, markets are still dominated by the wealthy elements of the modern sector—the "Canada" side of southern Africa—and the signs seem clear that major changes are perceived as destabilizing. The consequences that follow loss of market confidence, and erosion of the institutional base, could seriously compromise the potential for rapid growth.

Second, rapid growth is essential to produce the resources to attack poverty and bridge the huge service gap between rich and poor. Yet, public spending must be constrained both to curb deficits and to keep taxes at competitive levels.

Finally, the most imponderable ingredients in the mix are experience and common sense, which suggest that managing macroeconomic policy for growth and stability is much more difficult and risky in situations of pronounced inequality. A recent World Bank study found a strong correlation between ethnic diversity, accompanied by prejudices against minorities, and poor economic growth. The potential for populist forces, for unpredictable outbreaks, and for lack of public support seems to be greater in this scenario, creating a domino effect of calamities in the market.

Although exact knowledge and prediction are not possible, three imperatives do stand out: carefully conceived and executed information and education campaigns to bring economic policy to public attention; institutional and "governance" initiatives to demonstrate the intention to promote fairness, justice, and the rule of law; well-designed and creative efforts to address poverty issues, including quantifiable, measurable targets, and an emphasis on programs in education and health that build the future. Without an educated population, the prospects for a successful southern Africa in the next century are not favorable. Community development schemes, social funds, well-structured agricultural extension, and programs meant specifically for women and children are invaluable, and excellent starts already exist in several countries.

External Partnerships

The crucial theme of war and peace raises a host of questions for the international institutions that seek to support development in southern Africa. The number of roles that external partners can play is great, probably much greater than is widely recognized.

In some of the countries of the region, the "donor community"—an unfortunate name—carries an extraordinary weight, with few historical precedents: For instance, Mozambique depends on donor flows for almost 70 percent of its total budget; and Zambia has incurred an enormous debt, relying on several fragile packages to keep its economy afloat. So huge are the financial gaps forecast for Angola that it is difficult to envisage a lasting economic solution without much new aid from the outside. These situations contrast sharply with those of South Africa and other countries, where the external community is much less involved.

The spectrum of functions that external partners can be asked to assume runs the gamut from the detailed, elaborate agreements known as conditionality, to micro-level interventions at community level via philanthropic NGOs, to technically driven interventions in, say, universities. Even in a single setting, individual responsibilities can include those of an advisor and financier, purveyor of international knowledge, advocate, policeman (a duty thrust upon outsiders far too often), external analyst and diagnostician, and even scapegoat.

The multiple donors at work in many countries can complicate economic policymaking and become a management problem of substantial dimensions. One problem is what I term the "project patchwork"—the emergence of multiple projects at the local level, designed to avoid large central bureaucracies and effect tangible results. These programs are sometimes prone to external interference and overlapping goals, sapping efforts at coherent sector management. The sector investment approaches that are afoot in several countries, however, are an important step in the right direction.

A second difficulty turns around capacity building and technical assistance. Few would deny the perils and disappointments associated with traditional technical assistance. The image of well-paid foreign advisors beside poorly paid counterparts is all too common. Nonetheless, technical cooperation is one of the most vital and enriching means of development, and the continued exchange of ideas is of the utmost importance. It is also clear that the challenges of institutional development are as demanding and worthy today as ever. External partners must find better ways to promote the interplay, transfer, and adaptation of ideas and to support viable efforts to develop human capital.

The deteriorating aid climate may not be well understood in public and governmental circles. Constituencies for international aid are delicate. The pressure to support only successful programs and countries, the keen scrutiny of management and resource use, and the matter of how much aid is actually available are major concerns for those who are aware of the indispensability of aid to bring successful growth and alleviate poverty in the region for years to come, whether amid chronic social tension or, more hopefully, in rebuilding societies after conflicts.

There are important links between a nation's external assistance, its path of economic development, and its prospects for sustainable growth that fosters greater social harmony in the future. That said, there is room for considerable uncertainty. Is fast growth during an initial period needed to gain momentum, even if it accentuates inequality? How do participation and democracy relate to capacity for reform, especially in societies with extraordinarily high levels of inequality that fuel the potential for populist movements and policies? Where do social analysis and the resulting policies border on undue intervention in the affairs of sovereign states or "cultural imperialism"? These are just a few of the dilemmas that haunt the interaction between developing countries and their partners.

The connections between economic prosperity and stability are numerous and powerful: For southern Africa, perhaps more than any other region, the challenges of enhancing the quality of life and catching up on development demand immediate attention. Without social peace, the investment climate will worsen. The economic stability most conducive to poverty alleviation requires sound economic policies. They alone can promise low inflation and wide opportunity for entrepreneurship.

Moreover, everyone concerned needs to understand the causes and effects of conflict better, despite the modesty and distance that these complex issues seem to compel. For example, neither group interests—such as those of women, the urban poor, and others—nor ethnic forces can be ignored when it comes to locating investments and designing institutions. Discussions and analysis are essential, though there are not many tested, let alone proven, recipes for avoiding or detecting conflict in advance. Investment and expenditure policies can either calm or exacerbate tempers, but, as yet, few are as wise in prognostication as they are in hindsight.

Failing or struggling states have an urgent need for collaboration between a plethora of institutions, ranging from those that are purely humanitarian to those that specialize in practical development. Even in the midst of conflict, and particularly when the process of making peace is underway, evidence suggests that the socioeconomic agenda should come into discussion sooner than it generally has.

The supports are in place for effective bridges between humanitarian and development activities at the community level (for example, through social funds) and at the sectoral level (education, food-aid policies, priority drug procurement, water points, and communications), and "Marshall Plan"-style rehabilitation efforts may be appropriate in situations that call for the mobilization of funds and the coordination of multiple partners. Such special strategies may be the most apt in crisis situations, but the exigencies of poverty may also mandate the same kind of commitment.

8

Robert S. Gelbard

Drug Trafficking in Southern Africa

AFRICA DID NOT play a significant role in the international drug trade for a long time. A producer of neither opium nor coca, it was not a source for heroin or cocaine; and even though it has a long tradition of cannabis cultivation, with some export to Europe, it was never a significant international supplier, since virtually every other region of the world also produces marijuana. Not until the early 1980s, when a group of Nigerian naval officers undergoing training in India organized a trafficking ring to smuggle Southwest Asian heroin—then the world's leading heroin source—to Europe and, eventually, the United States, did the African continent began to fill an important niche in the international trade. Organized mostly around an "army" of couriers, this initial effort received a boost when the Nigerian economy collapsed in the mid-1980s, and more smugglers could be recruited cheaply. Other well-off Nigerians, who lost their lifestyles in the collapse, decided the drug trade was the route to riches. By the time that authorities had become fully aware of the Nigerian threat and method of operation, the organization had solidified its base of operations in West Africa and was branching out to acquire additional drug sources in Southeast Asia and Latin America.

Today, Nigerians run some of the premier drug trafficking and organized crime networks in the world. They still rely on couriers who typically ingest the drugs or conceal them in their bodies or in their belongings; this method precludes the seizure of large costly shipments, even if it means only relatively small amounts can be smuggled at any one time. But the Nigerians continue to make significant operational adjustments to avoid detection and apprehension. Nigerian trafficking cells, for instance, are located throughout Southeast and Southwest Asia, where they arrange purchases, recruit couriers, and plan routes. They frequently change courier "profiles"—apparently relying now, for instance, on young white women rather than on West Africans—and routes, avoiding direct flights from source areas to markets by making several intermediate stops. They have a reputation for carefully studying customs and security procedures in both transit and market-country ports of entry.

The prevalence of the Nigerian drug threat is best reflected in selected seizure-and-arrest statistics. Some 30 percent of the heroin seized at United States ports of entry in 1994 was taken from Nigerian-controlled couriers. As of December 1995, 700 Nigerian traffickers were imprisoned in Thailand. From 1993 to 1995, Brazilian authorities arrested 42 Nigerians in possession of a total of 266 kg of cocaine. Brazil is the primary staging area for Nigerian cocaine shipments because of its close historical ties to Africa and its large ethnic African population. Nigerian-controlled cocaine dealers have also been arrested recently in Colombia, Paraguay, and several West African locations. Nigerian organizations are largely responsible for creating a significant market for cocaine in Europe and for spreading illegal drugs throughout West Africa.

International efforts to stem the Nigerian threat have been disappointing so far, and, by all accounts, Nigerian traffickers are determined to expand their operations further, setting their sights specifically on southern Africa. The United States government and other members of the international community have tried to work with the Nigerian government to develop intelligence about the Nigerian drug trade, strengthen the government's counterdrug institutions, and conduct effective antinarcotics operations. But these efforts have been largely to no avail. Indeed, for four years running (including 1997), the United States has imposed congressionally mandated sanctions on Nigeria for its failure to cooperate in international narcotics-control efforts. Corruption has been a major barrier, impeding cooperation in

174 / ROBERT S. GELBARD

major cases and thwarting efforts to extradite important traffickers to the United States. Because anti-drug institutions are not adequately funded and staffed, investigative cases have targeted only marginal traffickers. The government's anti-corruption efforts, meanwhile, have been insincere, focusing only on low-level officials.

Against this backdrop of worldwide drug contacts with an operational sanctuary in Nigeria, Nigerian drug and other crime organizations are moving aggressively to exploit the rich trafficking opportunities in southern Africa. Nigerian heroin trafficking cells are already established in South Africa to facilitate transshipment of heroin and cocaine to other parts of the world and, probably, to distribute drugs in South Africa as well. In 1993, Nigerians were responsible for more than half the cocaine that was seized in South Africa, and that percentage may be rising.

Political Transition in Southern Africa

Opening the Door to International Criminals

Southern Africa is on a collision course with the expanding worldwide drug trade and can ill afford not to take corrective actions soon. The advent of majority rule and the abolition of apartheid, along with other political changes that have occurred in the region during the past several years, are inadvertently fostering the socioeconomic conditions that abet international crime and the narcotics trade. Fortunately, however, these very advances in democracy and open-market economy also offer the keys to a solution.

The global community recently applauded southern Africa for pulling itself out of a postcolonial morass of undemocratic practices and, in the face of adversity, setting out to rebuild its states. The area is now on a path to political and economic liberalization. Rapid transition to democratic government, however, produces political and institutional conditions that are also favorable to the interests of drug and organized crime syndicates.

Early stages of transition are usually accompanied by significant reforms, including the disbandment of the security forces that were used to maintain strict social order, and their replacement with new personnel and organizations that are not necessarily qualified, trained, or equipped to take on their new responsibilities. The same difficulties can be said to face the new judicial institutions, which must focus on protecting individual freedoms rather than on suppressing opposition. There is also widespread decentralization of business and commercial activity, as crumbling government regulation and oversight mechanisms give way to laissez-faire, free-market activity. As a result, nations in transition—and those of southern Africa are no exception—often find themselves beset with a number of institutional weaknesses, such as outdated or inadequate laws for dealing with complex crimes, inadequate financial regulations, weak judicial and police institutions, and lax border controls that nurture organized crime activity and focus government attention away from the crime threat onto other pressing issues.

Southern Africa's geography no longer offers it protection from traffickers who once plied direct routes from sources to markets. Indeed, its geographical location has become increasingly central for global commerce. The region also offers a sophisticated air, sea, and land infrastructure that makes it a prime conduit for moving illegal cargoes. Long, porous borders and weak border controls, including undermanned ports and numerous secondary airports, give drug traffickers nearly unlimited access through which to transport their goods. Police forces in the region are understaffed and undertrained. Current customs and immigration laws cannot adequately cope with the massive volume of international connections, and imperfect immigration controls allow criminals to purchase passports from corrupted officials.

Southern Africa has the potential to play a number of roles in the international drug trade. At this point, it is primarily a transshipment center for heroin, cocaine, and Mandrax—a synthetically produced sedative made from methaqualone powder and antihistamines—but it is a growing market. If the problem is left unchecked, the trend will almost certainly be for southern Africa to grow into a major support center, offering money laundering, chemical production and distribution, and shipping services, and eventually a base for powerful international narcotics brokers. Already a source of cannabis for regional consumption and limited export, it could also become a producer of other organic or synthetic drugs for the international market.

Most southern African nations are beginning to recognize that drug trafficking threatens their societies—an important first step for addressing the problem. They realize that more and more of the drugs entering their region are for local consumption, not just transshipment to remote markets. They are also beginning to get a sense of the ties between drug abuse and trafficking and increased violent crime, robbery, and general lawlessness.

A Regional Survey: South Africa and Its Neighbors

As southern Africa's largest, wealthiest, and most economically diverse country, South Africa is understandably at the hub of the region's drug trade. It began assuming this distinction after the institution of majority rule and the end of its international isolation in 1994. The Nigerians were the first to exploit these developments, capitalizing on South Africa's location, and advanced transportation, communication, and financial systems to establish heroin and cocaine transshipment operations through the country. By 1995, authorities estimated that some 136 drug networks—many of them Nigerian-controlled drug cells—were at work in the country. According to South African officials, 50,000 Nigerian immigrants were in South Africa in 1996, some with long histories of contraband smuggling out of Nigeria. Many enter as tourists, illegally acquire South African identification books, and then apply for South African passports.

Cocaine is currently the most serious drug problem that South African authorities face. Nigerians, who acquire the drug in Brazil and Argentina and smuggle it via Angola and Namibia, manage most of the trade. Although much of the product is destined for Europe, increasing amounts are slated for the domestic market. Rising cocaine seizures—up 200 percent in 1995—and low prices—approximately $18 per gram in 1996—signify a glutted market. The scenario is similar for the heroin trade that originates in Southeast and Southwest Asia, which the Nigerians also dominate. Once mainly in the business of transshipping the drugs to the United States and Europe, they are now stepping up their efforts to market it locally.

Indian traffickers, taking advantage of the long-established expatriate Indian population in Southern Africa, also figure heavily in the South African trade. They are particularly expert at smuggling heroin into the region from Afghanistan and Pakistan and are extensively involved in the Mandrax trade. Mandrax is very popular in South

Africa; indeed, the country may be the drug's largest market. Some shipments are smuggled directly from South Asia, but considerable amounts traverse various East African ports and countries before arriving in South Africa.

South Africa is one of the world's leading marijuana producers, distributing to both local and regional markets. Marijuana is available in ton quantities; some estimates put the retail value of the crop as high as $4.5 billion.

South Africa is already beginning to feel the sting of increased crime and violence associated with the drug trade. Authorities are dealing increasingly with drug-related robberies, turf wars, murder, and money laundering. One grave example of the threat involves the exchange of automatic weapons for marijuana in Pondoland and Soweto. The villagers use the weapons to guard their crops from theft and police seizures. Meanwhile, the growing concern in judicial and other government circles is that South Africa's position as the region's major financial center makes it a potential money-laundering base as well. There are already indications of drug traffickers illegally purchasing gold and diamonds and then selling them to buyers in Switzerland to legitimize their drug profits.

Other Nations

None of the other countries in southern Africa are so involved in the drug trade as South Africa, but, collectively, they offer substantial, additional opportunities and alternatives to the South African trade. Angola, Mozambique, Zambia, and Zimbabwe have already made their mark as significant transit points. Angola has emerged as an especially attractive center, owing to its accessible ports of entry and the breakdown of law-enforcement institutions, caused by two decades of civil war. Direct flights from Brazil to Angola have become a significant pipeline for the cocaine that is eventually distributed in the region or sent to Europe. Much of the "Angolan trade" is redistributed through Mozambique, where antiquated drug laws, widespread corruption, and ill-equipped police forces make the country an ideal conduit. In early 1996, Mozambique's judicial system released the sole remaining suspect from 1995's 30-ton hashish seizure and set free ten south Asians arrested in September of that year for attempting to manufacture Mandrax.

Zambia, lying astride the major East African trade routes, is a significant transit point for Indian-produced Mandrax destined for South Africa. The trade has almost certainly been abetted by corruption that has already taken a toll on the Zambian government. In 1993, just two years after Zambia's first free multi-party election in twenty years, senior government officials were tainted by credible reports of involvement in drug trafficking. In the wake of the allegation, a consultative group of donors threatened to withhold aid vital to Zambia's balance-of-payments situation, unless President Frederick Chiluba purged his cabinet of alleged drug dealers and corrupt politicians. Consequently, Vernon Mwanga, Zambia's foreign minister, and other senior officials resigned in January 1994, although Mwanga continued to maintain an influential position within the ruling party.

Zimbabwe, with its relatively developed infrastructure, is an active transshipment center for drugs flowing into and out of the region. Authorities report that significant amounts of Mandrax from India, heroin from Pakistan, and cocaine from Latin America transit Zimbabwe for other parts of southern Africa or for local consumption. The country is also a well-documented trans-shipment center for Malawi-produced marijuana destined for the Netherlands.

Of the remaining countries in the region, Malawi appears to harbor the most active drug trade. Until recently, authorities there thought that the country was relatively free of the drug threat, but recent large seizures point to an increasing effort by traffickers to shift operations formerly earmarked for surrounding countries to Malawi. Traffickers appear to be calculating that the country's new spirit of openness and its fledgling democratic institutions will divert the government's attention and resources from drug control onto other competing social and economic concerns. In the meantime, indigenous traffickers seem to be specializing in the production of high-quality marijuana, which is exported through Zimbabwe and Mozambique primarily to European markets.

Botswana, Lesotho, and Swaziland currently play only minor roles in the regional trade. Each, however, has admitted to low-to-moderate levels of drug use. Growing seizures, particularly in Swaziland—400 g of cocaine in 1994 and 2.7 tons in 1995—signal expanding transshipment through these countries.

The most widely abused drug in virtually every country of the region is locally produced marijuana. Southern Africa is rapidly becoming a poly-drug market; the trend will undoubtedly attract even more drug trafficking to the region. Cocaine, heroin, and Mandrax use are on the rise. Predictably, the problems are worse in the major transit countries. Cocaine and heroin use is escalating primarily among the wealthier segments of society—the social, economic, and political elites and the trendsetters. How they react as a class to these developments will likely have a significant bearing on how their countries respond.

Countering The Drug Trade: A Focused and Systematic Response

Southern Africa faces a formidable challenge in combatting the region's burgeoning drug and crime threat. Currently, the criminal elements seem to have the upper hand: They can operate when and where they want and with near impunity. The region's governments are starting from the disadvantage of having to work with weak information and institutional bases. Moreover, the world of international organized crime and drug trafficking is an environment rife with opportunity. Governments can quickly squander scarce resources and achieve only negligible results if induced to pursue elusive or irrelevant prey. Yet timely, systematic response stands a good chance of preventing drug trafficking and international organized crime from becoming the type of national-security threats that they are elsewhere in the world. Three broad areas of concentration are of particular importance: information development, institution building, and international cooperation.

From its conceptualization to its implementation, an effective and comprehensive counter-drug and counter-crime strategy is only so good as the reliability of its information. Governments must have enough data to identify the threat and assess its consequences so that they can both map strategies and convince the public to support them. Moreover, to save resources and avoid operational failures, governments need to determine which drug and crime targets are the most critical and vulnerable, which requires a heavy front-end investment in the collection and analysis of intelligence. The investment will pay dividends, however, only if it permits authorities to set their sights on targets that yield the most damage at the least relative cost. The leadership of the major organizations in southern Africa is a case in point: It is forced to operate in accessible venues; it can be identified with good intelligence; and it cannot hide from good police work. The successful investigation of a leader not only weakens an organization from the top and makes its entire criminal apparatus more vulnerable, it also serves as a deterrent, signaling the government's ability and commitment to respond.

Long-term, effective anti-drug programs are useless without strong institutions that can withstand and outlast the drug trade. Indeed, several institutions must link together to make law-enforcement efforts work, and, since the weakest link determines the outcome, progress must be even across all fronts.

Legislatures must pass strong anti-corruption measures and other laws that enable the police to conduct sophisticated investigations with state-of-the-art techniques. For instance, such laws should authorize conspiracy investigations, promote criminal asset seizure and forfeiture, and prohibit money laundering. In some cases, cadres of criminal investigators may have to be developed from scratch to take advantage of all the anti-criminal procedures permitted by law. The judiciary must also be skillful enough to prosecute, convict, and incarcerate. Many anti-drug efforts have failed in the past because antiquated procedures and incompetent or corrupt judges have combined to let powerful criminals go free.

Nations that will be effective in the struggle against drug trafficking must have an equable and efficient criminal justice system. The closest connection that most people have with a government is the police on the street. But citizens need to know that the laws will protect them, that the courts will be fair, and that they will be represented by an honest lawyer if circumstances so dictate. The legitimacy of a democracy often depends on how citizens perceive the justice system as a whole. If they have no faith that it is unbiased and capable of resolving conflicts, they will revert to violence as a way of protecting themselves and their interests.

For judicial and other institution-building measures to succeed, governments must be prepared to fight internal corruption. The blind eye or active participation of senior officials is an expensive insurance policy that allows traffickers to operate with impunity. Yet, it can be undermined cheaply with exposure and punishment. Similarly, authorities should seek to personalize the drug threat, that is, to make the identities of the major traffickers household names and to give the public faces to recognize. This strategy goes a long way toward enlisting public support for anti-drug efforts.

Because drug traffickers operate freely across continents, it takes more than the commitment of one or two countries to stop them. Without comprehensive regional and international cooperation, southern Africa runs the risk of creating more narco-democracies. Fortunately, there are well-established principles and mechanisms to guard against it. The 1988 Vienna Convention Against Illicit Traffic in Narcotic Drugs and Psychotropic Substances provides a comprehensive blueprint to address nearly all facets of narcotics control—from production to consumption, domestically and globally. Many countries in southern Africa have not yet acceded to the Convention—South Africa being one of them. Joining immediately would demonstrate a commitment to narcotics control and pave the way for greater regional and international cooperation. Adherence to the recommendations of the international Financial Action Task Force would enhance both domestic and international efforts to thwart money laundering by drug and other crime syndicates. The United Nations and other multilateral groups are promoting similar efforts to strengthen international cooperation to control precursor chemicals (those used to make illegal drugs) and maritime smuggling.

Countries that share borders must work together to distinguish legitimate commerce from contraband and to catch smugglers. Bilateral agreements to share information and cooperate on investigations and extraditions are also critical. One of the best ways to weaken the power and resiliency of drug organizations is to eliminate safe havens, so that traffickers have nowhere to hide. The most effective instruments for achieving this goal are strong bilateral extradition treaties and strong judicial systems.

The new democratic government in South Africa is demonstrating its awareness that only through international cooperation can governments succeed in eliminating trafficking organizations. Not only has it posted drug-liaison officials in countries from which it receives illicit narcotics—its neighbors, as well as Brazil, Thailand, India, and Pakistan; it has taken the lead in southern Africa by hosting a SADC-EU (Joint Southern African Development Community and European Union)

Conference on Cross-Border Drug Trafficking in 1995. The European Union helped with funding, and the United States sent an expert on corruption. The impetus behind the conference, however, was South Africa's concern that narcotics trafficking in the region was on the upswing. The conference adopted a regional draft protocol on combatting the illicit drug trade and offered valuable guidance for a uniform approach to the problem in southern Africa, and highlighted the need to address drug abuse in the region.

United States Aid to South Africa

The governments of the United States and South Africa are currently pooling their resources to fight international crime and drug trafficking. Beginning with the anti-crime agreement signed between Vice President Al Gore and Vice President Thabo Mbeki in 1996, the two governments have set out to update existing institutions, revise criminal codes, and provide training to a cadre of law-enforcement officials.

In late 1996, the United States government began a program with South Africa's Ministry of Safety and Security to promote skills in the areas of investigator training, police organization, prosecutor task forcing, and general professional development. The United States Marshall Service and South Africa are working together to establish a witness-protection program; the Drug Enforcement Administration was scheduled to open an office in Pretoria in 1997; and the Immigration and Naturalization and Customs Services are ready to train South African personnel in border and immigration controls if necessary.

The United States government is also providing several short- and long-term advisors to South Africa to help create a judicial infrastructure based on democratic principles, draft and implement procedures to facilitate criminal investigation and prosecution, introduce appropriate anti–money-laundering laws and regulations, and establish a national drug-control strategy and institutional framework. Regional training programs that the United States offers in other southern African nations are intended to assist in the control of such related problems as alien smuggling, gangs, organized crime, and financial crime.

Embracing Individual and Collective Commitments

Global problems require global solutions. The conception may seem simple, but the application is not. Success against a threat that transcends national borders requires countries to adopt common strategies that go beyond the traditional limits of national sovereignty. No one nation can beat the drug trade. Drugs of all kinds are rampant throughout Africa, Western and Eastern Europe, Asia, and the states of the former Soviet Union. The trade's devastating effects on governance and society during the last decade have been reflected in countries as diverse as Colombia, Nigeria, and even Italy where drug and organized-crime syndicates launched a wholesale campaign to assassinate the country's leading prosecutors and intimidate the entire judicial system. Individually, countries have the constitutional and moral authority—as well as the institutions and public support—to expose, isolate, and punish those involved. Collectively, they have the power to deny criminals, and their profits, sanctuary by pursuing good government and enforcing standards already established by international convention. If we fight criminal organizations on all fronts—while building strong, open democracies—we can reduce international crime and drug trafficking to the point where it no longer poses a serious threat to global security.

9

C. J. D. Venter

Drug Abuse and Drug Smuggling in South Africa

DRUG TRAFFICKING is a form of "commodity" trading conducted by transnational crime syndicates, generating an annual income of more than R1,800,000 ($500 billion) a year worldwide, of which R900 billion ($250 billion) may be a net profit. It is expanding at such an alarming rate that the United Nations General Assembly has begun to focus on it as a multidimensional threat. The illicit demand for, production of, and traffic in narcotic drugs and psychotropic substances has a negative impact on socioeconomic and political systems and endangers the stability, national security, and the sovereignty of an increasing number of countries in southern Africa, and in particular, South Africa.

Regional Overview

South Africa has become an attractive manufacturing alternative, transit route, and market for drug traffickers because of, among other things, its relatively good infrastructure and affluence, its inadequate border control, its inability to stem the tide of illegal immigrants, and its insufficient awareness of the risks of drug abuse.

The escalation in drug trafficking in South Africa can be attributed to such factors as stricter laws aimed at curbing smuggling and greatly improved control (with passports, for instance) at airports and harbors in Europe and the Americas; a renewed interest in South Africa on the part of international investors; South Africa's favorable geographical position on the major routes between the Far and Middle East, the Americas, and Europe; and South Africa's accessibility via land, sea, and air routes, especially since its re-entry into the international arena. The drug problem is exacerbated by southern Africa's ability to cultivate, manufacture, and process drugs—in some instances, even with the knowledge and participation of government officials. Mandrax is manufactured in Zambia, Mozambique, Swaziland, Kenya, Tanzania, and South Africa, and cannabis (marijuana) is cultivated in the mountainous areas of southern Africa, especially Swaziland, Lesotho, and South Africa.

During 1993, the South African Police confiscated and/or destroyed illicit drugs worth approximately R1,000 million. During 1994, illicit drugs valued at almost R7,500 million were confiscated and/or destroyed. In 1995, the figure dropped to R1,500 million (see table 9-1). The monetary value and quantity of illicit drugs confiscated and/or destroyed comprise approximately 10 to 15 percent of the estimated value of the illicit drug trade in South Africa, the monetary value of this trade in 1995 being double the allocated budget of the entire South African Police Service (SAPS) for the 1995/96 financial year.

The interrelatedness of criminal activities in South Africa has become increasingly evident: Motor vehicle theft/robbery is linked to the illegal arms trade and drug trafficking to motor vehicle theft and money laundering. Because of the well-established smuggling networks in the southern African region, the same routes are often used for such drugs as Mandrax, cannabis, heroin, and LSD as for weapons, cars, rhino horn, ivory, and gems. In the aftermath of its protracted civil war, Mozambique has emerged as a major transit facility for heroin, cocaine, hashish, and Mandrax to the southern African region, Europe, and the Americas, probably because of a lack of proper police expertise and legislation. Indications are that South Africa could become the southern end of a drug triangle joining Nigeria and Ghana in the northwest and Kenya and Sudan in the northeast, with Johannesburg the nerve center for syndicate operations.

TABLE 9-1. Detailed Statistics Pertaining to Drug-Related Offenses

Illegal drugs confiscated and/or destroyed, as well as arrests made	1 Jan.–31 Dec. 1992	1 Jan.–31 Dec. 1993	1 Jan.–31 Dec. 1994	1 Jan.–31 Dec. 1995	1 Jan.–31 Dec. 1996
Cannabis (Dagga)					
Arrests: Possession of	6,511	4,331	3,169	2,047	637
Mass confiscated and/or found abandoned	470kg000	5,891kg000	4,415kg000	1,470kg529	423kg071
Arrests: Dealing in	10,272	8,717	7,896	4,065	1,843
Mass confiscated and/or found abandoned	253,672kg000	841,445kg000	264,201kg000	237,342kg681	55,415kg647
Mass destroyed in cultivation areas	4,618,238kg000	860,471kg000	6,914,254kg000	1,188,018kg000	25,011kg783
Mandrax					
Arrests: Possession of	527	534	324	172	105
Tablets confiscated	34,819	26,879	27,121 + 4g	683	17,314 + 101.5g
Arrests: Dealing in	2,394	3,338	2,459	1,288	527
Tablets confiscated	3,761,526	3,511,349	2,641,100 + 57g + 2,085,000 in Swaziland	886,162.5 + 30kg008 powder	289,521.5 + 3.8kg powder
Cocaine					
Arrests: Possession of	17	28	28	23	27
Mass confiscated	0kg592	0kg895	0kg666	0kg110	0kg287
Arrests: Dealing in	108	236	266	269 + 2 for dealing in crack	65
Mass confiscated	11kg042	77kg493	68kg895	187kg505 + 0kg150 crack	77kg166

Heroin					
Arrests: Possession of	5	1	4	1	0
Mass confiscated	0kg003	0kg006	0kg078	0kg001	0
Arrests: Dealing in	7	14	29	21	7
Mass confiscated	1kg338	1kg840	24kg667	5kg941	0kg783.5
LSD					
Arrests: Possession of	12	22	23	4	1
Units confiscated	55	2,023	199	9	6
Arrests: Dealing in	54	78	65	54	31
Units confiscated	4,695	8,946	16,502	3,098	1,325 (10,000)
Hashish					
Arrests: Possession of	0	0	2	0	0
Mass confiscated	0	0	0kg008	0	0
Arrests: Dealing in	0	0	5	12	4
Mass confiscated	0	0	27kg078	7kg858	g065 + 3 pieces
Nexus					
Arrests: Possession of	0	0	0	0	0
Tablets confiscated	0	0	0	0	0
Arrests: Dealing in	0	0	0	2	0
Tablets confiscated	0	0	0	14	0
"Ecstasy"					
Arrests: Possession of	0	0	0	3	2
Units confiscated	0	0	0	4	8.5
Arrests: Dealing in	0	0	7	32	29
Units confiscated	0	0	1,262	2,117	2,746.5
Speed					
Arrests: Possession of	0	0	0		2
Amount confiscated	0	0	0		12

Origin, Extent, and Distribution

Cannabis is a naturally growing plant that contains tetrahydro-cannabinol (THC) as psychoactive ingredient. It is primarily smoked, but teas and cakes have also been made of this substance. It is known locally as *dagga* and has been grown for years by rural South Africans. The cultivation, possession, use, and sale of cannabis are still prohibited by law in South Africa. The surge in its cultivation there has been fueled, first and foremost, by its tremendous profitability. Many rural people who struggle to survive on migrant remittances and pensions do not regard cannabis cultivation and use as illicit activities; intelligence indicates that cannabis syndicates recruit the rural population to cultivate their crops. The profits gained in this way hamper the government's attempt to persuade the local farmers to consider crop substitution. In some areas, cannabis is the only cultivated crop because of its ability to grow in poor soil. The production of cannabis is maintained annually in similar quantities and in similar areas—in KwaZulu/Natal, the Northern Province, and extensively in the Eastern Cape (mainly the former Transkei), as well as in neighboring Malawi, Lesotho, and Swaziland (see table 9-2)

Cannabis is transported out of the mountains of the Eastern Cape and nearby Lesotho by individuals on horses and mules to lower-level staging areas where it is loaded onto vehicles and smuggled to consumer markets in, for example, Durban, Johannesburg, and Cape Town. Cannabis is also exported to the Netherlands and Britain by sea and air; on several occasions, South African cannabis has been seized in Britain, concealed in air freight.

Hashish is composed of resinous secretions, with added binding substances obtained from the cannabis plant. Hashish is cultivated mainly in Morocco, Lebanon, Afghanistan, and Pakistan. Recent reports indicate that southern Africa is being used as a conduit for transporting the substance to the European and North American markets. The seizure of 28,000 kg of hashish in Mozambique, which resulted from the close cooperation between SAPS and the Mozambican authorities, supports this theory. Seizures of hashish in South Africa have not been substantial—just under 35 kg during the 1994/1995 period. The major trafficking routes in cannabis and hashish are illustrated graphically in Figure 9-1.

TABLE 9-2. Cannabis

Cultivation areas	Respective Areas	Potential yield
KwaZulu-Natal	2,567 ha	5,442,040 kg
Northern Transvaal	167 ha	354,040 kg
Eastern Cape	40,000 ha	84,800,000 kg
Total area under cultivation in South Africa	42,734 ha	90,596,080 kg

Methaqualone (Mandrax) is the main psychoactive ingredient in a sleeping tablet that was originally marketed under the trade name Mandrax. The substance was banned in South Africa in 1977 due to abuse, but continues to be the major problem there now. A possible explanation for this phenomenon is that South Africa was the first country in which a subculture evolved in which Mandrax was ground into a powder, mixed with cannabis and smoked as a concoction known as "white pipe." Mandrax was traditionally manufactured in illicit Indian laboratories and transported from Bombay by air and sea freight to Kenya, Mozambique, Tanzania, Zimbabwe, or Zambia, and ultimately to South Africa (see Figure 9-2).

Because of the significant successes achieved by Indian authorities in detecting and closing down clandestine laboratories, the illicit manufacturing of Mandrax has shifted to Africa, especially southern Africa. Several Mandrax laboratories in Africa were shut down in Kenya, Tanzania, Zambia, and South Africa in recent years. Twelve clandestine Mandrax factories have been identified and terminated since the South African Narcotics Bureau (SANB) closed down its first in 1987. In September 1996, a laboratory capable of producing half a million tablets was discovered in a rural area. Citizens from Britian, Portugal, Botswana, and South Africa were arrested on the scene, indicating the international nature of the trade.

Designer drugs comprise all the synthetic stimulants/hallucinogens, specifically LSD, the "ecstasy (or XTC) group" (MDMA, MDEA, etc.), Methamphetamine (speed), and 2C-B (nexus). Traditionally, South Africa has had a core user group of LSD to which the problem of abuse was confined. However, the emergence of the "rave scene" has exposed South African society to the full complement of designer drugs. The ecstasy drugs were first seized in 1994; in 1995 the seizures doubled.

FIGURE 9-1. Major Drug-Trafficking Routes: Hashish, Cannabis

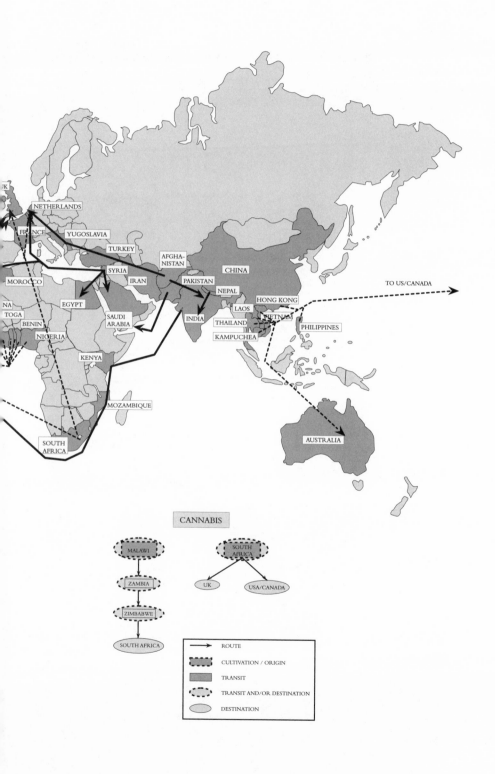

UK

NETHERLANDS

FRANCE   YUGOSLAVIA

TURKEY

AFGHA-
NISTAN

SYRIA

IRAN   PAKISTAN

CHINA

MOROCCO

NEPAL

HONG KONG

LAOS

VIETNAM

NA
TOGA

EGYPT

SAUDI
ARABIA

INDIA

THAILAND

PHILIPPINES

BENIN

KAMPUCHEA

NIGERIA

KENYA

TO US/CANADA

MOZAMBIQUE

AUSTRALIA

SOUTH
AFRICA

CANNABIS

MALAWI

SOUTH
AFRICA

ZAMBIA

UK   USA/CANADA

ZIMBABWE

SOUTH AFRICA

→ ROUTE

CULTIVATION / ORIGIN

TRANSIT

TRANSIT AND/OR DESTINATION

DESTINATION

FIGURE 9-2. Major Drug-Trafficking Routes: Mandrax, LSD, "XTC"

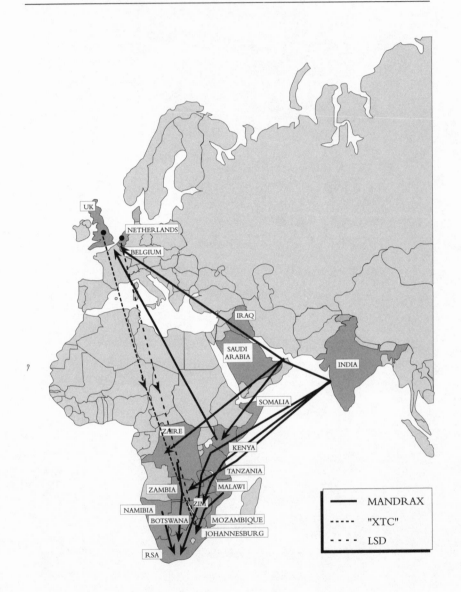

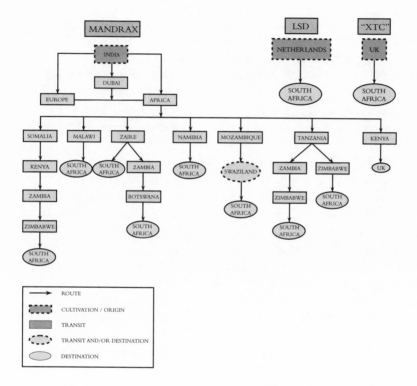

In 1996 they were expected to double again. The lesser known 2C-B also has appeared in South Africa. Intelligence reports indicate that the designer drugs are manufactured in Europe, mainly Britain and the Netherlands, and then smuggled into South Africa (see Figure 9-2). Reports further reveal that cannabis is often bartered for the designer drugs in Europe.

The threat that the new designer drugs hold for South Africa cannot be underestimated; in contrast with LSD, they have found their way quickly to a wide cross-section of society, particularly those in the sixteen to twenty-four age group. The popularity of raves—4,000 to 5,000 people not being unusual in the larger metropolitan areas, such as Johannesburg, Durban, and Cape Town—increases the user base dramatically.

Cocaine is a stimulant of the central nervous system, derived by extraction of the raw material from the leaf of the coca plant. During the 1970s and 1980s, cocaine was considered a "status" drug in South Africa, since it was confined to the middle- and upper-class suburbs, where it fetched prices averaging between R300 to R400 per gram ($75 to $100). The purity levels were low because of the cutting agents used in the marketing process. A few hundred addicts were spread throughout South Africa. Cocaine was smuggled either through the postal system (in letters or parcels) or by couriers organized by local drug traffickers.

In 1992, West African nationals (WAN) started arriving in South Africa, immediately introducing high-quality cocaine. The cocaine initially retailed at R300 per gram, but constant supply dropped the price to c. R180 per gram. The existing local cocaine traffickers found it more cost-effective and convenient to obtain their supply from Nigerians wholesale, at a rate of c. R120 per gram. Cocaine was no longer a "status" drug; a slump in prices made it affordable even in the less affluent areas. All racial groups have started abusing the substance.

A cause for grave concern is the free availability of "crack" cocaine—also called "rock," "freebase," or "wash" in South Africa; it is highly addictive, easy to obtain, and simple to manufacture. A crack manufacturing facility was recently discovered in the kitchen of a Johannesburg dwelling. The drug is smoked or inhaled with immediate euphoric effects, quickly followed by depression and paranoia. Crack smoking is associated with violence, especially with adolescent abusers.

Crack is starting to compete with Mandrax as the drug of choice among users in the major metropolitan areas. Studies of the American experience with crack demonstrate the inherent dangers of the substance for society. The major cocaine trafficking routes for cocaine are graphically illustrated in figure 9-3.

Heroin is a depressant of the central nervous system, derived by chemical processing of raw opium obtained from the opium poppy. It is becoming one of the most popular and profitable drugs of the 1990s. Many of the cocaine drug lords in Colombia and other coca-producing countries are beginning to focus their attention on manufacturing and dealing heroin. The implication for South Africa is that established routes for cocaine trafficking can now be used by heroin syndicates. WAN groups now participate actively in these operations, acting as conduits for sales in both Western Europe and the United States. The WAN involvement is a further cause for concern when seen against the backdrop of United Nations (UN) estimates that approximately 51 percent of the world heroin market is controlled by these syndicates.

Heroin abuse in South Africa has been limited, primarily due to the fact that a synthetic pain killer, dipipanone, is available on the legitimate market. Dipipanone produces the same effects as heroin when taken intravenously, but users prefer it because its production in clinical conditions and its diversion from legitimate consignments into the illegal market make it cheaper than heroin. The major heroin trafficking routes are graphically illustrated in Figure 9-4.

The Socioeconomic and Political Implications of Drug Trafficking

In countries most affected by drug trafficking, the destabilizing impact of the drug industry constitutes a serious threat to security, sovereignty, and the effective functioning of democracy. The loss of superpower benefactors, declining rates of per capita GDP, unstable commodity prices, and rising domestic and foreign debt make the hard currency and profits connected with drug trafficking almost irresistible, especially to marginalized African countries.

The drug business is invariably accompanied by social disorder in both producer and consumer countries. However, the social and economic cost has yet to be quantified. Social disorder creates mass anxiety, which is rarely without political consequences. Moreover, the increased ability of drug traffickers and criminal organizations to operate internationally is a potential danger for social and economic order in every country. The exorbitant profits from drug trafficking are encouraging criminals already involved in more orthodox crimes— such as robbery, extortion, gambling, and prostitution—to extend their activities to drug trafficking on a national and international scale. This dimension is even more disturbing than drug-related delinquency. Socially, it has a negative impact on community structure, not only with regard to criminality but also the need for stricter border control, which affects the movement of both trade and individuals.

The large-scale presence of illegal immigrants in South Africa, apart from its role in crime (including drug trafficking), has led to an

FIGURE 9-3. Major Drug-Trafficking Routes: Cocaine

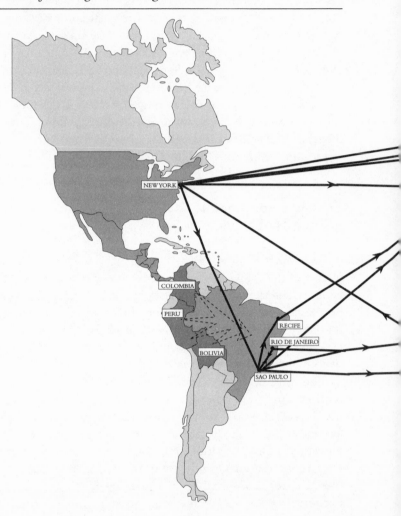

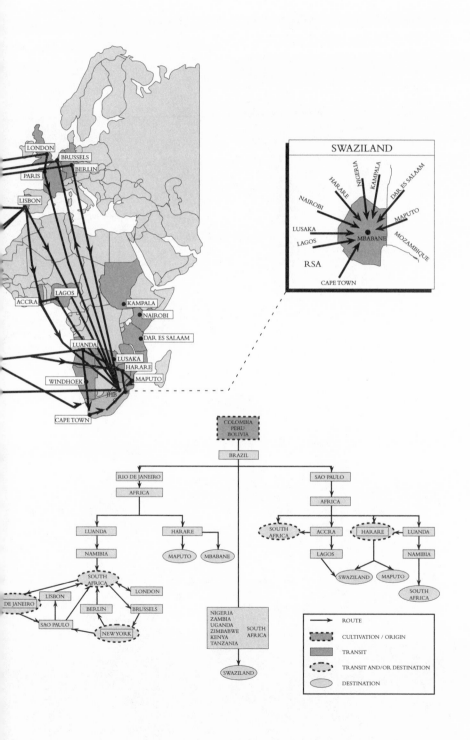

SWAZILAND

NAIROBI
HARARE
NIGERIA
KAMPALA
DAR ES SALAAM
LUSAKA
LAGOS
MBABANE
MOZAMBIQUE
MAPUTO
RSA
CAPE TOWN

LONDON
BRUSSELS
PARIS
BERLIN
LISBON
LAGOS
ACCRA
KAMPALA
NAIROBI
DAR ES SALAAM
LUANDA
LUSAKA
HARARE
WINDHOEK
MAPUTO
JHB
CAPE TOWN

COLOMBIA
PERU
BOLIVIA

BRAZIL

RIO DE JANEIRO

AFRICA

SAO PAULO

AFRICA

LUANDA

NAMIBIA

HARARE

MAPUTO   MBABANE

SOUTH
AFRICA

ACCRA

HARARE

LUANDA

LAGOS

NAMIBIA

SWAZILAND   MAPUTO

SOUTH
AFRICA

SOUTH
AFRICA

DE JANEIRO
LISBON
BERLIN
SAO PAULO
NEW YORK
LONDON
BRUSSELS

NIGERIA
ZAMBIA
UGANDA
ZIMBABWE
KENYA
TANZANIA
SOUTH
AFRICA

SWAZILAND

→ ROUTE

CULTIVATION / ORIGIN

TRANSIT

TRANSIT AND/OR DESTINATION

DESTINATION

FIGURE 9-4. Major Drug-Trafficking Routes: Heroin

ROUTE
CULTIVATION / ORIGIN
TRANSIT
TRANSIT AND/OR DESTINATION
DESTINATION

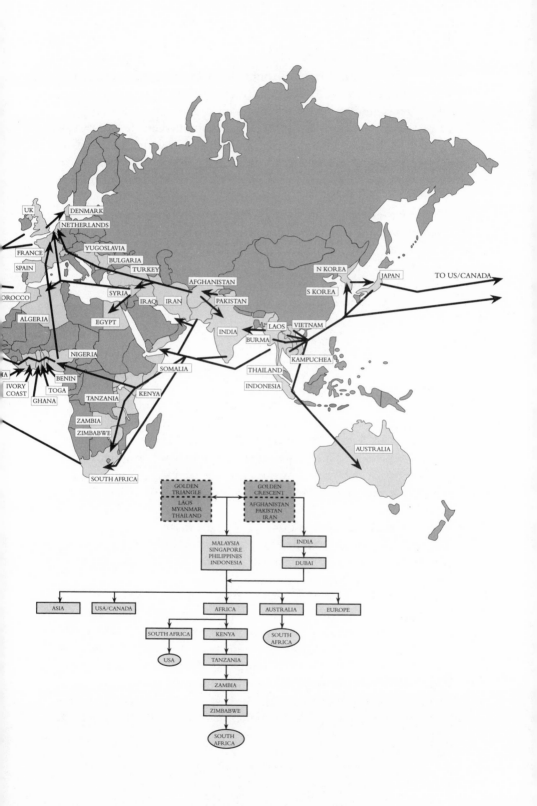

UK
DENMARK
NETHERLANDS
FRANCE
SPAIN
YUGOSLAVIA
BULGARIA
TURKEY
OROCCO
SYRIA
IRAQ
IRAN
AFGHANISTAN
PAKISTAN
ALGERIA
EGYPT
INDIA
BURMA
LAOS
VIETNAM
N KOREA
S KOREA
JAPAN
TO US/CANADA
NIGERIA
SOMALIA
KAMPUCHEA
MA
BENIN
IVORY
COAST
TOGA
GHANA
TANZANIA
KENYA
THAILAND
INDONESIA
ZAMBIA
ZIMBABWE
AUSTRALIA
SOUTH AFRICA

GOLDEN
TRIANGLE
LAOS
MYANMAR
THAILAND

GOLDEN
CRESCENT
AFGHANISTAN
PAKISTAN
IRAN

MALAYSIA
SINGAPORE
PHILIPPINES
INDONESIA

INDIA

DUBAI

ASIA
USA/CANADA
AFRICA
AUSTRALIA
EUROPE

SOUTH AFRICA
KENYA
SOUTH
AFRICA

USA
TANZANIA

ZAMBIA

ZIMBABWE

SOUTH
AFRICA

increase in the already intense competition for scarce resources. The influx of immigrants into South Africa is expected to increase even further, compounding most current socioeconomic problems, not the least of which is crime. Owing to concern about the role of firearms in criminal activity, including drug trafficking, more effective combatting of the illegal import, use, distribution, trade, and possession of firearms/ammunition/explosive devices was an integral part of the Ten Point Plan created by the SAPS to combat crime and violence.

The drug industry is also one of the most unstable. The drug-trafficking networks, extremely well financed and superbly armed, can buy the susceptible and terrorize the honest. The vulnerability of state institutions to corruption and intimidation because of drug trafficking, which is increasing at an alarming rate, also undermines public faith in democratic institutions and imperils governability.

Enforcement Initiatives

The Government of South Africa is a signatory to the United Nations Single Convention on Narcotic Drugs (1961), the 1970 Protocol, and the United Nations Convention on Psychotropic Substances (1971). In 1992, South Africa entered into an agreement with the government of Britain concerning mutual assistance with drug trafficking. South Africa also has the following initiatives and treaties with neighboring governments: adherence to the Protocol on Cross-Border Control Measures of the Southern African Development Community (SADC), signed August 1994; a formal agreement with Mozambique to cooperate and to render mutual assistance in combatting crime, signed March 1995; an informal agreement with the government of Swaziland, made August 1995.

In 1996, the SADC drafted a protocol on the combatting of illicit drug trafficking, providing for areas of cooperation between the members. The protocol also commits the member states to the establishment of a regional institutional framework to combat illicit drug supply, demand, and corruption through legislation and social policies. The members are convinced that a joint concerted effort is necessary to eradicate illicit drug trafficking. South Africa also has a 1947 Extradition Treaty with the United States that covers drug trafficking, though it has significant gaps in its coverage, including divergent definitions of conspiracy.

The SAPS, in pursuance of its counter-narcotics strategy, has introduced a multidimensional approach to the escalating drug problem, tasking all governmental and nongovernmental organizations to utilize their individual expertise for the furtherance of drug and drug-related investigations. It has also restructured itself to allow investigators to specialize in specific fields, thus improving the professional capabilities of members and the effectiveness of the service as a whole. In addition, the SANAB has been divided into provincial and national units. The provincial units are responsible for localized drug matters, and the national units, which operate under the head, Organized Crime, are responsible for drug matters on a national and international scale.

Since the SAPS realized that the South African borders were not patrolled effectively, it has established a new Border Policing Unit to guard against the smuggling of contraband at all ports, airports, and border posts. The SAPS also works closely with INTERPOL, which disseminates information about couriers and assists with international enquiries. Consequently, in 1995, the police stopped twenty couriers, made five arrests, and seized 36.5 kg; in 1996, the numbers were fifty-six couriers, six arrests, and 14 kg. The SAPS also run Crime Stop, an anonymous information network, which acquires information from concerned citizens by telephone via a toll-free number, and offers rewards for positive information.

Although the efforts of the SAPS are aimed primarily at the reduction of drug supplies, significant steps have been taken to reduce demand as well. Captain Crime Stop is an educational program for children that treats all aspects of crime but mainly the areas of child and drug abuse, and SANAB units present lectures at schools, churches, and other civic institutions in an attempt to educate both young and old about the drug situation in South Africa.

The drug-trafficking issue not only harms interstate relations in Africa; it also has a particularly deleterious effect on the political and economic stability of South Africa, especially with regard to the successful implementation of the Reconstruction and Development Program (RDP). Community structure suffers from drug abuse as well as the need for stricter border and visa control, which affect individuals' freedom of movement. Moreover, policy programs for the prevention and interception of drug trafficking place a severe financial burden on governments.

There is no quick solution to drug trafficking and abuse. The processes and factors that contribute to the problem will have to be addressed in such a way that the vicious spiral of drug-related crime can be checked. The problem of drug abuse comprises two main components, namely supply and demand. Any successful strategy against drugs will have to reduce both. To combat drug-related crime effectively, a multidimensional approach, with multiprofessional assistance, may be what is necessary—in other words, a close relationship between the control, intelligence gathering, and law enforcement concerned with the problem. This collaboration should come as a result of the responsibility, direct or indirect, that every party has in the prevention of drug abuse and trafficking.

10

Steven Metz

The Conceptual Transformation of the South African Military
Changing Strategy, Ethos, and Civil–Military Relations

THE SECURITY ENVIRONMENT of southern Africa is undergoing revolutionary change. With the end of the Cold War and the demise of apartheid, two of the forces that stoked armed conflict in the region faded from the scene. The result has been a winding down of some of the region's debilitating wars and an even more widespread decompression of political tension as a new spirit of cooperation emerged. All things considered, the security environment of southern Africa shows greater promise for peace and security than it has for decades. Many states in the region are undertaking extensive military downsizing. Between 1995 and 1999, for instance, South Africa expects to reduce its military from 131,000 to about 70,000. Other nations are taking similar measures.[1]

Major military demobilization is always difficult, particularly in the absence of rapid economic expansion to provide opportunities for those released from service. Success requires strong political leadership. But if the goal is the actual transformation of the security environment, rather than simply a diminution of defense budgets, the shrinking of armed forces alone is not enough. Transformation, as Griffiths suggests, is an extraordinarily complex and sequential process in which demobilization and disarmament must be followed by institutional restructuring and—most difficult of all—conceptual and attitudinal change. This is the situation in southern Africa today. Demobilization and disarmament are underway. Restructuring is likely to follow. But only conceptual transformation can complete the transformation and offer hope that it may become permanent.[2]

For a military, conceptual transformation entails a fundamental shift in the basic ideas that shape when, where, and how armed forces perform their functions. In the broadest sense, there are four forms of such conceptual transformation. Although they are all complex, the easiest is *operational* change, which alters the way military units fight. A second and more complex form is *strategic* change, which affects basic military roles and missions, redefining the security threats against which the armed forces are to defend, and often causing a realignment of partners or allies. The third form of conceptual transformation involves *civil–military relations*. The fourth form concerns the *ethos* of a military—the basic values that define and shape it.

All four forms of military conceptual transformation are challenging, sometimes even politically dangerous. Each requires changing such essential elements of a military organization as its structure, doctrine, and training. Furthermore, the forms are not mutually exclusive, but may take place in combination. Today, for instance, that the South African National Defense Force (SANDF) is undergoing conceptual transformation in the realms of strategy, ethos, and civil–military relations has immense implications. Because of South Africa's economic, political, and military power, the success or failure of this transformation will shape regional stability for years to come and may help determine the course of post-apartheid reconciliation within South Africa itself. As goes South Africa, so goes the southern Africa sub-region and perhaps sub-Saharan Africa as a whole. The ultimate outcome of the SANDF's conceptual transformation remains uncertain.

Strategy

Every nation that takes security seriously has a national-security strategy to integrate the elements of national power and a military strategy to guide the development and the actual employment of the armed force. These strategies may not be formal, but, to be effective, they must be understood by civilian and military leaders and, in the case of democracies, by the public. Since military strategy helps translate political objectives into military roles and missions, it exists at the intersection of the political and military realms. National leaders define interests, objectives, stipulations, and priorities. In an extremely important part of strategy formulation, national leaders and military strategists usually work in conjunction to assess and rank security threats. The military's own capabilities, or perception of its capabilities, also shape strategy by defining the limits of the feasible. Finally, a nation's history—particularly its military history—and strategic culture influence how leaders think about the use of force, and thus play an important role in shaping military strategy.

Generally, the more developed the political and military institutions of a state, the more formal is its process for formulating, adjusting, and promulgating a national military strategy. States with well-developed procedures for making and explaining strategy often have an advantage over states with informal or ad hoc strategy systems. As might be expected, South Africa has one of the more elaborate and formal strategy-formulation systems in sub-Saharan Africa. The result has been a tradition of clear and refined military strategy. To a large extent, it was a reaction to the threats that the political system based on white minority rule had to face. Decolonization in Africa, and the subsequent entry of the Soviet Union into the continent's politics, prompted Pretoria to refine, expand, and formalize what had previously been a rather loose military strategy. The fear among the leaders of the minority government was that pressure growing from decolonization, black nationalism, and political radicalism would lead to the downfall of apartheid and, the argument went, endanger white culture and values. In response, they lavished resources and attention on national security.[3]

Because South African–occupied Namibia, white-ruled Rhodesia, and the Portuguese colonies of Mozambique and Angola seemed to provide a buffer against black nationalism and radicalism until the mid-1970s, Pretoria supported the counterinsurgency campaigns there. But in the late 1970s, South Africa faced a broad-based and precipitous erosion of its security situation. Angola and Mozambique became independent and radical. The entry of a large number of Soviet advisers and Cuban troops in Angola was particularly threatening. Southern Angola quickly became a basing area for the South West Africa People's

206 / STEVEN METZ

Organization (SWAPO), which had begun guerrilla attacks against South Africa's administration of Namibia in 1966; and, within South Africa, a period of relative quiet ended with the Soweto riots of 1976. As anti-apartheid violence spread across the country, many black youths abandoned peaceful resistance to apartheid and provided recruits and support to the guerrilla campaigns run by the African National Congress (ANC) and Pan-Africanist Congress (PAC).[4]

This disintegrating security situation led many white South Africans to conclude that they were the target of a "total onslaught" orchestrated by the Soviet Union. According to this view, the anti-apartheid movement both inside and outside South Africa had been co-opted by Moscow. Hence, the issue was not the resistance of the white minority to the rights of the majority, but the global struggle between communism and free-enterprise democracy. Within the rigid Cold War weltanschauung of South Africa's political and military leaders, this view made perfect sense. Since the North Atlantic Treaty Organization (NATO) and the United States had thwarted direct Soviet expansionism in Europe and Asia, Moscow was resorting to an indirect strategy, namely, the use of third-world nationalism and radicalism to weaken the West by eroding its morale and political will, draining human resources, and ultimately, strangling its economies. "In its indirect onslaught against Western capitalism," stated a South African defense white paper, "Soviet strategy is aimed at denying essential natural resources to the West." South Africa was a high priority target because of its mineral wealth, industrial base, and location on vital shipping routes. Since Western interests in South Africa and the prowess of the South African Defense Force (SADF) prevented outright invasion by communists, the Soviets had to rely on proxy aggression.[5]

Pretoria responded to the "total onslaught" with what became known as the "Total Strategy." South African strategists were convinced that in the face of Soviet-engineered aggression, defense required a carefully integrated political, ideological, economic, and military counter-strategy. The Total Strategy had several overlapping objectives, all designed to protect the white-dominated system. One was the mobilization of support for the effort, particularly within South Africa but also, to the extent possible, in the world community. The architects of the Total Strategy—like their counterparts in the United States of the 1940s and 1950s—believed that the most insidious elements of

Soviet aggression—its subtlety and indirectness—could prevent victims from recognizing their plight until it was too late. The Total Strategy sought to rectify this situation with public education. Another objective was the development of a more efficient system for strategy formulation and of more effective means for the actual use of available power resources, which involved both improvements in the capabilities of the SADF and a major contribution from the military in the formulation of national policy and strategy, to assure a seamless integration of the military and nonmilitary elements of national power.[6]

The Total Strategy also sought to divide the forces that Pretoria saw as its enemies; it led to such creations as the "tribal homelands" program and others to dilute the black community. Finally, the Total Strategy entailed a careful blend of carrots and sticks. Those who cooperated with Pretoria, both inside and outside South Africa, were rewarded, often using economic inducements; those who supported the anti-apartheid forces were punished. The preferred method for dispensing punishment was through proxies—whether insurgents, such as Jonas Savimbi's Union for the Total Independence of Angola (UNITA) and Afonso Dhlakama 's Mozambique National Resistance (RENAMO), or the governments of the tribal homelands. When proxies failed, Pretoria was willing to strike directly at its enemies and their supporters, sometimes far from the borders of South Africa itself. Because South Africa—like most third-world states—did not have much long-range capability, this action usually took the form of commando raids on places like Cabinda, Maputo, and Lusaka, or terrorist attacks, such as the letter bomb that killed Ruth First, the scholar and political activist.

By the 1980s, South African military strategy had totally abandoned its earlier emphasis on defense against conventional invasion from outside the Republic's borders to focus on counterinsurgency (including community support activities aimed at "winning hearts and minds"), proinsurgency in Angola and Mozambique, support to police during internal violence, and small-scale direct strikes. Despite facing an arms embargo and isolation from most of the international military community (Israel and Taiwan being important exceptions), the SADF became the most professional, well-led, and well-trained armed force in Africa. Though it relied heavily on whites (particularly for leadership functions), it did make use of a wide range of non–whites. Domestic production and cooperation with Israel and Taiwan allowed Pretoria to reach self-sufficiency in most types of armaments. (An exception—and one that proved important in Angola—was the failure to develop modern fighter aircraft).[7]

The notion that impeccable logic based on flawed premises always leads to flawed conclusions holds true for the case of South African strategy. Despite the skill of the SADF, particularly in counterinsurgency, the nation's wider national strategy suffered debilitating flaws. For starters, the assumption that Pretoria was the target of a deliberate, Moscow-controlled offensive appears to have been naive. Without this foundation, the rest of the Total Strategy's political logic eventually collapsed. Pretoria found it more and more difficult to sustain public support for the use of military force, especially in Namibia. An important segment of the white South African population concluded that the political, economic, and human costs of the war there could not be justified by the security threat which a majority-ruled Namibian state would pose. Domestically, the use of the SADF to support the police also grew increasingly unpopular, even within the military itself. Even though the SADF often supported civil-action projects in the black townships and thus had a relatively positive image among the black population, many soldiers (and their families) felt that domestic stability operations were not what the military was designed to do. In time, Nathan argues, the SADF's "credibility amongst large sections of the population was destroyed" as a result of internal deployments and other apparent police functions.[8]

By the end of the 1980s, the political objectives of the Total Strategy had become clearly unattainable. The "carrots"—mostly promises of economic cooperation with African states who abandoned the antiapartheid movement—had not paid the expected dividends. Global opposition to apartheid proved much too strong to be swayed by Pretoria's arguments that South Africa's strategic minerals were threatened by the Soviets and that apartheid was actually based on the principle of "separate but equal." Only a small group of extreme conservatives in the West accepted the notion of the "total onslaught" and the strategy that emanated from it. The end result was similar to that faced by Napoleon, Hitler, and other failed strategists throughout history: A skilled, professional military force and a coherent military strategy proved unable to compensate for a defective grand strategy based on faulty assumptions and unrealistic political objectives. Yet, as happened with Napoleon and Hitler, the proficiency of the military persisted long after the political component of the national security strategy proved bankrupt. Luckily, South Africa's leaders proved wiser than Napoleon and Hitler; they were able to change their political strategy radically rather than suffer total defeat.

The adaptation of South Africa's strategy to the new political and strategic environment is still underway. An important part of this adaptation has been a realignment of strategic relationships and security ties. Apartheid-era South Africa became virtually isolated in the security sphere once Zimbabwe and the Portuguese-speaking colonies moved to majority rule. Post-apartheid South Africa has greatly improved cooperation with the other states of southern Africa. In 1996, for instance, South Africa supported the creation of a new security organ as part of the Southern African Development Community (SADC). Soon after, South African Defense Minister Joe Modise called on the SADC states to arm themselves heavily in order to stave off any external threat to the region.[9]

Pretoria's strategic shift has included the renewal of long-dormant ties with Western Europe and the United States; it sent the first-ever South African student to the U.S. Army War College during the 1995/96 academic year. The 1996 visit to Washington, D.C. of SANDF Chief of Staff Gen. Georg Meiring was seen as a symbol of a "new relationship" between the South African and American militaries.[10]

The shift also led to relations of various kinds with nations never heavily involved in southern Africa, such as Iran, Palestine, India, Ukraine, and Malaysia. In what was probably the most dramatic (and controversial) turnaround, President Nelson Mandela's government severed ties with Taiwan and opened them with the People's Republic of China.[11]

The realignment of security relations is important, but the alternation of the basic concepts undergirding South African strategy is even more vital. For instance, South Africa has taken a much more holistic view of security than its predecessor. According to the 1996 defense white paper, "In the new South Africa national security is no longer viewed as a predominantly military and police problem. It has been broadened to incorporate political, economic, social and environmental matters." Ironically, the Total Strategy prepared South Africans for thinking about security in a broad and holistic fashion; that breadth has become part of South Africa's strategic culture. According to Defense Minister Modise, "The root causes of insecurity are primarily non-military by nature and require a range of non-military measures to deal with them." The post-apartheid government has defined the threat to national security differently than its predecessor did. As the defense white paper states, "The Government of National Unity recognizes that the greatest threats to the South African people are socio-economic problems like poverty, unemployment, poor education, the lack of housing and the absence of adequate social services, as well as the high level of crime and violence."[12]

The stress on crime is central. By 1996, crime had reached such epidemic proportions that President Mandela identified it as a threat to South Africa's fragile democracy. Modise added an even more radical twist to the new thinking about the purposes of South African power when he announced that protection of foreign investment was one of the major reasons for improving the SANDF:

> The gap between those people who are deprived and those who are not is very big. Statistical surveys show 43 percent of South Africa's population is without formal employment. What South Africa needs to address this problem is investment, and no right-thinking person is going to invest in a country that is not militarily strong enough to defend those investments.[13]

Although South Africa's broadening of what constitutes national security reflects a general trend around the world, it places a great strain on the senior leaders of the military. It diminishes the importance of the military relative to other state agencies that deal with the promotion of security. During the final stages of apartheid, the South African military played a preeminent role in national security that the government's redefinition of security explicitly seeks to change. So far, the SANDF has shown remarkable discipline in accepting this decline in stature. However, the process of adjustment is slow and remains incomplete. Some analysts go so far as to label it a failure and to argue that the SANDF is as involved in policymaking as the SADF was. Although this is an overstatement, the military certainly retains a highly influential position in South African policymaking.[14]

Nonetheless, resentment of a decline in political influence is not the only problem that involves the SANDF: The wider definition of national security will tempt the military to assume functions previously beyond its purview, which can be dangerous in even the most stable political settings. In South Africa, which is definitely not the most stable political setting, political leaders have redefined security without undertaking either adequate institutional reform or across-the-board conceptual reform.[15]

The formulation of military and national-security strategy is always easier in the presence of an obvious threat. Today, South Africa does not have an enemy amenable to traditional military force. As a result, the emerging strategy has several potentially debilitating contradictions, tensions, or dilemmas. The first concerns the balance between offense and defense. The orientation of the Total Strategy was explicitly offensive; it sought to interdict or preempt opponents as far from South Africa's borders as possible. The government, however, has adopted a defensive strategy as part of its rapprochement with the former Front Line States. The defense white paper states that "the SANDF shall have a primarily defensive orientation and posture." But the SANDF still retains many of its offensive operational capabilities. Combining strategic initiative with operational defense—the opposite of the current South African stance—is a time-tested technique for a state with multiple enemies. The Prussia of Frederick the Great, for instance, mastered it. But blending an essentially defensive strategy with an offensive operational capability is much trickier. For South Africa, the capability to project power might deter potential enemies or, at least, limit the damage that they could do to South Africa, but it also risks intimidating neighbors, stoking an arms race, and increasing regional tension.[16]

Another dilemma concerns determining the appropriate role of the SANDF in nontraditional military missions such as internal security, nation building, and social engineering. The new strategy admits that the shortcomings of South African Police Services (SAPS) may force the military to undertake internal-security missions for some time. The goal, though, is to improve the SAPS sufficiently to permit the SANDF to become involved in internal security "only under the most exceptional circumstances." The new strategy also uses the SANDF to help integrate the former guerrillas of the ANC (Umkhonto we Sizwe, or MK) and PAC (Azanian People's Liberation Army, or APLA) into civil society. A national service brigade was created to teach job skills, but it has been woefully inadequate in light of the problem. According to Griffiths, "Returning from exile, MK soldiers often faced economic hardship, including recession and unemployment, as well as public hostility and a less-than-enthusiastic welcome from some internal ANC leaders." As a result, some of the disgruntled ex-soldiers have drifted into criminal activity, thereby contributing to one of South Africa's most pressing problems.[17]

Defense Minister Modise also committed the military to participation in South Africa's Reconstruction and Development Program and National Growth and Development Strategy, but did not explain precisely what the SANDF's function would be or why the military was the appropriate organization for these projects. Use of the military for nonmilitary political purposes or for security functions that probably should be police matters is certainly nothing new. Even the United States military performed such service throughout its history. It promoted internal security during the expansion of the frontier and the military occupation of the South after the Civil War; and it has served as a tool of social engineering during the quest for racial and gender equality. But such nontraditional missions can erode a military's ability to perform core functions or turn the military into a political arm. Hence, the SANDF would probably prefer to extricate itself from internal security as rapidly as possible.[18]

Lt. Gen. Wessel Kritzinger, SANDF chief of staff for operations, has argued that the SANDF should be involved only in "serious crimes that threatened the country's constitutional dispensation." It may be years, however, before the SAPS are strong enough and South Africa stabilized enough for the military to be extricated significantly from internal-security functions. The charge by such critics as Frederik W. de Klerk, leader of the National Party, that the SAPS is dangerously demoralized due to low salaries, overwork, and the travails of affirmative action suggests that the involvement of the SANDF in internal security may actually increase in the short term. The only long-range solution is to produce strategy that specifies when and how the military should be used for internal defense.[19]

The same argument applies to the use of the military for social engineering. South Africa has made a substantial investment in its military, and the SANDF could serve a vital function in the crucial process of racial reconciliation. But the nation's political leaders must see this role as an aberration—an extraordinary response to extraordinary conditions—if the military is to retain its professionalism and prowess over the long term.

Another point of contention revolves around how the SANDF is to be used in multinational peace-support operations. The end of the Cold War prompted attempts to settle many long-standing conflicts around the world, but also allowed others to blossom. The result has been a dramatically renewed interest in multinational peace operations, many of them under the aegis of a United Nations reinvigorated by the lifting of the Cold War stalemate in the Security Council. Although a number of states like Canada, Sweden, Ghana, Nigeria, and Nepal had long experience in multinational peacekeeping, others were new at it. Nations seeking to take a larger share in multinational peace-support operations could find themselves drawing time, talent, and money away from other tasks. The objective is balance, to determine the appropriate place for peace operations within a wider strategy.

In response to countervailing pressures and considerations, South Africa has vacillated about its commitments to multinational peace operations. Some leaders, both civilian and military, who favor an active role, perhaps even a leading one, stress South Africa's skill at planning and supporting complex military operations, as well as its moral obligation to employ it in behalf of regional stability. As Cilliers and Malan put it, "South Africa is an African leader, and the dominant state in Southern Africa. Inevitable responsibilities and commitments flow from its position of economic and moral strength. . . . [P]eace-keeping in Southern and even Central Africa, therefore, may be considered as action in direct pursuit of its national security and economic interests." Most South Africans support this position in principle: A 1995 poll showed that about 67 percent wanted a military force that could help other countries maintain peace. The rub is in the cost of translating this principle into policy.[20]

Turning the SANDF from traditional national defense to peace operations will entail military complications, economic costs, and political risks. Troops would have to be retrained and officers reeducated (no easy task for a military strongly indoctrinated in the "warfighter" mentality). As nations heavily ensconced in multinational peace operations, like Canada, are finding, long and frequent deployments can be quite burdensome on relatively small armed forces and can hinder recruitment and retention. Peace operations always risk creating new enemies and turning peacekeepers into targets of terrorism. According to opponents of increasing SANDF participation in multinational peace operations, the problems of building a post-apartheid society and a post-apartheid military are so great for South Africa that all such distractions should be avoided. Military leaders in particular are aware of the extent to which peace operations would require new skills at precisely the time when the SANDF is focused on the complexities of the integration process. In many ways, South Africa's emphasis on multinational peace operations reflects the attitude of the United States, namely, that power brings a moral responsibility incompatible with a cold-hearted isolationism that considers promoting world peace not worth the costs in blood or money.[21]

In this mélange of argument and counterargument, the first real test of South Africa's position on regional peacekeeping came during discussions about what to do in Burundi during 1996. Pretoria seemed unable or unwilling to clarify its position. At the same time that President Mandela announced his support for a South African contribution to a multinational force for Burundi, Deputy Foreign Minister Aziz Pahad issued a formal statement withholding SANDF troops.[22]

Events later in 1996 intensified the debate over South African involvement in peace operations. In October, United States Secretary of State Warren Christopher proposed the formation of an African Crisis Response Force, which was to consist of 5,000 to 10,000 troops from African states who were to be trained, equipped, and sponsored by the United States and other developed nations and used for rapid deployment into African conflicts. Although the United States was able to muster some support for the proposal before Christopher's October trip to Africa, South African participation was "regarded as crucial." Within South Africa, however, the proposal met a lukewarm reception. President Mandela, though not opposed in principle, strongly urged that the initiative for such a force come from the United Nations rather than from the United States. By contrast, *The Star* of Johannesburg, one of the influential publications that supported Christopher's proposal—argued that "this may be South Africa's moment to step out of the wings and begin to play its proper role in Africa." The debate between those favoring activism and those favoring a more restrained regional policy showed little sign of resolution.[23]

A few weeks later, a crisis that exploded in eastern Zaire quickly developed the potential to engulf much of central Africa in violence and generate a massive humanitarian disaster. France, stung by charges that it had abetted the 1994 violence in Rwanda, advocated a Western intervention force, but could not get the immediate American commitment that it considered vital. Most African states also supported a multinational force, but preferred that Africans, not Europeans or North Americans, lead it. Attention naturally fell on Pretoria, but South Africa's response again wavered, indicating deep fissures within the nation's leadership. On November 1, Foreign Affairs Minister Nzo urged an international effort to restore peace in Zaire, but when a summit of regional leaders opened in Nairobi a few days later, South Africa sent only an observer rather than a full participant. According to Stefaan Brummer of the Johannesburg *Mail and Guardian*, this behavior "underscored South Africa's relatively passive role in Africa's latest crisis." On November 12, the Organization of African Unity endorsed a multinational force with African participation. Three days later the United Nations Security Council approved the idea and Canada volunteered to lead the force.[24]

While these events were taking place, South Africa still failed to clarify its position. On November 7, Deputy Foreign Minister Pahad stated that the SANDF was not prepared to send ground troops to Zaire, and an official announcement on November 15 said so again. At a meeting in Rome, Executive Deputy President Thabo Mbeki stated, "[W]e do not proceed from the principle that South Africa has a special role....We reject the idea of South Africa as an African superpower." Almost simultaneously, however, President Mandela was expressing South Africa's determination to send troops to Zaire, claiming that they could be ready for deployment within a day or two. In what may have been a compromise between those advocating activism and those urging caution, Jakes Gerwel, a presidential aide, announced that the SANDF would provide "technical assistance" to the Canadian-led multinational force, but would not play a more high-profile role. This stand presumably meant no use of SANDF combat forces.[25]

The confusion surrounding participation in multinational peace operations may be the most obvious evidence of the incomplete transformation of South African strategy, but the other contradictions, tensions, and dilemmas remain as well. The result is a polyglot that obstructs the decisiveness needed by military leaders for force development, training, refinement of doctrine, equipment acquisition, and operational planning. On one hand, traces of the apartheid-era strategy linger, primarily in the major role accorded military power in the broader national-security strategy, the use of the military for internal security, and the stress on initiative and offensive actions. On the other hand, new elements, including active involvement in peace support and social engineering, are emerging. Until South Africa's civilian leaders establish a clear priority among what seem to be the major mission areas for the SANDF—regional peace operations, traditional defense against external enemies, internal security, and such nontraditional missions as nation building—it will be extraordinarily difficult for political leaders to decide what the proper size of the military should be, or for military leaders to craft coherent programs and plans.

Ethos

A military's ethos is composed of the core values that hold it together, give it coherence, define its institutional culture, distinguish it from the rest of society, undergird its morale, and structure its relationships with political leaders and civil society. Changing and rebuilding a military ethos is a vital part of the postrevolutionary transformation that South Africa is undertaking. If the process fails, other changes may become moot. But the importance of ethos is easy to misunderstand, particularly for civilian leaders not intimately familiar with the military.

To a large extent, military ethos derives from history and tradition. A military draws from its collective experience—its defeats and its victories—in order to construct a value system. The lessons drawn from history and tradition are often more influential than what historians consider "the facts." A military ethos also mirrors a nation's wider political culture, worldview, and social history, but it is also somewhat distinct, reflecting the military's position as both part of wider society and separate from it. The fact that armed forces are designed for organized violence is the most important reason for the cultivation and development of a strong ethos to link members of the military and give them a framework for making personal and professional decisions.

One essential component of a military ethos is a norm-based system for establishing priorities among the various missions, tasks, and roles. These responsibilities can be in conflict, particularly when the military has internal duties—preserver of law and order or guarantor of good government, as in many Latin American militaries, etc.—and external ones aimed at defense of national sovereignty, borders, and territory. Furthermore, ethos helps a military force to establish priorities among the characteristics that it wants its members to have, whether loyalty to the military or to a specific segment of society, obedience to civil authorities, pursuit of a distant goal (for instance, the establishment of socialism or the spread of a religion), service to the nation, or a war-fighters' mentality.

A military ethos must also shape the relationship between its members—including that between commissioned officers and other ranks. In most Western military systems, this relationship is paternalis-tic. American officers are trained and educated to serve as mentors to their subordinates and to show concern for their well-being. In other less humane systems, the relationship of superiors and subordinates is more that of patron and client than mentor and student. The Nigerian military provides one of the more pathological examples of this type of hierarchy. The late 1980s and the 1990s witnessed the emergence of a system in which corrupt senior "military godfathers" built networks of lower-ranking clients to enrich themselves. Many junior officers without patrons were unhappy with this system, not necessarily because it did not serve the national interest but because it did not serve their own. For enlisted personnel, conditions were dire. While most senior leaders were multimillionaires living in mansions and driving Mercedes, the lower ranks took the brunt of the crushing poverty that followed Nigeria's economic collapse.[26]

Reflecting the cultural complexity of South Africa, the ethos of the SADF was based on two traditions. One was the British, characterized by high levels of professionalism— particularly in the standing forces—the camaraderie that grows from a regimental system, careful and formal programs of leader development and education, and a paternal-istic relationship between superiors and subordinates, including units that paired white officers and black troops. The British tradition also imbued the SADF with an appreciation for civilian control of the military and for the military's limited role in the making of national policy, which eroded precipitously after former Minister of Defense Pieter W. Botha became prime minister (later president) of South Africa in 1977. As the white-dominated state faced mounting challenges, the military's influence on policymaking became so pronounced that scholars wrote about the "militarization" of South African politics. But even at the height of the crisis, the British tradition remained strong. The ethos of the SADF retained the feeling that military involvement in crafting national policy was undesirable and temporary.[27]

The second tradition that contributed to the ethos of the SADF was the "citizen soldier" mentality, which originated with the Afrikaner tradition of local self-defense commandos, which each shared responsibility for defending their community. The Afrikaner tradition gave the SADF ethos a Manichean, "us against them" worldview that could always envision enemies willing and able to eradicate the community that the military served. It also gave the SADF a sense of loyalty to a specific community defined by culture, race, and language, as opposed to a more abstract entity like the state. The preservation and protection of culture, which is not a major part of the traditional British military ethos, became preeminent objectives for the SADF. Even though the Afrikaner tradition was different from the English in many ways, the two proved complementary. The blend led to one of the most effective ethos in Africa (and, perhaps, in the world), at least as far as military objectives were concerned.[28]

The SANDF ethos has been able to assimilate certain venerable military qualities, such as discipline, respect for civil authorities, and overall professionalism. But, as Williams argues, these alone cannot provide an institutional culture acceptable to a multiracial South Africa or South African military. Hence, the government has devised a program to craft a new ethos that seeks to combine the best of the SADF tradition with the values and perspectives of the former liberation movements and homeland armies. The 1996 defense white paper, *Defence in a Democracy*, cites "professionalism" as the bedrock of the military ethos, defining it as (1) acceptance of civilian control; (2) maintenance of requisite technical, managerial, and organizational skills and resources; (3) strict adherence to the constitution, to domestic legislation, and to international law; (4) operation according to established policies, procedures, and rules; (5) commitment to public service; and (6) nonpartisanship in party politics. On that note, the new constitution of South Africa is in full agreement about the responsibility of the military to the law: "The security services must act, and must teach and require their members to act, in accordance with the Constitution and the law, including customary international law and international agreements binding on the Republic."[29]

To create and cultivate these characteristics, Williams recommends an institutional culture for the SANDF based on four "legs," the first being the old regimental system, albeit one not based on ethnicity or regionalism. As Williams recognizes, a strong regimental system is an outstanding way to cultivate and disseminate the military ethos, especially when joined with a well-developed program of professional military education. The second leg of the new institutional culture would consist of units and regiments to embody the non-SADF traditions. The third leg would include regional units drawing on the traditions and strengths of the former homeland armies. The fourth leg would be composed of functional corps that are technocratic rather than regimental, including artillery, engineer, and signal. Along these same lines, Williams advocates disbanding the local commandos and transferring their personnel to the police reserves.[30]

Whether Williams' plan is ever translated into official policy, the government has begun efforts to transform the ethos of the SANDF. As Nathan notes, officer education is pivotal in the transmission of values during the SANDF's transition. The current educational program on the proper role of the military in a democracy stresses respect for the constitution, international law, and multicultural diversity. The goal is to integrate these topics into training as a whole rather than to treat them as an isolated issue.[31]

Finding a workable blend of the diverse traditions that compose the SANDF and building a coherent ethos from them will be difficult. As Williams writes, "Caught between the 'professional-constitutional' model of the armed forces in Western democracies and the nation-building tradition of armed forces in developing democracies, the South African armed forces will exhibit a hybrid identity.[32]

The broadest view seems to suggest three possible outcomes. One is that the non-SADF forces—which include the former guerrillas of MK and APLA as well as the "TBVC" (Transkei, Bophuthatswana, Venda, and Ciskei) forces—will take on characteristics of the SADF ethos rather than inspire some sort of synthesis. Analysts from the political left who assume a unitary body of military attitudes that overrides distinctions among various armed forces hold this position. A second alternative is that attempts to synthesize the diverse traditions that now compose the SANDF will fail, and the military will either split into factions or will have to be rebuilt from scratch. The third option—the one preferred by most South Africans and most supporters of stability in southern Africa—is that the program of synthesizing the diverse traditions will succeed. Although such a synthesis would be historically significant and almost without precedent, the difficulties that it would entail must not be underestimated.[33]

Civil–Military Relations

As the conceptual foundation of South African strategy and the ethos of the SANDF are changing, so are the country's civil–military relations. At the core of these relations is the way a state and society answer two crucial questions: (1) Should the military reflect the composition and values of the wider society; and (2) What is the appropriate role of the military in the creation of national policy?

Leaders do not always seek a military force that mirrors the composition and values of society. Elites often prefer their soldiers to be distinguished from society at large, whether on the basis of ethnicity or some other factor, so that empathy will not prevent them from using force. In sub-Saharan Africa, for example, many of the contemporary armed forces grew from colonial militaries. In Zaire, the Belgians based the security of their colony on the Force Publique, which combined Belgian officers with enlisted personnel usually composed of troublemakers whom local chiefs wanted out of the way, thus inaugurating a pattern of antagonistic relations between the security forces and the Zairian public. The army was more a repressor of the citizens than a protector.[34]

Most modern democracies seek to forge a bond between their populaces and the military. The American military ethos holds that the military is "of the people," reflecting a heritage of local militias. State-based national-guard units and reserve components remain important even today. Even in democracies without a strong reserve or militia tradition, a civil–military equilibrium requires that the armed forces reflect society in whatever criteria are deemed important, whether ethnicity, race, religion, or language. This complex process often has a profound impact on the armed forces. It has both an "input" dimension, in which recruitment is structured by the desired social criteria, and a "procedural" dimension, which involves promotion, retention, and the dissemination of socially approved values through training and education.[35]

Transforming the South African military into an organization that reflects its society has been an important part of post-apartheid reconciliation. The apartheid-era SADF was never intended to mirror the full scope of South African society accurately since, according to Howe, its express purpose was "maintaining white hegemony." The move from a nonreflective to a reflective military, could well have entailed starting from scratch and building an entirely new force. But the government recognized that this approach would have eroded, perhaps destroyed, the most professional and proficient armed force in Africa. For a nation in the midst of revolutionary transformation and extensive internal violence, it was an unacceptable risk.[36]

Although almost everyone recognized the need for a new armed force blending MK, APLA, and the TBVC forces with the old SADF, the main issue was how much influence the SADF and MK should have in the new organization. Both sides moved toward compromise. The leaders of the SADF recognized the need for affirmative action, and MK underwent programs to improve the training and professionalism of its members. Eventually, a workable compromise was reached, the SADF becoming the model for the SANDF, which retained many of the senior leaders, and MK being assigned to manage the integration process. An Integration Oversight Committee, composed of members of Parliament, the secretariat of the Department of Defense, and leaders of the SANDF, provided high-level guidance.[37]

From the start, a few white military leaders were hesitant about accepting soldiers with little or no training solely to meet integration requirements, but most of the senior SADF leaders accepted the need for affirmative action. Some of the MK cadres have also been dissatisfied with the process, expressing discontent about their promised financial rewards, as well as their status in the new SANDF. More than 5,000 MK soldiers went absent without leave during their basic training period, thus proving an embarrassment to the ANC-controlled government. Yet, integration has proceeded fairly well. Although the government does not anticipate completion until 1999, by the end of 1996, approximately 16,000 of 34,000 MK and APLA had reported; 4,000 of them opted to demobilize. Officers appointed numbered 1,700 (along with 500 from the TBVC forces)—eleven of them generals.[38]

Despite this initial success, the Mandela government eventually may have to choose between speeding the integration process and dropping SANDF standards, and maintaining an efficient, tough security force capable of controlling the ever-present threat of political violence. If affirmative action is pushed too hard in the SANDF, talented whites may leave or avoid the service. The expense of integration is also a great burden for a state facing immense demands on its financial resources. In late 1996, Deputy Defense Minister Ronnie Kasrils estimated the total cost at c. R3 billion.[39]

The fact that South Africa has no imminent external threat and no immediate internal problem beyond the powers of the SAPS gives the government breathing room to pursue military integration. But it must be consolidated quickly; the security environment could become more threatening at any moment. Even Defense Minister Modise recently admitted that the SANDF is "virtually powerless to deter attacks," because of drastic budget cuts. If the SANDF has not been transformed into an integrated organization that reflects the ethnic composition and values of South Africa, South Africa may face disaster, if or when the next threat emerges.[40]

Post-apartheid South Africa has done much to make the SANDF responsive to society, but less to deal with the second vital issue in civil–military relations—defining the appropriate role of the military in the making of national policy. The initial tasks were to diminish the extensive political power that the military held during the apartheid era, to reinvigorate civilian supervision of the military, and to clarify the military's responsibility for adherence to national law, civil rights, and international law.

The 1995 draft defense white paper, *Defence in a Democracy*, stated that the military "remains an important security instrument of last resort but it is no longer the dominant security institution." To institutionalize the diminution of the military's policymaking role and consolidate civilian control, the government created a defense secretariat through which the uniformed head of the Defense Force was to report to the minister of defense. Lt. Gen. (retired) Pierre Steyn, a relatively liberal Afrikaner, became head of the Defense Secretariat and was assigned to work on budgetary issues and long-term policy, leaving the head of the Defense Force to concentrate on military operations, intelligence, training, and discipline. Although the defense secretary and head of the Defense Force are technically equals, this fledgling bureaucracy further diluted the policymaking role of the military and forced the heads of the Defense Force to report to the head of the Defense Secretariat for the first time.[41]

Even given these structural adjustments, analysts such as Kynoch contend that the political influence of the military has not been significantly reduced. South Africa's internal and regional policies still feature the use of force. Although Kynoch's view may overstate the case, in light of the military's power during the apartheid period, SANDF is and undoubtedly will remain a important player in policy formulation, if for no other reason than the time needed to develop a corps of civilian defense experts to staff the secretariat. Tradition takes time to change, particularly in an environment that, contrary to Kynoch's position, is rife with security threats (albeit nontraditional ones).[42]

As a general rule, the more intense the security threat, the greater is the role of a military in making national policy. Civil–military relations are usually more placid when both sides understand and accept the distribution of responsibility for specific issues and functions. Three variables can upset this balance: a perception by one side that the other is unable or unwilling to fulfill its responsibilities; deliberate encroachment by one party on an issue or function considered the prerogative of the other; or the emergence of new issues or functions not yet allocated to one party or the other. In South Africa's case, the greatest risk is that the military may become frustrated if the nation's security situation worsens, and the SANDF perceives its civilian masters as unable to deal with it. Healthy exchange between civil society and the military depends on both inculcating new values throughout the SANDF, primarily through military education and the continuation of professional, competent civilian direction, including the cultivation of a corps of civilian defense managers.

The program for the conceptual transformation of the SANDF, designed with civilian and military input (and crucial help from a number of outside analysts), is sound. South Africa's defense establishment has been rich in that most elusive and vital resource—talented leadership. The nearly miraculous ability of such ANC leaders as Modise to transcend their revolutionary heritage once in power is one reason that the transformation has proceeded as smoothly as it has. The professionalism of SADF's senior officers and their willingness to adapt to political changes is another. The visionary leadership of the SANDF has been particularly instrumental in the process of changing the organization's ethos. Altering strategy and civil–military relations, however, is trickier. Leadership will be decisive, but the ultimate success or failure of the SANDF's transformation will be decided not by the SANDF itself, or even the Ministry of Defense, but by South Africa's other civilian authorities.

What, then, will determine the outcome? One of the most important factors will be the ability of South Africa to develop a coherent foreign policy. In the final years of apartheid, an effective military strategy faltered because it was built on an untenable grand strategy. Today, South Africa may be in a similar situation. Although the changes underway in the nation's military strategy are generally well designed and logical, South Africa does not have a refined grand strategy, relying instead on an ad hoc, astrategic approach.

Some South Africans feel that "South Africa has not found its role in the world, and furthermore, that its leadership is either not competent (in the case of its foreign minister) or ill-informed and driven by an antiquated understanding of global affairs (in the case of its president)." According to McNeil, South African foreign policy is running on two different tracks. The first comes from the formal processes of the Foreign Ministry, in which experts are consulted and congruence with other policies considered. The second is whatever President Mandela decides to announce. Vacillation and confusion result.[43]

There is no sign of consensus about South Africa's interests and objectives at an even deeper level. Government statements about foreign policy do little to define national interests or set priorities. This is a very serious problem; effective military strategy is impossible without a coherent set of foreign-policy objectives. If South Africa does not rectify this shortcoming soon, the process of military transformation will falter.[44]

The transformation of civil–military relations depends on competent civilian defense experts who can instill confidence in the military that national policy is in good hands. South Africa needs both a corps of civilian defense professionals and elected civilian officials who understand the use of military power. Simply to inculcate a military with a belief in the undesirability of political intervention on its part is not enough. The weakness of civilian leadership is at least as responsible for military intervention in politics as is the aggression of the armed forces.

In South Africa, if internal instability becomes a problem, military intervention could conceivably result in a temporary direct take-over of the state or some form of extensive control over a weak civilian government. South Africa's leaders must both cultivate civilian expertise and improve the SAPS in order to forestall the sort of internal disorder that the SANDF could interpret as a threat to national security.

The transformation of the SANDF—which is vital to the future of South Africa, as well as the southern Africa region as a whole—is in the hands of South Africa's elected leaders. If they craft a coherent foreign policy, cultivate civilian administrators and elected officials with expertise about defense, and maintain internal stability by augmenting the capabilities of the SAPS, the transformation will probably succeed. If not, dangerous times lie ahead.

Notes to Chapter 10

1. Only Botswana, apparently concerned that instability in South Africa might spill over its borders, is enlarging its armed forces and upgrading its major equipment. See Stefaan Brummer, "Defence Force Rapidly Expanding," *Mail and Guardian*, 4 Apr. 1996, distributed via Africa News Online; South African Press Agency, "Canadian Fighter-Bombers Delivered to Botswana," African National Congress electronic newswire, December 21, 1996; Norman Chandler, "MK to Chair Integration of SADF into New Armed Forces," *The Star* (Johannesburg), 16 Apr. 1996, 11, reprinted in Foreign Broadcast Information Service (FBIS) report *FBIS-AFR-96-075* (electonic edition).

2. Robert J. Griffiths, "Democratisation and Civil-Military Relations in Namibia, South Africa, and Mozambique," *Third World Quarterly*, XVII (1996), 474.

3. Deon Geldenhuys, *The Diplomacy of Isolation: South African Foreign Policy Making* (New York, 1984); James M. Roherty, *State Security in South Africa: Civil-Military Relations Under PW Botha* (Armonk, N.Y., 1992); Metz, "Preto-

ria's 'Total Strategy' and Low Intensity Warfare in Southern Africa," *Comparative Strategy*, VI (1987), 437-440.

4. Robert Jaster, "South Africa's Narrowing Security Options," in *idem* (ed.), *Southern Africa: Regional Security Problems and Prospects* (New York, 1985), 47-48; Gail M. Cockram, *Vorster's Foreign Policy* (Pretoria, 1970); Al J. Venter, *Vorster's Africa: Friendship and Frustration* (Johannesburg, 1977); Christopher Coker, "South Africa: A New Military Role in Southern Africa, 1969-1982," in Jaster (ed.), *Southern Africa*; Christopher R. Hill, "UDI and South African Foreign Policy," *Journal of Commonwealth Political Studies*, VIII (1969), 96-103; Richard Leonard, *South Africa At War* (Westport, 1983); Thomas G. Karis, "Black Politics: The Road to Revolution," in Mark A. Uhlig (ed.), *Apartheid in Crisis* (New York, 1986).

5. Republic of South Africa, Department of Defense, *White Paper on Defence and Armaments Supply* (Pretoria, 1979), 1; Robert J. Hanks, *Southern Africa and Western Security* (Cambridge, Mass., 1983); James E. Dornan, "The Strategic Importance of South Africa," in Robert L. Schuettinger (ed.), *South Africa—The Vital Link* (Washington, D.C., 1976); South African Embassy, *South Africa: The Persian Gulf of Minerals* (Washington, D.C., 1980); idem, *The Cape Route—Passageway to Survival* (Washington, D.C., 1980).

6. Kenneth W. Grundy, *The Militarization of South African Politics* (Bloomington, 1986).

7. Helmoed-Römer Heitman, *South African War Machine* (Novato, Calif., 1985).

8. Laurie Nathan, "The Restructuring and Reorientation of the South African Defence Force," in *Towards Sustainable Peace and Stability in Southern Africa* (New York, 1994), 133.

9. "SADC Organ on Politics, Defence, and Security," Communiqué issued by the summit of government heads of state in the Southern African Development Community, Gaborone, June 28, 1996, reprinted in *FBIS-AFR-96-127* (electronic edition); Panafrican News Agency electronic newswire, "Southern Africa Creates Defence and Security Body," June 29, 1996. For analysis, see Jakkie Cilliers, *The SADC Organ For Defence, Politics, and Security*, Institute for Defense Policy Papers, 10 (Halfway House, 1996). Christo Retief, "Modise: Arm Yourselves to the Teeth," *Die Republikein* (Windhoek), 9 July 1996, 1-2, reprinted in *FBIS-AFR-96-137* (electronic edition).

10. South African (SA) radio broadcast, "'New Relationship' Cited with U.S. Armed Forces," Johannesburg, March 22, 1996, transcription in *FBIS-AFR-96-057* (electronic edition).

11. SAPA broadcast, "Military Cooperation Agreement Signed With Malaysia," Johannesburg, November 12, 1996, transcript in *FBIS-AFR-96-220* (electronic edition); Jericho Voice of Palestine broadcast, "Defense Minister,

Other Officials Receive Palestinian Team," November 17, 1996, transcript in *FBIS-AFR*-96-223 (electronic edition); Sidarth Bhathia, "'Warming Relationship' With India on Defence, Security," *Sowetan* (Johannesburg), 13 Dec.1996, 36, reprinted in *FBIS-AFR*-96-241 (electronic edition); *Interfax* broadcast, "Delegation Signs Bilateral Accords in South Africa," Moscow, November 26, 1996, transcript in *FBIS-SOV*-96-230 (electronic edition); Iranian News Agency (IRNA) broadcast, "Visiting Rafsanjani—Iran Ready to Improve Ties with South Africa," Tehran, September 13, 1996, transcript in *FBIS-AFR*-96-180 (electronic edition); SA radio broadcast, "Deputy Pahad Cites Reasons for Breaking Links With Taiwan," Johannesburg, November 28, 1996, reprinted in *FBIS-AFR*-96-231 (electronic edition). This decision about China was criticized by much of the white community. See "New Direction on China 'Abrupt,' 'Unexpected,'" *Mail and Guardian* (Johannesburg), 6 Dec. 1996, reprinted in *FBIS-AFR*-96-236 (electronic edition); South African Press Agency, "SA Military Veterans Reiterate Friendship Bonds With Taiwan," 11 Dec. 1996 (electronic download).

12. SA Department of Defense, *Defence in a Democracy*, white paper on defense for the Republic of South Africa, May 1996 (electronic download), chap.2; "Defence Minister Briefs Media on 'Challenges,'" *Salut* (Pretoria), April 1996, 19, 20, reprinted in *FBIS-AFR*-96-100, May, 22, 1996 (electronic edition).

13. SA radio broadcast, "Mandela—Crime, Gangsterism Threat to 'Fragile' Democracy," Johannesburg, October 29, 1996, reprinted in *FBIS-AFR*-96-211 (electronic edition); Chandler, "Defence Force Revamp to 'Protect Foreign Investment,'" *The Star* (Johannesburg), 16 Aug. 1996, reprinted in *FBIS-AFR*-96-161(electronic edition).

14. Gary Kynoch, "The 'Transformation' of the South African Military," *Journal of Modern African Studies*, XXXIV (1996), 446-450

15. Charles J. Dunlap, Jr., has warned that making the American military responsible for such nontraditional missions as counter-narcotrafficking could upset civil–military relations in the United States and, in the most extreme case, actually spark military intervention in politics. See "The Origins of the American Military Coup of 2012," *Parameters*, XXII (1992/93), 2-20.

16. Charles Knight and Carl Conetta, *Key Issues in Current South African Defense Planning* (Cambridge, Mass., 1996), 1.

17. William Gutteridge, "South Africa's Defence and Security Forces: The Next Decade," in Jack E. Spence (ed.), *Change in South Africa* (New York, 1994), 59; "Defence Minister Discusses SANDF Transformation Process," *Mail and Guardian* (Johannesburg), 8 Nov. 1996, reprinted in *FBIS-AFR*-96-218 (electronic edition); interview with Defense Minister Joe Modise, the *Sowetan* (Johannesburg), 24 May 1994, 9, reprinted in *FBIS-AFR*-94-101, 25 May

1994 (electronic edition). See also Jacklyn Cock, "The Social Integration of Demobilized Soldiers in Contemporary South Africa," *South African Defence Review*, XXII (1993), 1–17; Griffiths, "Democratization," 477.

18. "Defence Minister Briefs Media on 'Challenges,'" 19, 20.

19. SAPA broadcast, "General Urges the Use of Military Only With 'Serious Crimes,'" Johannesburg, February 14, 1996, transcription in *FBIS-AFR*-96-033 (electronic edition); Linda Ensor, "De Klerk Says Police Services in 'Demoralized State,'" *Business Day* (Johannesburg), 27 Nov. 1996, reprinted in *FBIS-AFR*-96-230 (electronic edition); SAPA broadcast, "Mbeki Opens Defence Policy Review Conference," Johannesburg, August 12, 1996, transcription in *FBIS-AFR*-96-157 (electronic edition).

20. Cilliers and Mark Malan, "A Regional Peacekeeping Role for South Africa: Pressures, Problems and Prognosis," *African Security Review*, V (1996), 23; Greg Mills, *War and Peace in Southern Africa: Crime, Drugs, Armies, and Trade*, WPF Reports, 13 (Cambridge, Mass., 1996) (part of which comprises the introduction of this volume), 33.

21. For discussion, see Malan (ed.), *New Partners in Peace: Towards a Southern African Peacekeeping Capacity* (Halfway House, 1996).

22. Brummer, "Daily—'Mixed Signals' on Sending Troops to Burundi," *Mail and Guardian* (Johannesburg), 19 July 1996, reprinted in *FBIS-AFR*-96-140 (electronic edition). See also SA Network broadcast, "Deputy Pahad—Troops Not on Standby To Go to Burundi," August 1, 1996, reprinted in *FBIS-AFR*-96-149 (electronic edition).

23. Warren Christopher, "Remarks at the Organization of African Unity," Addis Ababa, October 10, 1996 (electronic download from the Office of the Spokesman, U.S. Dept. of State); *idem*, "Address at the South African Institute of International Affairs," Johannesburg, October 12, 1996 (electronic download from the Office of the Spokesman, U.S. Dept. of State); Lionel Williams, "South Africa Not Against African Peacekeeping Force," Panafrican News Agency electronic newswire, October 13, 1996, 1; report on SAPA, "Mandela—UN Must Initiate African Peacekeeping Force," Johannesburg, October 12, 1996, transcription in *FBIS-AFR*-96-200 (electronic edition); editorial in *The Star* (Johannesburg), 10 Oct. 1995, reprinted in *FBIS-AFR*-96-198 (electronic edition).

24. Alfred Nzo, address to the International Diplomatic Association, Pretoria, reported in a SAPA broadcast, Johannesburg, November 1, 1996, transcription in *FBIS-AFR*-96-214 (electronic edition); AFP broadcast, Paris, November 5, 1996, transcription in *FBIS-AFR*-96-216 (electronic edition); Brummer, "Country Said 'Standing on the Sidelines' in Zaire Issue," *Mail and Guardian* (Johannesburg), 8 Nov. 1996, reprinted in *FBIS-AFR*-96-218 (electronic edition); resolution of November 12, 1996, distributed by Africa News Online; Resolution 1080, S/RES/1080, November 15, 1996.

25. SAPA broadcast, "Pahad: RSA Armed Forces Not Prepared for Zaire Problem," Johannesburg, November 7, 1996, transcription in *FBIS-AFR*-96-218 (electronic edition); Thabo Mbeki, interview by Ugo Tramballi, *Il Sole-24 Ore* (Milan), 17 Nov. 1996, 3, reprinted in *FBIS-AFR*-96-223 (electronic edition); SA radio broadcast, Johannesburg, November 17, 1996, transcription in *FBIS-AFR*-96-223 (electronic edition); L. Williams, "South African Troops for Zaire Soon," Panafrican News Agency electronic newswire, November 18, 1996.

26. *Africa Confidential*, 27 Sept. 1991, 4; *ibid.*, 2 July 1993, 1.

27. Grundy, *Militarization of South African Politics.*

28. Hebert M. Howe, "The SADF Revisited," in Helen Kitchen and J. Coleman Kitchen (eds.), *South Africa: Twelve Perspectives on the Transition* (Westport, 1994), 85.

29. Rocklyn Mark Williams, "The Institutional Restructuring of the South African Armed Forces," *Strategic Review for Southern Africa*, XXV (1993), 70; Constitution of the Republic of South Africa, as adopted by the Constitutional Assembly, May 8, 1996, amended October 11, 1996, chaper 11.

30. R. M. Williams, "Institutional Restructuring," 70.

31. Nathan, "Who Guards the Guardians? An Agenda for Civil-Military Relations and Military Professionalism in South Africa," *Strategic Review for Southern Africa*, XVII (1995), 65.

32. R. M. Williams, "South Africa's New Defense Force: Progress and Prospects," *CSIS Africa Notes* (March 1995), 7.

33. Kynoch, "Transformation," 441-457.

34. Sandra W. Meditz and Tim Merrill (eds.), *Zaire: A Country Study* (Washington, D.C., 1994), xxxviii.

35. There is a historical tradition of democracies relying on mercenary forces for security. This model may reappear in the future.

36. Howe, "The South African Defence Force and Political Reform," *Journal of Modern African Studies*, XXXII (1994), 31.

37. For brief desriptions of the MK, APLA, and TBVC forces at the start of the integration process, see Mills, "Armed Forces in Post-Apartheid South Africa," *Survival*, XXXV (1993), 79-83. Griffiths, "South African Civil-Military Relations in Transition: Issues and Influences," *Armed Forces and Society*, XXI (1995), 402-403; Chandler, "MK to Chair Integration of SADF into New Armed Forces," 11; "Defence Minister Discusses SANDF Transformation Process," *Mail and Guardian* (Johannesburg), 8 Nov. 1996, reprinted in *FBIS-AFR*-96-218 (electronic edition).

38. Interviews with military analysts and U.S. embassy personnel by Kent Butts of the U.S. Army War College, Johannesburg and Pretoria, August 1994; Gutteridge, "South Africa's Defence and Security Forces," 53; Bill Keller, "Can

a Post–Apartheid Army Ever Get In Step?" *New York Times,* 14 Oct. 1994, A4; Joseph Conteras, "Unrest in Mandela's Ranks," *Newsweek,* 14 Nov. 1994, 43; "Defence Minister Discusses SANDF Transformation Process"; Lindiz Van Zilla, "Former MK Soldiers Opt Not To Join Integrated SANDF," *Cape Times* (Capetown), 30 Jan. 1996, 3, reprinted in *FBIS-AFR*-96-025 (electronic edition).

39. Reuters reported that 122 people died from violence in Natal between October 6 and 13, 1995 (Reuters electronic newswire, October 13, 1995). SA radio broadcast, "Defence Force Transformation Reportedly to Cost R3 Billion," Johannesburg, October 23, 1996, transcript in *FBIS-AFR*-96-207 (electronic edition).

40. "Modise says Country 'Virtually Powerless,'" *Cape Times* (Capetown), 5 Jan. 1996, 5, reprinted in *FBIS-AFR*-96-008 (electronic edition).

41. SABC TV 1 Network broadcast, Johannesburg, August 4, 1994, transcription in *FBIS-AFR*-96-151, August 5, 1994, 20; *Africa Confidential* (London), 26 Aug. 1994, 7.

42. Kynoch, "Transformation," 450–457; R. M. Williams, "South Africa's New Defense Force," 7.

43. Anthoni van Nieuwkerk, "SA's Foreign Policy Challenge," *Mail and Guardian* (Johannesburg), 20 Dec. 1996, distributed by Africa News Service online; Donald G. McNeill, Jr., "South Africa's Foreign Policy: A Tough Balancing Act," *New York Times,* 3 Jan. 1997 (electronic edition).

44. For an example of an inconclusive foreign-policy statement, see Department of Foreign Affairs, *South African Foreign Policy: Discussion Document* (Pretoria, 1996).

11

Jeffrey Herbst

African Armies and Regional Peacekeeping
Are There African Solutions to African Problems?

THE BURGEONING number of states in Africa that are failing has led
to an extended and agonized search for new international mechanisms
to prevent the complete collapse of government structures and begin
the rehabilitation effort. The transition in South Africa and the considerable debate both within and without that country about what its
role in Africa should be has, perhaps ironically, given new impetus to
the idea that the solutions to regional conflicts can be subcontracted.
Indeed, President Nelson Mandela has encouraged this optimism.
Writing in *Foreign Affairs*, he stated, "South Africa cannot escape its
African destiny. If we do not devote our energies to this continent, we
too could fall victim to the forces that have brought ruin to its various
parts."[1]

Partially as a result of the prospect of the new South Africa policing
the continent, "African solutions for African problems" is a phrase
widely heard across a continent where many are well aware of the disastrous consequences of foreign meddling. Shifting the responsibility
to Africa for resolving conflicts is undoubtedly attractive to the world's
great powers, which, after Somalia, are desperate to embrace almost any
strategy to avoid placing their own troops at risk in Africa.

This chapter argues that "African solutions to African problems" is
no answer to the complex human disasters currently threatening a

number of countries. Although maximum African involvement is welcome, there is reason to be skeptical about the willingness and ability of African countries—including post-apartheid South Africa—to resolve conflicts, especially once warfare has broken out. Indeed, South Africa lacks both the desire and the capability to intervene in African conflicts to an extent that would justify faith in the viability of "African solutions for African problems."

The chapter also suggests that the traditional African approaches to sovereignty, now embraced by the new South Africa, are bankrupt, blocking more innovative strategies to address the unique problems of failed states. In the end, the forces that propel states to fail are so great that any solution must rely on the military, financial, and analytical resources of the entire world.

African Solutions for African Problems

The forces favoring Africans taking the lead in confronting Africa's problems are many and vary considerably in their legitimacy. In light of Africa's history of colonization and division symbolized by the Congress of Berlin, it was inevitable that, after independence, the Organization of African Unity (OAU) would make it a priority to try to solve conflicts without involving outsiders. As General R.P. Mboma, Chief of the Tanzania's People's Defense Force noted, "At the time of the OAU's inception in 1963, the heads of African states were convinced that Africans had an '*inalienable right*' to control their own destiny." This sentiment has been greatly strengthened by evaluations of the post–Cold War world. According to William Nhara, coordinator of conflict prevention and research in the OAU's Division of Conflict Management, "Regional organisations should realise that there is a need to take on the primary responsibility for their own problems, especially those relating to issues of peace, security and stability. This is necessary as Africa's external partners are increasingly less enthusiastic about sharing its problems." The setting of Africa as a clear priority in South Africa's new foreign policy and the energy of the new, nonracial government has re-energized hopes in Africa that the continent can develop its own solutions to the problems of conflict.[2]

At least as important is the idea, increasingly common in Western policy circles—especially in the United States after its trauma in Somalia—that conflict management can be subcontracted to regional organizations. There is a strain in American foreign policy, emphasized by the "regionalist" versus "globalist" debate during the Reagan administration, that has always placed considerable hope in the ability of regional organizations to guide American foreign policy. However, it is also clear that "African solutions" is a convenient cover for those who simply do not want to become entangled in more African problems. The rise of South Africa has fed the view that Africa can solve its own problems. South Africa is seen in some circles as able, and because of the sacrifices made by many countries during the liberation struggle, obliged to address Africa's problems. Indeed, when asked in 1995 what the United States would do if the remnants of the Hutu army tried to cross the Rwandan border to finish the genocide that they began in 1994, a senior State Department official hoped that South Africa and the Southern African Development Community (SADC) would respond. Yet, neither South Africa nor the SADC can muster the force needed to stop such an attack.[3]

The Cause of State Failure in Africa

To understand the prospects for peacekeeping and peace enforcement in Africa's current and future conflicts, it is important first to understand the nature of the problem of state failure. Conflict in Africa today does not come from the more traditional problem of separating warring states that have resolved to end hostilities. Indeed, one of the remarkable aspects of post-independence Africa has been the absence of interstate war. Rather, the threats to peace in Africa, as in much of the world, come from conflict within nations. The virtual disappearance of interstate conflict in Africa and the rest of the world is a relatively recent development; yet, in the bloody twentieth century, more people have been killed by their own governments than by foreigners. Hence, even though the problems of state failure in Africa are particularly severe, they are by no means unique or exotic.[4]

When the decolonization of Africa began in the late 1950s, the United Nations General Assembly—the gatekeeper to statehood—

immediately declared the new countries to be sovereign and ratified their borders. The General Assembly was encouraged to do so by the new states themselves, who soon constituted a large percentage of that body, and by the considerable anxiety worldwide to avoid the violence that accompanied the division of the Indian subcontinent in the late 1940s. However, the United Nations' granting of sovereignty by administrative fiat was a revolutionary departure from the usual practice, whereby sovereignty had to be earned. In point of fact, Africa was never composed of sovereign units, classically defined as states possessed of a monopoly on force within their own boundaries. Most colonial states did not make any effort to extend the administrative apparatus of government much beyond the capital city. In the words of Jackson, "In most cases they [the colonial governments] were little more than elementary bureaucracies with limited personnel and finances and were more comparable to rural country governments in Europe than to modern independent States." After independence, African countries attempted to extend the administrative reach of the state, but they were always more focused on the urban populations.[5]

The central paradox of the international treatment of African states is that, although sovereignty was granted as a result of simply gaining independence from colonialism, the immediate assumption was that the new states would somehow take on the characteristics that normally characterize sovereignty—most notably, unquestioned physical control over the defined territory, but also an administrative presence throughout the country and the allegiance of the population to the idea of the state. Indeed, the principal criteria for state recognition in the modern world are a permanent population, a defined territory, and the ability to enter into relations with other states; demonstrable control and allegiance of the population are, at best, secondary considerations.[6]

Although sovereignty in the strict sense was a legal fiction for many countries, appearances were relatively easy to maintain in the 1960s and 1970s. Most African economies were growing, buoyed by relatively high prices for their basic commodity exports. Moreover, the global strategic competition between the United States and the Soviet Union discouraged threats to the design of states in Africa or elsewhere. One of the implicit rules of the Cold War was that supporting efforts to change boundaries was not part of the game. In fact, the great powers usually intervened (as was the case with Zaire, Chad, and Ethiopia) to protect the integrity of existing states.[7]

Finally, there was no intellectual challenge to the immediate assumption of sovereignty by African states. Decolonization happened so quickly, and Africans were so intent on seizing power, that interested parties had neither the time nor the motivation to develop a well-rehearsed response to the method of national political organization. Once the dozens of newly independent states became established, leaders found that the window of opportunity for instituting revolutionary change in political structures was closing.[8]

The Facade of Sovereignty Overturned

As a result of numerous changes, the actual nature of sovereignty in at least some of these African countries is now being exposed. The long economic crisis that many of them have experienced has caused a profound erosion of their governments' revenue bases. Even the most basic agents of the state—agricultural extension agents, tax collectors, census takers—are no longer to be found in many rural areas. As a result, some states are becoming less able to exercise physical control over their territories. As Thom, the U.S. defense intelligence officer for Africa, has written,

> Most African state armies are in decline, beset by a combination of shrinking budgets, international pressures to downsize and demobilize, and the lack of the freely accessible military assistance that characterized the cold war period. With few exceptions, heavy weapons lie dormant, equipment is in disrepair, and training is almost nonexistent. . . . the principal forces of order are in disorder in many countries at a time when the legitimacy of central governments (and indeed sometimes the state) is in doubt.

Low, or negative, per capita growth in many African countries suggests that this gradual dissolution will become more common in the future.[9]

The extremely limited revenue base of many African countries is also partially responsible for one of the most significant developments on the continent during the last thirty years, namely, the change in the military balance between state and society. Whatever their other problems, African states at independence were usually Weberian in that they had control over the few weapons in society. However, as states atrophied, private armies—for example, in Rwanda, Ethiopia, and Chad—have been able to challenge them from the inside, helped by the spillover from conflicts throughout the region and the cheap price of weaponry after the Cold War. Private security outfits, such as the South African-based Executive Outcomes, have had to come to the rescue of beleaguered governments. Weak states currently face unprecedented threats to their continued existence from their own citizens.

International assistance to many African states is stagnant or in decline. Donors are redirecting their aid from Cold War proxies to countries that are achieving success with their economic and political reform, leaving countries that are continuing their fall. Somalia entered its particularly sharp downward trajectory in part because it could no longer pit the United States and the Soviet Union against each other in order to receive aid.

The decline in aid is not only a short-term problem. It represents a fundamental break with the practice of the past 100 years, which saw international actors offer support to the African state system, first through the creation of colonies, then by the enshrinement of sovereignty, and finally by the provision of financial resources without regard to domestic economic or political performance. Thus, it is hardly surprising that so many African states have suffered since the Berlin Wall fell; those that collapsed include a significant number of states (for example, Ethiopia, Liberia, Somalia, and Zaire) that were richly rewarded by international patrons because of their strategic position during the Cold War but were subsequently abandoned when donors became more concerned with economic and political performance.[10]

The combination of these forces has caused the centers of certain states—Liberia and Somalia, for instance—to collapse because the contending parties therein could not break a military stalemate. More common are the states that simply contract: Their centers may still exist, but they cannot extend their power very far over the territory that they nominally control. Zaire under Mobutu Sese Seko probably has the dubious distinction of pioneering this type of national fragmentation. A number of countries are slowly merging into a web of informal business associations, instituted by rulers who have less interest in carrying out the traditional functions of the state than in enriching themselves through trade, even if it means illegal trade across their own borders.[11]

State failure in Africa should be seen as the result of structural forces that have been at play for decades. Neighbors often have only a limited ability to influence events in a failing state via regular diplomacy or other peaceful means. Everyone's favorite example of African intervention—the effort led by President Mandela and other southern African leaders in 1994 to prevent the royal coup by Lesotho's King Letsie III—does not hold out as an easily transferable lesson about how Africans can stop state failure in its tracks. That initiative was successful because Lesotho is a landlocked country unusually vulnerable to outside pressure. Indeed, Mandela was simply continuing an old South African policy of dictating decisions to Lesotho.

The leverage of African countries with their neighbors is extremely limited. A more typical story than the Lesotho one starts with Zambian President Frederick Chiluba's mocking response to Botswana President Sir Ketumile Masire's call for regional consultations about Zambia's foolhardy attempt to keep the opposition leadership, including former President Kenneth Kaunda, from running for president in 1996. Chiluba called outside pressure "indecent curiosity," asking, "Are we also going to discuss the crisis between Botswana and Namibia, President Nelson Mandela's problems in KwaZulu/Natal, how [President Robert] Mugabe ran against himself in Zimbabwe's last elections or the definitely volatile situation in Angola?" By the same token, a great deal of preventive diplomacy before the genocide in Rwanda also came to nothing.[12]

The point is not to argue that Africans should not exert maximum effort to find solutions to African problems. The OAU can be successful, as Mandela was in Lesotho, and Africa has a long history of regional assistance in solving minor conflicts. However, the prospects for diplomacy resolving the profound problems affecting failing states are not favorable.

The Challenge of Africa's Problems: Peacekeeping and Peace Enforcement

It seems almost inevitable that more profound domestic failures will threaten the lives of many Africans and demand some kind of action by the regional and international community. Exactly where these problems will originate is difficult to predict. Indeed, even in the late 1980s, relatively few foresaw that Somalia would quickly become the paradigm of a failed African state. The prevailing wisdom now is that the type of peacekeeping required in the context of failed states is radically different from the notion that emerged after World War II, which focused primarily on keeping combatants apart. Yet, little work has been done on what constitutes legitimate policies for African armies, or any others, that intervene in the affairs of other states. These policies must be clear if the slogan, "African solutions for African problems," is to be meaningful.[13]

One feature of many African crises is that they demand open-ended intervention. African countries that collapse normally have endured at least a decade of structural declines and conflict. Those who intervene will often be forced to make an indefinite commitment to the operation. Indeed, one of the problems with the intervention in Somalia was that President Bush's goal of removing the troops in six weeks was so at odds with his stated evaluation of the problem that the American initiative was probably doomed from the beginning. The short time frame made it difficult for the United States to take the credible steps necessary to promote reconciliation. It was unreasonable to expect that, after years of civil war, the combatants could resolve their differences in a few months. Groups who were not prominent because they did not control large stocks of weaponry could not possibly come to the forefront; a much longer time frame was needed to cultivate those elements of Somali society that were forced to disappear during the long years of warfare.

Given that resuscitating a failed state often involves rebuilding basic state structures—including the police, the courts, and the entire system of local and provincial government—there is no reason to believe that intervention in a failed, or failing, state can be planned with the sort of precision that Western and African military planners would prefer. Because some conflicts do not have immediate solutions, intervenors should not assume that a quick exit is always indicated. Contrary to both Western and African ideals, not all conflicts have solutions that can be reached through a combination of goodwill and persuasion.

The idea of open-ended intervention is at odds with traditional peacekeeping in which the blue helmets remain for a defined period to help build the confidence that will allow them a relatively easy exit. There is no evidence that African governments or, more important, their armies, will be more accepting of uncertain commitment than Western countries are. Several West African countries pulled out of the Economic Community of West African States Cease-Fire Monitoring Group (ECOMOG) intervention in Liberia because of their frustration with the time scale involved. The South African draft white paper about defense suggested that South Africa would participate in a peace operation only if it had a "clear mandate, mission, and objectives," and "realistic criteria for terminating the operation."[14]

These conditions make sense, but it is hard to see how they could be applied to the confusing and unsettled politics of a failing state. For instance, what would have been the "realistic criteria" for terminating the intervention in Somalia—the restoration of order to Somali institutions and the end of the threat presented by the warlords? Such a day would have come only at the end of a difficult process involving many unclear mandates and ill-defined tasks. Indeed, as Clarke and Gosende have stated, none of America's wars actually met the detailed criteria for interventions first enunciated by Secretary of Defense Casper Weinberger.[15]

Well-defined schedules in the topsy-turvy world of failed states are probably counterproductive. The humanitarian needs may not evolve according to a timetable developed in New York, Pretoria, or any African capital. Declarations of limited involvement, as in Somalia, only serve to encourage militants whose ambitions require more fighting and more hostilities. Force-deployment schedules should be flexible and applied realistically to the political goals of an operation; any form of reconciliation in a failed African state, in the Balkans, or elsewhere in the world will take more than a year. The size and nature of the force should reflect the stages of the peace process and the level of threat that remains. There is little evidence that African armies will do worse than Western armies in situations with largely theoretical timetables, but no evidence, to date, that they would do better.

Even if African governments are committed to long-term intervention, they may not have the funds to complete such an operation. Tanzania's intervention in Liberia was persistently hampered by an inability to secure outside funding from the United States or the United Nations. No doubt, other African armies will also be deterred from long-term exercises because of the cost, especially when they are under pressure from donors at home to reduce the military budget. Thus, the new type of peacekeeping differs fundamentally from African— notably Ghanaian—experiences on behalf of the United Nations in the Golan Heights, where the safe job of peacekeeping was extremely remunerative, thanks to high United Nations per diems and relatively high levels of operational support.[16]

Nor does it appear that the new South Africa has the resolve or institutional capabilities to face the challenge of African peacekeeping in a manner that will significantly change the current situation. First, foreign policy writ large is not a priority in South Africa, given its long list of domestic problems. President Mandela's opening address to the third session of the first post-apartheid parliament did not mention foreign policy until the eleventh page of twelve, after speaking to the importance of the Youth and Gender Equality Commissions. Although Mandela expressed South Africa's desire to contribute to the building of a better world, he also added, "We should always be mindful of limitations we have as a nation, as well as the constraints of the real world we have to deal with."[17]

Furthermore, southern Africa, where the new South Africa has its most clearly defined set of interests, appears less likely to have failed states in the near future (with the possible exception of Angola) than other parts of Africa, where South Africa's own interests are less compelling. The new South Africa will undoubtedly contribute to peacekeeping in the future, but its domestic constraints make it unlikely that Pretoria will change the fact that Africa's ability to keep its own peace is inadequate and ultimately dependent on support from the international community.

A second characteristic of state failure in Africa is that all intervention is inherently political. African states fail because they are unable to solve political conflicts by themselves. Hence, any intervention will be seen domestically as a political act and the intervenors as one more set of domestic players to be coopted or coerced. Of course, this perception departs radically from the customary view that the peacekeeping force is neutral, not to be swayed by any of the parties involved in the conflict.[18]

The emphasis on neutrality created a problem in Somalia; it impeded the attempt to promote the kind of wholesale restructuring of Somali society that was necessary to defeat the warlords. The implication of calls for neutral intervention—in Somalia or elsewhere—is that the dire circumstances encountered—like starvation—are caused by nature. In fact, the famine that gripped Somalia in 1992 was fundamentally the result of how the country's political economy had evolved. As Natsios, the former assistant administrator of the U.S. Agency for International Development during the Somalia relief operations, described the situation,

> [F]ood imported through the relief effort became an enormously attractive objective of plunder by merchants, by common working people without a source of income, by organized gangs of young men, and by militia leaders in need of the wealth represented by food aid which they would use to purchase more weapons and keep the loyalty of their followers.... Merchants would actually request the local militia or bands of thieves to steal more food as their stocks diminished each day.

The entire country revolved around the plunder of food.[19]

When United States troops intervened in December 1992 to stop the theft of food, they immediately disrupted the entire political economy and stepped deeply into the muck of Somali politics. By supplying some semblance of order, the United States inevitably helped to provide the basic framework for future Somali politics; that is, it was involved in nation building. At a practical level, it is hard to see how anyone could believe that landing 30,000 troops in a country was anything but a gross interference in major aspects of its politics. The "Mogadishu line"—the notion coined by Lt. Gen. Sir Michael Rose, the former UNPROFOR commander, to describe the need to maintain absolute neutrality in the face of all provocation—was crossed as soon as troops were sent.[20]

Similarly, the notion put forward by Cilliers and Malan, South African analysts, that peacekeeping forces cannot engage a particular faction in battle because it will undermine their moral authority is simply unrealistic in situations like that in Somalia, where one party was causing many of the problems and threatening to disrupt the peace process. In failed states, the parties that benefit from the absence of a centralized state must often be fought; there is no reason to believe that they will suddenly succumb to sweet reason and put down the guns that have brought them so far.[21]

From this perspective, the most vicious insult that a peace operation can hear—that it is the victim of mission creep—is widely misunderstood. The highly political nature of intervention means that it is only natural that missions evolve. For instance, humanitarian relief and resettlement—key aspects of intervention in its early stages—must be protected by force, as the experiences in Somalia and the three other major post–Gulf War interventions by the United States (northern Iraq, Rwanda, and Haiti) demonstrate. Response to urgent requests by relief agencies for logistical support cannot be cited as evidence of mission creep (as was sometimes charged in Somalia), especially when such requests are entirely predictable and intrinsic to mission success. Other actions that intervenors take also may be susceptible to the charge of "nation building." Nonetheless, intervenors will have to discard the fiction that a large military force can or should be apolitical when faced with a crisis originated by politicians.

African armies probably cannot perform any better than Western ones when intervention means immediate interference in domestic politics. Indeed, neighbors often carry considerable baggage which compromises them before they even enter an arena. Many Liberians immediately viewed Nigeria, because of President Ibrahim Babangida's relationship with President Samuel Doe, as part of the problem once ECOMOG began. Similarly, a large sector in Mozambique opposed the presence of even the "new" South African army during the peace process there because of bitter memories about the white regime's record of destabilization, undoubtedly implemented by many of the officers still serving in the new, nonracial army. It may well take much of the southern African region a considerable amount of time to become comfortable with the intervention of South Africans, even in a good cause. Likewise, all sides in Burundi have made it clear that they view intervention, even by exclusively African armies, as direct interference in their domestic affairs, fearing that the planned African intervention will cause a change in the balance of power. The evolution of the situation in Burundi should dispel any notion that African intervention is somehow less "foreign" than intervention by Western armies.

Western countries can become involved in a country's domestic politics to disastrous consequences, as did the Americans in Mogadishu. However, relatively disinterested foreigners who are adept at understanding a country's nuances can, in fact, do just as well as African armies. For instance, the Australians in Baidoa, Somalia, successfully developed a comprehensive civil-affairs program to restore order:

Initially, the Australians set up an auxiliary police force in Baidoa, using former members of the Somali National Police Force whose names were vetted through the Police Committee in Mogadishu. The elders proposed a police commander for Baidoa acceptable to the community at large, who was first investigated by the Australians.... The Australians set up Police units throughout the Bay Region. Former Judges and court workers, who had survived the civil war in the Bay Region, were selected with the approval of the community. . . . The Australians rebuilt the Police Station, the Court and a small prison, all part of the same compound. At the end of the Australian Unit's tour of duty, the Bay Region was "completely secure" with approximately 260 Somali Police, a functioning court system, and the community had confidence in the system of law and order.

Certain African armies, notably the unit from Botswana, did perform as well in Somalia but it certainly does not appear to be a requirement that an army be African to get the politics right.[22]

In highly political intervention operations, certain "force multiplier" units, such as civil affairs and psychological operations, are absolutely vital. Few armies in the world have cadres well trained in such areas, and it is unlikely that many African armies will soon. It is still too early to see if the South African army will acquire the capabilities needed for intervention, but it is not a good sign that early discussions have centered around the procurement of equipment. For instance, the recent high-profile purchases of *Rooivalk* helicopters and submarines by the South African National Defense Forces (SANDF) are not at all what a military would purchase if peacekeeping were its priority. An allotment for the specialized forces just described, as well as for force projection—especially airlift—would be at the top of the list. These specialized forces are particularly important if, once peace is restored, the fundamental institutions of order—including the police and the courts—are to be restored, too.

The Challenge of Africa's Problems: Diplomacy

Given the powerful forces at work supporting state sovereignty, it is no surprise that the prevailing wisdom permits no alternative status for countries that fail besides the current conception of a "nation-state." For instance, even though it was obvious that Somalia had collapsed by December 1992, when the intervention force was being planned, no one seriously considered trusteeship or any legal standing other than the continuing fiction that Somalia was still a sovereign entity. Hence, Omar Arteb Ghalib, a former Somali prime minister, proposed the resolution on intervention to the Security Council so that the United Nations could pretend that Somalia was asking for the foreign troops.

Few, especially in Africa, entertain the idea that it might be better to redesign some African states rather than attempt to resurrect them after a profound failure. For example, there has been little discussion of alternatives in post-genocide Rwanda, despite the country's obvious structural problems and the obvious drawbacks of its current situation (the government's only constituency is the minority Tutsi). Nor has there been any discussion of alternatives for Congo, despite the fact that Kinshasa's writ has not always extended very far.

African states are outspoken that the continued sovereignty of all states guides their foreign policy. The decisions made by the General Assembly in the early 1960s regarding sovereignty are an essential part of the power base of many states in Africa. The July 1994 Windhoek Declaration, which formed the Association of Southern African States—the political arm of the Southern African Development Community (SADC)—included among its principles "the sovereign equality of all Member States" and "respect for the sovereignty and territorial integrity of each State."[23]

One of the stunning developments in the evolution of South Africa's foreign policy is how soon the country reverted to the old emphasis on sovereign equality and the distrust of intervention after the innovations of the liberation struggle. Despite the fact that South Africa under apartheid was an unmistakably sovereign state with physical control over its territory, the African National Congress (ANC) successfully argued that events within the country could justify international sanctions. It also consistently tried to interfere with the foreign policy of a number of Western states—the United States, in particular—in order to promote the global movement to punish Pretoria. The ANC was so successful that South Africa was one of the few places where gross human-rights violations were not allowed to hide behind the shield of sovereignty. Nonetheless, the new South Africa has quickly gone back to the traditional way of thinking on the part of African states stressing sovereign equality and the impossibility of interference in domestic affairs. Thus, even American criticisms of South Africa's relations with Iran are seen as violations of sovereignty—a far cry from the years when the ANC was lobbying the councils of many American cities to punish firms that had business in South Africa.

The problem with devotion to sovereignty is the concomitant assumption that the only remedy for states that have failed is to rebuild them. For instance, Aziz Pahad, the South African deputy foreign minister, correctly recognized that the collapse of the nation-state often involves a total collapse of all structures of government and civil society in conflict situations, but the only response to it that he acknowledged was the rehabilitation of the old institutions. If the failure is total, why is rebuilding on top of the ruins the only answer? African countries loom as the chief barrier to a better and more nuanced perspective on state design that would allow for experimentation. At this point, "African solutions to African problems" is, more than anything else, a recipe for stagnation.[24]

Despite African reluctance, after thirty years of assuming that the boundaries of even the most dysfunctional African state are inviolable, the world should at least consider the possibility of creating new sovereign states; the reality of disintegrating, crippled African states stands in such contrast to the legal fiction of sovereignty that innovation may be all but inevitable. The commonly heard argument in Africa that the establishment of new states is the first step down the slippery slope of microstate creation gives the international community and, especially, Africans, no credit to discern the specifics of situations on a case-by-case basis. The call for new states does not mean the abolition of the criteria for state recognition, only that the criteria have yet to be determined and that dogmatic devotion to the current boundaries is no longer useful. The disruption caused by state creation will have to be balanced against the profound harm that no longer viable states do to their populations everyday.

The international community—albeit in a halting, incomplete, and often incompetent manner—has offered bolder solutions to the new post–Cold War conflicts. Former Secretary General Boutros Boutros-Ghali wrote, "The time of absolute and exclusive sovereignty . . . has passed; its theory was never matched by reality." The flux induced by the end of the Cold War opens up the possibility for new organizational forms. Already, "Kurdistan" in northern Iraq, Palestine—the new type of political organization now taking shape in the West Bank and Gaza—and the "one country, two entity" creation in Bosnia are challenging the monopoly of the nation-state. That these options were brokered largely by the great powers, previously among the most conservative forces in the international community, suggests a willingness of those outside Africa to move beyond the warhorse of sovereignty.[25]

Workable new solutions, however, must emanate from the Africans themselves. The rest of the world does not care enough to develop new alternatives for Africa and is wary of imposing anything on Africa, given the history of colonization. Indeed, the international community is waiting for Africa to take the lead on these issues. To date, the new South Africa has shown neither the interest nor the inventiveness to do so. In no other area does Africa more clearly need leadership, and in no other area is South Africa, given its relative depth of human resources, more worthy of leading. Still, for South Africa to realize its potential, it must relinquish the old precepts of African diplomacy and embrace new norms.

Global Solutions for Africa's Problems

In a perfect world, regional powers, such as South Africa, would respond in a nuanced and effective manner to help settle the conflicts that erupt in their neighborhoods. However, the crises that often arise in Africa are particularly difficult for African armies—including South Africa's—to resolve. Relying on Africa alone to address the diplomatic issues surrounding state failure may result in few experiments, but also a dogmatic devotion to current boundaries—which is not to imply that African intervention does not have its benefits under certain circumstances. Sometimes, Africans may do an excellent job in preventing conflict, especially when the target group or country is unusually vulnerable to pressure. African armies also may play an important role in peacekeeping, as Botswana's did in Somalia. Still, the day when there will be an exclusively African answer to all of the conflicts in Africa seems far away.

The goal of many Africans to regionalize conflict, and the related hope of many Western countries to subcontract the dirty work of resolving domestic wars, should be rejected in favor of a partnership between African and Western countries that would allow global solutions to African problems. Indeed, the Western countries should continue to develop new diplomatic responses and try to convince African countries that the old reliance on sovereignty is outdated and counterproductive. All parties must work to find better modalities for intervention—the area in which South Africa's potential is greatest.

Finally, the heartfelt desire for "African solutions to African problems" should not allow the West to ignore the profound humanitarian disasters that may visit Africa in the future. The genocide in Rwanda was correctly called a crime against humanity, not simply a crime against Africans. Thus, there is a strong moral argument against "African solutions for African problems"; such partitioning is anachronistic in a world too interconnected for people not to be concerned about human tragedy wherever it occurs.

Notes to Chapter 11

1. Nelson Mandela, "South Africa's Future Foreign Policy," *Foreign Affairs*, LXXII (1993), 89.

2. R. P. Mboma, "The Role of Regional Bodies in Preventive Diplomacy and Peacekeeping," in Jakkie Cilliers and Greg Mills (eds.), *Peacekeeping in Africa* (Johannesburg, 1996), II, 109; William Nhara, "The OAU and the Potential Role of Regional and Sub-Regional Organisations," in *ibid.*, 100. South Africa's foreign-policy direction is set forth in Department of Foreign Affairs, *South African Foreign Policy: Discussion Document* (July 1996), 14, located at http://www.polity.org.za/issues/foreign.html.

3. For the subcontracting of conflict management, see Michael C. Lemmon, "The Role of the US in Peacekeeping," in Cilliers and Mills (eds.), *Peacekeeping in Africa*, II, 227. See Mark Shaw, "The Future of Peacekeeping in Africa," paper presented at the conference, "The SA Army—Futures and Forecasts," Institute for Defense Policy (Pretoria, 1994), 1, for the notion of "African solutions" as a convenient cover for the unwillingness to intervene.

4. See Herbst, "War and the State in Africa," *International Security*, XIV (1990), 117-139, for discussion about the absence of interstate war in Africa. Charles Tilly, "State-Incited Violence, 1900-1999," in Diane E. Davis and Howard Kimeldorf (eds.), *Political Power and Social Theory* (Greenwich, Conn.,

1995), IX, makes the point about the greater number of people killed by their governments than by foreigners.

5. The point about sovereignty by fiat is made well by Robert H. Jackson, *Quasi-States: Sovereignty, International Relations and the Third World* (Cambridge, 1990). His description of colonial governments as "elementary bureaucracies" appears in *idem* and Alan James (eds.), *States in a Changing World: A Contemporary Analysis* (Oxord, 1993), 139.

6. John Dugard discusses the principal criteria for state recognition in *Recognition and the United Nations* (Cambridge, Mass., 1993), 7.

7. The argument about Cold War intervention is developed in Herbst, "The Challenges to Africa's Boundaries," *Journal of International Affairs*, XLVI (1992), 17-31.

8. This point about newly independent states is made well by Julius K. Nyerere, *Uhuru na Ujamaa* (Oxford, 1968), 28, 209.

9. Quotation from William C. Thom, "An Assessment of Prospects for Ending Domestic Military Conflict in Sub-Saharan Africa," *CSIS Africa Notes*, 177 (1995), 3. Across sub-Saharan Africa, gross national product declined at an average rate of .8 % from 1980 to 1993 (World Bank, *World Development Report 1995* [Washington, D.C., 1995], 163).

10. From 1962 to 1988, six countries—Ethiopia, Kenya, Liberia, Somalia, the Sudan, and Zaire—accounted for most of the United States foreign aid to Africa, despite their exceptionally poor economic and political performances. All but Kenya can be considered failed states. See Michael Clough, *Free at Last: U.S. Policy toward Africa and the End of the Cold War* (New York, 1992), 77.

11. William Reno, "War, Markets and the Reconfiguration of West Africa's Weak States," unpub. paper (Florida International Univ., 1995), 1.

12. Joe Chilaizya, "U.S. Cuts Aid, While Japan Steps in," InterPress Service, 18 July 1996, provided the quotation from Chiluba.

13. Concerning peacekeeping in the context of failed states, see the good essay by John Chipman, "What Do We Understand by Peacekeeping Today?" in Cilliers and Mills (eds.), *Peacekeeping in Africa*, II, 11.

14. South Africa, *Defence in a Democracy: Draft White Paper on National Defence for the Republic of South Africa* (June 1995), 18, located at http://www.polity.org.za/govdocs/white_papers/defence.html.

15. Walter Clarke and Robert Gosende, "Keeping the Mission Focussed: The Intelligence Component in Peace Operations," *Defense Intelligence Review*, V (1996), 57.

16. Mboma, "Role of Regional Bodies," 116, makes the point about Tanzania.

17. Mandela, "Opening Address by President Nelson Mandela to the Third Session of Parliament" (February 1996), reprinted at http://www.polity.org.za/govdocs/speeches/parlopen.96.html, 3.

18 See, for instance, Cilliers, "Peace Support Operations," in *idem* and Mills (eds.), *Peacekeeping in Africa*, II, 59.

19. Andrew Natsios, "Humanitarian Relief Interventions in Somalia: The Economics of Chaos," in Clarke and Herbst (eds.), *Learning from Somalia* (Boulder, 1997), 83.

20. John Darnton, "U.N. Buildup in Bosnia Eyes 'Mogadishu Line,'" *New York Times*, 7 June 1995, A18, discusses the "Mogadishu line."

21. Cilliers and Mark Malan, "South Africa and Regional Peacekeeping," *CSIS Africa Notes*, 187 (1996), 6.

22. Martin R. Ganzglass, "The Restoration of the Somali Justice System," in Clarke and Herbst (eds.), *Learning from Somalia*, 28, is the source for the passage about the Australians in Baidoa.

23. Aziz Pahad, "South Africa and Preventive Diplomacy," in Cilliers and Mills (eds.), *Peacekeeping in Africa*, II, 156.

24. *Ibid.*, 163, is the source of Pahad's statement.

25. The quotation about sovereignty is from Boutros Boutros-Ghali, *An Agenda for Peace 1995* (New York, 1995), 44.

12

Mark Malan

Prospects for Keeping the Peace in Southern Africa

BEFORE DELIBERATING on the prospects for keeping the peace in southern Africa, we must bring some clarity to just what is meant by peace and peacekeeping. Peace does not imply the absence of conflict, for conflict is generic to politics and is as ubiquitous as politics itself. It means, rather, the absence of violent means of reconciling such conflicts. According to the International Peace Academy (IPA), peace is: "A condition that exists in the relations between groups, classes or states when there is an absence of violence (direct or indirect) or the threat of violence." Direct violence is, in turn, defined as "a condition that exists when human beings deliberately kill or physically injure other human beings"; and indirect violence is "a condition which exists when the physical and psychological conditions of some groups, classes or states is inferior to that of others." At the conceptual level, it is hard to improve on these definitions. However, there is a problem of utility when addressing a topic such as "keeping the peace in southern Africa." The direct article before peace in this instance implies a qualitative element, that peace in southern Africa may be somewhat different to peace in North America, and that peace (like democracy) is more an ideal than an observable end state. It is therefore necessary to examine briefly the nature of the peace to be kept in southern Africa, before commenting on the prospects for keeping it.[1]

250

Similarly, the very concept of peacekeeping is open to contention. We have entered an era when international interest and participation in a variety of third-party multinational interventions in order to help terminate intrastate wars has spawned a plethora of conceptual issues that were foreign to the "classical" notion of United Nations (UN) peacekeeping during the Cold War era. The contemporary debate revolves around concepts such as multifunctional peacekeeping, partial consent, the use of force, standby arrangements, and the civilian nature of peacekeeping. The IPA has defined peacekeeping as "The containment, moderation and/or termination of hostilities between or within states, through the medium of an impartial third party intervention, organised and directed internationally, using military forces and civilians to complement the political process of conflict resolution and to restore and maintain peace." UN Secretary General Boutros Boutros-Ghali's somewhat controversial definition sees peacekeeping as "The deployment of a United Nations presence in the field, hitherto with the consent of all the parties concerned, normally involving United Nations military and/or police personnel and frequently civilians as well. Peace-keeping is a technique that expands the possibilities for both the prevention of conflict and the making of peace." In the absence of any reference to peacekeeping within the UN Charter, even such widely accepted and utilized definitions tend to elicit lengthy and inconclusive debates. For the purposes of avoiding the conceptual ambiguity, an overview of peacekeeping, as it has recently been applied in southern Africa (Mozambique and Angola), serves as a second point of departure for examining the prospects for keeping the peace in the sub-region.[2]

Peace and Peacekeeping in (Southern) Africa

The Nature of the Peace

In southern Africa, countries such as Namibia, South Africa, Mozambique, and Angola have at last emerged from Cold War politics and internal strife, which has created an impression that peace has come to the region at last. However, pernicious internal struggles still plague Sierra Leone, Somalia, the Sudan, Zaire, Rwanda, Burundi, and

Liberia to the north, and the threat of internal war haunts a number of others. Some of these states border on Southern African Development Community (SADC) member states, and African borders are notoriously permeable. War and its effects continue to inflict immeasurable human and material losses to society and economy in Africa. It is virtually impossible to describe or quantify the suffering, pain, anguish, and trauma faced by so many Africans, and it is hard to imagine that these effects do not cast a shadow over whatever kind of peace prevails within southern Africa. Aside from any other differences that may prevail, the states of southern Africa remain *African* states, despite the anomalous identity of the southern-most country and the weight of its presence.

In a world where an estimated 90 million land mines are spread across 64 countries, killing 24,000 people each year, 20 million are concentrated in half of the countries in Africa. Angola alone has an estimated 8 to 10 million mines, and unexploded ordnance (UXO) which threaten life and limb. In Mozambique, the "guesstimate" is 2 million mines and UXO. The mere threat of mines hampers market forces—the movement of people, goods, and services—and the resettlement of large tracts of arable land, constraining the type of development that is generally deemed essential to maintaining a condition of peace. Nearly half the population of sub-Saharan Africa, 250 million people, are living below the poverty line, many of them homeless. During the past decade, Africa has hosted c. 50 percent of the world's displaced people. By 1994, 21.4 million Africans had fled their homes because of violent conflict; 6.2 million were living abroad—38 percent of the world's refugees. Violent internal conflict, rather than natural disasters, is now the leading continental cause of emergencies, human suffering, and displacement.

Although some may enthuse about the new wave of African democracy, poverty, inequality, and ethnic discrimination continue to undermine the authority of many states; and the often life-threatening social fragmentation has led to the privatization of violence, as armed factions fill the vacuum left by failing state security and administrative apparatus. Previously, local power factions or entire countries were armed by Cold War principals. Internal factions now rely on the control and sale of precious natural resources (such as forest wood, rubber, diamonds, and oil) to sustain arms acquisition, at the expense of urgent developmental priorities. In such circumstances, it does not require the efforts of large, well-trained armies to terminate a condition that may loosely be described as "peace." Witness the destruction of the Liberian state that began in 1989 when Charles Taylor invaded the country from the Ivory Coast with a Libyan-trained force numbering 100 men, roughly the equivalent of an infantry rifle company.

There have been many calls for the demilitarization of the African continent and the demobilization of armed forces as a prerequisite for peace. However, the disbanding of organized military forces does not necessarily lead to a decline in the violent use of armed force. Unless conducted effectively, demobilization fuels small-arms proliferation. There are, for example, an estimated 70,000 to 100, 000 AK-47 assault rifles in private hands in the Angolan capital of Luanda. Moreover, demobilized soldiers who have not been effectively reintegrated into civil society have turned to armed banditry to survive the advent of peace in such countries as Angola and Mozambique. Some have managed to find more respectable employment in the private-security industry, which may offer little solace for those who wish for true peace.

Thousands of former African soldiers and policemen are now for hire as security guards; the security companies that employ them exploit fears about rising crime and the perceived inability of governments to protect their citizenry. That private security is one of Africa's few vibrant growth industries is a sad indication of the health of the African state. Indeed, the privatization of security grew at its most obvious in such countries as Angola and Zaire (renamed Democratic Republic of Congo in 1997), where the state had all but collapsed. The number of security companies in Luanda grew from two in 1992 to more than 70 in 1997; many more were operating like private armies in the diamond-rich provinces to the north. Many of the security companies in Angola, and elsewhere in Africa, are managed by former South African Defense Force (SADF) soldiers. In Sierra Leone, the head of the National Provisional Ruling Council enlisted the services of several "security firms" to help train the Republic of Sierra Leone Military Force. One was the South African–based Executive Outcomes, which rose to infamy in support of the Popular Movement for the Liberation of Angola (MPLA) forces, and took a "proactive approach" to military training in Sierra Leone—a thinly disguised euphemism for direct participation in combat operations against insurgents.[3]

Just as democracy in South Africa is marred by the "legacy of apartheid," peace has left other countries with a terrible legacy of war. In Rwanda, for example, a four-year UN peacekeeping operation failed to halt an ethnic genocide that resulted in 500,000 to 1 million deaths. During the holocaust that lasted from April to July 1994, Hutu extremists "systematically hacked down, shot and blew up tens of thousands of Tutsis and Hutu moderates." In spite of the UN's efforts to restore peace, a silent genocide reportedly continues in Rwanda. About 70,000 people have been jailed for the massacres, but there is no functioning legal system in place to deal with them. Women and children suffered most from the aftermath of the genocide: An estimated 47,000 children were orphaned, 250,000 to 500,000 women were raped or forced to have sex with a relative; and 2,000 to 5,000 children were outcast because they were conceived as a result of rape.[4]

More than 600,000 people died and more than 3 million were forced from their homes during twenty years of Angolan civil war. According to the UN High Commissioner for Refugees (UNHCR), since the government and the Union for the Total Independence of Angola (UNITA) signed a peace accord in 1994, 14,500 people have been repatriated. There are still 200,000 Angolan refugees in Zaire, 96,000 in Zambia, 12,000 in Congo, 1,000 in Namibia, and a further 15,000 scattered in 32 different countries. Angola illustrates the tenuous nature of peace in southern Africa and the immense developmental problems that accompany the process of establishing peace. Its infrastructure is nonfunctional, and inflation is rampant (between 3,000 and 4,000 percent) in an economy dominated by corruption and organized crime.[5]

Conditions were not much better in Mozambique, where 494,000 children younger than five had died, and one out of every four children could expect to die before the age of five when the peace accord was signed in 1992. The military and police forces seemed to have abdicated all sense of responsibility for the security of the state and its citizens, in favor of the profit motive. Senior military and police officials were reportedly engaged in the bulk sale of state-owned weapons to anyone who could pay the price. Nor was the price too high. It was possible to buy an AK-47 for a bottle of cheap whiskey from the guard at the weapons depot in Maputo.[6]

For many of southern Africa's people, the nature of the state must approximate Thomas Hobbes' state of nature, in which everyone lives in fear, and lives are "solitary, nasty, brutish, and short." The tentative peace falls far short of the IPA's ideas about absence of violence (direct or indirect) or the threat of violence. Nevertheless, it must represent an objective improvement in the conditions that existed prior to the signing of peace accords in Mozambique or Angola, for the international community, through the UN, has invested millions of dollars and tens of lives in trying to keep it. Or perhaps the very concept of peace-keeping is a misnomer, and the real object of contemporary UN operations has been to establish a modicum of stability as the essential basis for the gradual development of peace.[7]

The Nature of Peacekeeping

MOZAMBIQUE. The United Nations Operation in Mozambique (UNOMOZ) lasted from December 1992 to January 1995. It has been widely lauded as the success story of contemporary, multifunctional UN peacekeeping in Africa. At peak strength, UNOMOZ employed 204 military observers, 941 soldiers, and 918 civilian police. The peacekeepers suffered a total of 17 fatalities.

After almost thirty years of civil war, centered initially on the liberation struggle and subsequently on the conflict between the Front for the Liberation of Mozambique (FRELIMO) and the Mozambique National Resistance (RENAMO), the establishment of UNOMOZ was precipitated by a General Peace Agreement (GPA) signed in Rome, October 1992, by Joaquim Chissano, President of the Republic of Mozambique, and Afonso Dhlakama, President of RENAMO. The agreement provided for, among other things,

1. UN participation in monitoring the implementation of the Agreement and specific functions relating to the cease-fire, the elections, and humanitarian assistance;
2. a cease-fire to come into effect not later than October 15, 1992 (E-Day);
3. the separation of RENAMO and government forces and their concentration in assembly areas soon after E-Day;
4. withdrawal of foreign troops (Malawi and Zimbabwe guarding transport corridors) following E-Day;
5. demobilization of government and RENAMO soldiers who would

not serve in a unified Forças Armadas de Moçambique (FADM), to be completed six months after E-Day;

6. establishment of a police commission; and

7. the forming of new political parties and conduct of elections not later than October 15, 1993.

Elections were finally held October 27-29, 1994, monitored and verified by 900 UN observers and 1,400 various international observers. The results of the Mozambican elections were endorsed by Security Council resolution 960, which also called on all parties to accept and abide by the results, and continue the process of national reconciliation through democratic processes.

Many observers feel that the peace in Mozambique became possible because both parties were exhausted and had no alternative, and that the UNOMOZ force was unnecessary, since both sides had firmly committed themselves to the peace process. Lacking diamonds, oil, or new funds from Cold War sponsors, Mozambique had no alternative but to accept peace. Perhaps this criticism is too harsh. UNOMOZ had a clear mandate, and carried it out almost to the letter. However, the issue of demobilization, reintegration, and the reconstitution of a unified armed force continued to threaten the prevailing order. At the conclusion of the war, the UN expected that 30,000 of the 90,000 government and RENAMO soldiers would want to remain in a new, integrated army, which presently numbers only 10,000 personnel. That there is little parity between former RENAMO and former FAM officers is a result of both numbers and training. Moreover, because the FAM was historically dominated by southerners, whereas most RENAMO commanders were of the Ndau ethnic group from the center and west of the country, there is the potential for intramilitary conflicts grounded in ethnic/regional differences. Internal deterioration, divisions within the elite, inter-service rivalries, and inherited structural weaknesses have combined to create an army totally lacking in military culture. Gun-running via Swaziland or directly into South Africa is commonplace—a legacy of ineffective disarmament and a miserable reintegration package for former combatants.[8]

A Western-style democracy, based on a winner-takes-all system and little or no accommodation for the loser, has also done little to raise hopes for sustainable peace. Despite the fact that RENAMO was nar-

rowly defeated by FRELIMO at the polls, it has had minimal accommodation in government. Consequently, RENAMO is highly disillusioned
and disgruntled, and there are signs of political fragmentation rather
than much-needed national unity. Dhlakama feels sidelined, and was
believed in 1996 to be supporting civil disobedience and attacks on
FRELIMO representatives in areas still under his control. Although there
may not yet be a general desire to "go back to the bush," this threat
remains, and there is already a major security threat from increased
armed banditry in areas such as Manica Province.

ANGOLA. The United Nations Verification Mission in Angola
(UNAVEM) was created in December 1988, not to keep any peace in
that country, but to monitor the withdrawal of some 50,000 Cuban
soldiers as part of the settlement that led to Namibia's independence.
The operation was staffed by seventy military observers and twenty
officials from ten different countries, and was given a thirty-one-
month mandate. Just before the expiry of UNAVEM's mandate, the
Bicesse peace accord between the Angolan government and UNITA was
signed on May 31, 1991. Like the Mozambican GPA, the accord provided for a cease-fire; the banning of external military assistance to the
MPLA and UNITA; the confinement of troops from both sides to assembly areas; the restoration of government administration in rebel-con-
trolled areas; internal security during the transition period before the
elections; the disarmament and demobilization of surplus troops; the
creation of a new, unified 50,000-strong armed force; and the holding
of free and fair multiparty elections before the end of November 1992.

The main difference between the beginning of the peace process in
Mozambique and that in Angola was the level of UN involvement. On
the eve of the signing of the Bicesse accord, the Security Council
extended UNAVEM's mandate. UNAVEM II—with a budget of $132.3
million and consisting of a mere 350 military observers and 90 civil
police from 24 different countries—began deployment in July 1991. Its
purpose was to ensure that the provisions of the peace accord, especially those regarding the encampment of government troops in
twenty-seven zones and UNITA in twenty-three others, were honored.
Military observers were also deployed in twelve critical areas for the
purpose of conducting patrols over the entire country.[9]

On March 24, 1992, the Security Council approved the expansion of
UNAVEM II and its mandate. A 400-strong electoral division was subse-

quently deployed, with an additional budget of $18.8 million, in order to monitor and evaluate the conduct and impartiality of the presidential and legislative elections. It was expected to operate in all eighteen provinces during the three phases of the electoral process: voter registration, the election campaign, and the poll itself. The outcome should have been predicable. The under-resourced UNAVEM II was not able to defuse escalating tension in advance of Angola's first multiparty elections; nor was it able to deal with pre-electoral clashes between government and UNITA forces, to assemble, disarm, and demobilize the belligerents, and create a new army. Despite the fact that only 37 percent of government troops and 85 percent of UNITA's were in the forty-eight cantonment centers established for them, elections were held on September 29-30, 1992. The governing MPLA won 53.7 percent of the parliamentary seats; UNITA achieved 34.1 percent. In the presidential elections, Jose Eduardo dos Santos, the incumbent, won 49.7 percent of the vote compared with Savimbi's 40.1 percent. The results were validated by UN and other international observers, but UNITA rejected the outcome and launched an assault on Luanda on October 30, once again plunging the country into full-scale civil war. Under such circumstances, it is difficult to refute UNITA's charges of electoral fraud, which provided the rationale for the resumption of the war.[10]

After two more years of fighting, the government and UNITA eventually signed a UN-brokered peace accord in Lusaka in December 1994, which provided once again for the formation of a national government and a new Angolan army, and allowed for the establishment of another UNAVEM mission. The mandate of UNAVEM III includes verifying, monitoring, reporting, and investigating any incidents linked with the Lusaka protocol and relevant Security Council resolutions. The total strength of the military and police personnel of the Mission stood at 7,071 as of March 29,1996, making UNAVEM III the largest current UN peacekeeping operation.

Although it may be unfair to prejudge an ongoing peacekeeping operation, there is ample evidence that the much stronger UNAVEM III mission will not end in success. Continuing rivalry over Angola's oil reserves constantly jeopardizes the chances of ending the civil war. This rivalry includes not only the government and UNITA, but also the Front for the Liberation of Cabinda, which is demanding secession for northern Angola, where offshore installations produce

60 percent of the country's oil and account for 80 percent of Angola's revenue.

The nagging mercenary issue continues to place doubt on the parties' true commitment to peace. Despite official government assurance in December 1995 that the contract with Executive Outcomes would be terminated with immediate effect, in the first quarter of 1996, 800-strong battalions of Angolan Armed Forces (FAA) soldiers were reported to have been rushed through intense three-month Executive Outcomes training courses to make them battle-ready within the next six months or so. UNITA was also allegedly recruiting mercenaries and transport aircraft pilots in South Africa, while other foreign specialists were training UNITA forces in northern Angola and in Zaire itself.[11]

Major setbacks have also occurred in the assembly, disarmament, and demobilization of the warring forces. Early in April 1996, UNAVEM reported that 1,716 UNITA soldiers had deserted from unsupervised encampment sites where they were due to be disarmed. UNITA blames poor accommodation in the camps for the desertions. In his April 1996 report to the Security Council, Boutros-Ghali stated that progress had been "limited and has not fulfilled the hopes generated." He added that "implementation is once again behind schedule. Further delays and procrastination could still jeopardize the peace process." According to the secretary general, the success of the peace process depends on "complete and fully verifiable quartering by UNITA of its troops," as well as withdrawing government troops to the nearest barracks, completing the quartering of the government's rapid-reaction police, disarming the population, and integrating UNITA elements into the new army.[12]

Although the Angolan government has announced plans to launch a program to disarm the civilian population (the majority of Angolans living in Luanda were armed by the government in 1992 after UNITA rejected the outcome of the elections), it had no fixed plan about how to proceed, apart from talk of a "food for weapons" program. By the end of May 1996, the security situation in Luanda was so tense that riot police were deployed to prevent demonstrations, amid fears of a military coup. The three-month extension of the deadline for the demobilization of troops, set for May 8, 1996, was extended for two months, until the end of July. By the beginning of June 1996, the cantonment of UNITA forces had virtually ground to a halt, with some 35,000 men and boys registered in 11 UN assembly areas. At least half were considered not to be soldiers by UN officials, and only two-thirds arrived with any type of small arms. No heavy weapons were surrendered, very few munitions were registered, and new arms supplies had been flown into UNITA via Zaire.[13]

As of February 1, 1997, 70,660 UNITA troops were registered in the fifteen UN quartering areas. Of this number, 22,686 had deserted or were temporarily absent from the camps. The growing number of deserters was a major source of concern to UNAVEM III, and by March 1997, there were reports of strong contingents of UNITA soldiers being deployed in Zaire in support of Mobutu Sese Seko's ailing forces. To exacerbate matters, the Angolan government was also reported to have sent over a thousand troops to Rwanda and eastern Zaire to back Laurent Kabila's rebel army.[14]

Whatever the outcome of the UNAVEM III operation, both Angola and Mozambique will clearly be engaged in a process of post-conflict peacebuilding for decades to come, hopefully with the continued assistance of the international donor community and their regional neighbors. However, even the longer-term developmental challenges associated with a comprehensive peace process are dependent upon an initial and appropriate response to complex emergencies created by violent conflict in Africa, a response that cannot be taken for granted.

Future Prospects for Keeping the Peace

Weakness of International Response to African Problems

The UN's response capacity depends, at this stage, on the Stand-By Forces Arrangement, which has proven to be totally inadequate for meeting contemporary peacekeeping challenges. For example, when the UN needed 5,500 soldiers for its operation in Rwanda in 1994, it approached the nineteen countries that, at the time, had pledged a total of 31,000 peacekeepers for future UN operations; all declined to participate. UN member states also show a lack of enthusiasm for the implementation of the secretary general's idea of earmarking and training battalion-size units for rapid deployment in future UN peace operations, and even less enthusiasm for accepting the costs of more ambitious proposals for the creation of a standing UN force. For the foreseeable future, the UN Security Council is likely to continue routinely passing resolutions without being obliged to provide the soldiers to implement them.

The political will to commit resources—especially of the human variety—to UN peacekeeping missions still leans heavily upon the perceived *national interest* of the potential contributors. By all indications, the major powers and most of the traditional troop contributors to UN peace operations have reached the conclusion that the costs—in domestic political capital—of further engagement in "new generation" peace operations in African countries simply outweigh the altruistic benefits of potentially contributing to the cause of world peace. The United States, for example, has replaced the stringent cry of "no more Vietnams" with an equally stringent cry of "no more Somalias." Aside from the unique case of the former Yugoslavia (where the major powers have powerful vested interests), the contemporary literature on peace operations is dominated by "lessons learned" from the intervention in Somalia, lessons that repeatedly stress the perceived futility of future involvement in such missions.

Apart from gloomy forecasts for the future of the Angolan peace process and the much-publicized failure in Somalia, Rwanda provides the most recent and vivid example of an inadequate and inappropriate international response to an African disaster. A report entitled *The International Response to Conflict and Genocide: Lessons from the Rwanda Experience*, the first multinational evaluation of the response to the Rwandan massacre, blames the failure to prevent the 1994 crisis on a lack of political action and a reluctance by UN members. The report described the Security Council's decision to pull most of its troops out when killings started in April 1994 as "fateful," and claimed that a case could be made that thousands of people would not have been killed if the force had been expanded. (Despite calls from the force commander for UN reinforcements to protect Rwandan civilians, the Security Council, on April 24, 1994, cut the UN peacekeeping force from 2,500 troops to 270.) It also accused the Security Council of avoiding action as recently as March 1996 when, in spite of fears of a similar genocide, it asked the UN to prepare only for humanitarian action in neighboring Burundi. According to Tardif-Doughlin, one of the report's principal authors, "There were significant signs that Hutu extremist forces in Rwanda were preparing the climate and structures for a genocide of Tutsis and moderate Hutus. . . . But the states, the international organisations and other parties . . . ignored, discounted or misinterpreted these signs, indicating an inability or unwillingness to intervene."[15]

On June 12-14, 1996, the United Nations Department of Peacekeeping Operations (UNDPKO) convened a seminar about lessons to be learned from the United Nations Assistance Mission to Rwanda (UNAMIR), with the intention to formulate recommendations for improving ongoing peacekeeping operations, as well as to consider better ways to prepare for future deployments. Thus far, however, the lessons extracted from the experience of peacekeeping missions in Somalia, Rwanda, Mozambique, and Angola seem to do nothing to boost the waning enthusiasm of the major powers and the traditional troop-contributing member states for deploying soldiers on African soil. Much of the ambivalence about Rwanda, for example, stemmed from the interpretation of President Clinton's directive that United States contributions to peacekeeping would be limited by time and that United States troops provided for peacekeeping operations would remain under the control of the president. Moreover, peacekeeping operations are extremely expensive, and the costs are unevenly distributed throughout the international community, having risen dramatically at a time when the UN is in a state of severe financial restraint. It has also proved extremely difficult for the UN to move beyond the role of "classical" Chapter VI peacekeeping toward something that approximates Chapter VII, but falls short of peace enforcement. The conceptual confusion has led to a complete lack of consensus about the UN's obligations in messy and indistinct intrastate conflicts.[16]

Not surprisingly, the UN and a number of foreign governments have recently become strong advocates of the position that African countries should accept a greater degree of responsibility for peacekeeping in Africa. The French government proposed the establishment of an African intervention force at a summit of francophone states in November 1994. The British government convened seminars about African peacekeeping in Accra (October 1994), Cairo (January 1995), Gaborone (August 1995), and Harare (January 1996), with the purpose of investigating doctrinal issues, training requirements, and the establishment of a regional early-warning system. The main thrust of both the British and French projects related to the creation of a Multinational African Rapid Deployment Peace Force, for which Africa would supply the personnel and the American and European participants the logistics. A host of less ambitious peacekeeping initiatives from Denmark, Norway, and Sweden, as well from such organizations as the Global Coalition, the African Leadership Forum, the Carter Center, and the UN African Regional Center for Disarmament, were also in the offing to help Africans to manage conflict. Although there is often fair warning of impending crises (such as in Burundi), peacekeeping in Africa now depends upon the creation of a viable capacity to respond rapidly to emergent crises, not only with preventive diplomacy, but also with the timely deployment of adequate numbers of trained and equipped peacekeepers to maximize the chances of preventing killing where diplomacy has failed, and of upholding fragile peace accords in the wake of brutal and ruinous conflict.

In October 1996, U.S. Secretary of State Warren Christopher undertook a sudden, five-nation tour of Africa, during which he promoted a proposal to set up an all-African military force under the supervision of the UN Security Council—The African Crisis Response Force (ACRF)—to deal with insurrections, civil wars, or genocidal conflicts that threaten mass civilian casualties. According to Christopher, the purpose of the force would not be to intervene in hostilities but to protect designated safe areas where civilians could receive humanitarian assistance. The intermediate objective of the ACRF would be to develop a rapid-reaction capability for such contingencies. The United States offered to fund half of the cost—estimated at $25 to $40 million, depending on whether the force would be operational by 1997.[17]

If time permitted, proponents envisaged the ACRF assisting humanitarian relief in Burundi. However, Christopher's idea met with a cool response in Africa; only Ethiopia, Mali, and Tanzania agreed, in principle, to contribute troops. Moreover, when the international media spotlight on Africa switched to the Rwandan refugees, shortly after Christopher's African tour, the problems of Burundi were all but forgotten, and with them any enthusiasm that may have been generated for the ACRF. The lack of interest is regrettable; the ACRF attempted to address an important gap in the hierarchy of responses to African crises, albeit in a somewhat unilateral and hasty fashion.[18]

Nonetheless, the clear signal being sent to the countries of Africa is that they will have to prepare to staff future peace operations on the continent with African peacekeepers. The countries of Africa have the biggest stake in stabilizing the region, and they alone can justify to a domestic constituency the human costs of involvement in local peace operations. With a few praiseworthy exceptions, however, African countries have not numbered among the traditional troop-contributing countries for UN peace operations. Indeed, the inadequate training of units from countries other than the traditional troop-contributing ones has been cited as a major challenge to the effectiveness of contemporary UN peace operations.

The African Response

The peacekeeping issue was discussed during the sixty-second ordinary session of the Council of Ministers of the Organization for African Unity (OAU) in June 1995. The Council felt that despite the fact that the UN Security Council had primary responsibility for the maintenance of peace and security in the world, the OAU, should seriously endeavor to develop and enhance its capacity to keep the peace. Salim Ahmed Salim, secretary general of the OAU, encouraged member states to set aside or earmark ready contingents for specialized training in peace-support operations, with a view to participating in peacekeeping operations "either under the aegis of the United Nations or in exceptional cases that warrant the involvement of the OAU in some limited peace-keeping and observation missions." Little progress was made during the following year. However, the chiefs of staff of member states of the Central Organ of the OAU's Mechanism for Conflict Prevention, Management, and Resolution, met in Addis Ababa, Ethiopia, June 3-5, 1996, for the first time since the Organ was established in 1993, to determine the feasibility of establishing an African capability for peacekeeping. The secretary general hoped that the meeting would "come up with concrete and practical recommendations on such issues as logistics and administrative arrangements, command and control, standby arrangements, training, and funding as they relate to peace support missions in Africa." The ultimate objective was to "adopt a set of guidelines which could ensure that Africa and the international community are not caught unprepared in the face of tragic developments on our continent."[19]

After much tiresome deliberation and speech making, which extended the meeting an extra day, the chiefs of staff managed to come up with the following confirmations and recommendations:

1. The meeting recalled the principle that the primary responsibility of the OAU should lie in the anticipation and prevention of conflicts in accordance with the relevant provision of the 1993 Cairo Declaration. It also recognized that the primary responsibility for the maintenance of international peace and security particularly in the area of peacekeeping rests with the United Nations Security Council. At the same time, the meeting recognized that certain exceptional circumstances can arise and lead to the deployment of limited peacekeeping or observation missions by the OAU.

2. In order to equip the OAU to undertake peace support missions better, the meeting saw the need to strengthen the existing military unit of the General Secretariat subject to further study.

3. For purposes of strengthening the coordination between the OAU and the UN in peace-related issues, the meeting recommended that the relationship between the two organizations should be formalized. It was also recommended that the OAU should continue to coordinate closely with subregional organizations in its peace-support operations taking advantage of existing arrangements within the subregions.

4. The meeting accepted the principle of standby arrangements and earmarked contingents on a voluntary basis. Such earmarked contingents could serve either under the aegis of the United Nations or the OAU or under subregional arrangements. In this regard, the meeting recognized the need for proper preparation and the standardization of training.

5. In order to provide further clarity and to come out with practical and realistic recommendations on the technical issues raized in the working document, and the meeting's report, especially those relating to logistics, it was recommended that a working group of military experts from member states of the Central Organ be set up.

6. The meeting recommended that there should be meetings of the chiefs of staff of member states of the Central Organ as and when the need arises.

7. The meeting recognized the need for further clarity with regard to the guidelines that apply to possible OAU peacekeeping operations.

The meeting therefore called upon the OAU secretary general to take the necessary action so that a clear position in this regard is formulated at the highest level.

Salim's hopes were not to be fulfilled: Apart from reiterating certain points made in his opening address, the meeting managed to refer the most pressing problems regarding lack of resources and the role of the UN back to the secretary general and an ill-defined "working group of military experts."

The OAU's lack of resources, especially finances, deny it the freedom to decide unilaterally the strategic, tactical, and operational aspects of the peace operations that it wishes to initiate. If it is unable to fund such operations itself, whoever does fund them for the OAU will have a large impact on the objectives and operational procedures of the mission. Reliance on foreign funding means that donors can influence which missions the OAU initiates and which it does not. Based on their own interests, donors can determine the duration of a mission, and place terms and conditions on continued funding—or even withdraw funding if the OAU wishes to amend the scope of the mission.

A central problem within the OAU has been the continued lack of adequate human resources within the General Secretariat to deal appropriately with all the conflict situations in Africa, and to service the Mechanism adequately. When the Conflict Management Division was created in 1994, it was staffed by three officers. Since then, this resource base has been strengthened somewhat with the recruitment of three senior political officers and one senior military officer. By July 1996, the division was staffed by a total of nine professional officers (two of whom were military), plus supporting staff and three consultants. The ongoing restraints on the effectiveness of the continental organization coexist with an emerging conviction that the enhancement of capabilities for participation in peace operations could best be achieved through cooperation and action at a subregional, as opposed to a continental, level.

The Southern African Response

Following the resolutions and recommendations of the SADC Workshop on Democracy, Peace, and Security, which was held in Windhoek on July 11-16, 1994, SADC appeared determined to enter the fields of security coordination, conflict mediation, and military cooperation. Among a multitude of recommendations, the Windhoek Working Group on Disarmament and Demilitarization called for the "development of regional mechanisms for peacekeeping and peace enforcement activities" and the "equipping and training of national forces for peace keeping roles." These goals have subsequently been the subject of lengthy debate at a number of meetings of the Heads of State and Council of Ministers, but little progress was made until the meeting of the SADC ministers of Foreign Affairs, Defense, and Security, which was held in Gaborone in January 1996. The ministers agreed to recommend to their heads of state the creation of an SADC Organ for Politics, Defense, and Security, which "would allow more flexibility and timely response, at the highest level, to sensitive and potentially explosive situations." A number of objectives were defined for the Organ, including security and defense cooperation through conflict prevention, management, and resolution; mediation of disputes and conflicts; preventive diplomacy and mechanisms, with punitive measures as a last resort; sustainable peace and security through peacemaking and peacekeeping; development of a collective-security capacity and a mutual defense pact, and regional peacekeeping capacity; coordination of members' participation in international and regional peacekeeping operations; and addressing extraregional conflicts that impact on peace and security in southern Africa.[20]

As of March 1997, the Organ still existed only at the level of the heads of state and the Inter-State Defense and Security Committee (ISDSC). The ISDSC is composed of a ministerial council, three subcommittees—dealing with defense, security, and intelligence, respectively—and three sub-subcommittees concerned with operations, maritime affairs, and aviation. It convenes in the various SADC countries on a rotational basis, chaired by the host country's minister of defense.

Despite its lack of a permanent structure, the ISDSC is helping to build confidence in the region. However, its predominant representation from military, security, and intelligence departments limits its scope. It provides the Organ with no clear mechanism for the pusuit of foreign-policy and human-rights objectives—a glaring omission given the widespread perception of the SADC as the regional model for Chapter VII of the UN Charter, as well as the Organ's supposed focus on preventive action, which would seem to entail the resources peculiar to departments of foreign affairs.

Morever, the fact that the Organ functions only at the summit level leaves the exact duties of the SADC chair (President Nelson Mandela) and the Organ chair (President Robert Mugabe) unclear, possibly creating an insurmountable barrier to "addressing extraregional conflicts that impact peace and security in southern Africa" in a timely and effective manner. It also means the exclusion of vital diplomatic and technical inputs from SADC ministers of foreign affairs and line functionaries in such departments as foreign affairs, defense, and security, essentially relegating the Organ to the role of a fire brigade—the heads of state and government reacting to, rather than preempting, crises that affect the region.

A number of pertinent questions remain unanswered at the conceptual level: What is the regional vision of "peacekeeping capacity" in southern Africa? As yet, there are no clear indications of the size and configuration of the peacekeeping assets to be developed by the countries of southern Africa, the doctrine according to which the various elements are to be trained, the type of equipment to be used, and the upper management of such capacity (within the SADC, OAU, or the UN).

For which types of contingencies and in which geographical areas should such a capacity be established? Certain countries reject outright the prospect of becoming involved in complex emergencies that require a Chapter VII mandate; others express a preference for participating only in those peace operations conducted within the region, which is also variously defined as either Africa or southern Africa.

What are existing, or potential, national military capacities for involvement in peacekeeping operations, in terms of equipment, finances, force levels, units and formations, level of military cohesion, etc.? As yet, there has been no attempt to formalize standby arrangements within the SADC framework, and to provide a rough inventory of what assets individual countries might be willing to commit to future efforts to keep the peace (although Tanzania, Zambia, and Zimbabwe have confirmed their willingness to provide standby resources to the UN).

How much, and what type of, dedicated peacekeeping training is currently available from national armies of the various SADC countries? There is presently a lack of baseline information about the type of peacekeeping training that the various countries in southern Africa are offering (content, duration, standard, and compatibility with that given elsewhere).

Could existing training capacity—institutions, time, and resources, be redirected toward peacekeeping training without drastically impairing the ability of national forces to execute their constitutionally defined and de facto roles? The military often regards training for peace operations as a detraction from its primary (war-fighting) role and as a drain on resources and combat readiness. These perceptions may be fallacious, given that appropriate training for peace operations may indeed enhance certain facets of military professionalism, and that none of the SADC countries faces a conventional military threat for the foreseeable future.

What is the potential contribution of the civilian police (CIVPOL) in the various SADC countries to future peacekeeping operations, and how can it be enhanced? Few countries in southern Africa have spare policing capacity—human resources that are appropriately trained and available for CIVPOL monitoring and training duties in peace operations. This aspect of peacekeeping has been largely ignored in the current debate about regional peacekeeping capabilities.

Which nongovernmental organizations (NGOs)/private voluntary organizations (PVOs) are operative in, or indigenous to, the countries of the region, and how can they be expected to help in future peacekeeping operations? The expanding civilian component of contemporary multifunctional peacekeeping increasingly involves not only UN specialized agencies, but also international and local NGOs, which should be incorporated into the evolving southern African peacekeeping framework.

Tentative answers to some of these questions may be provided by further research and analysis, but the more fundamental questions can be answered only by the SADC heads of state and government. Underlying the uncertainty is the fact that some of the larger potential SADC troop contributors are wrestling with the problem of controlling the military under conditions of fundamental and rapid domestic political change—conditions that are associated with the revolution in the post–Cold War strategic environment. In a number of cases, political reform has entailed a complete break with the old political order, necessitating the creation of entirely new civil–military relations. In

Angola, Mozambique, Namibia, South Africa, and Zimbabwe, armies inherited from an era of armed struggle over political dispensations are being reconstituted through a fusion of many different military groups and the creation of a unified defense force. Integration, or the process of organizational and normative fusion, has encountered resistance and tensions that are rooted in recent historical events. The process of force transformation is at an advanced stage in Zimbabwe and Namibia, although intramilitary ethnic tensions are still evident in Zimbabwe. Mozambique and South Africa have barely completed the first phase of force integration, and the real challenges of creating effective and cohesive armies still lie ahead. Angola still has to run the full course of post-conflict transition under extremely adverse circumstances. Thus, three SADC countries, which previously boasted the largest armies in the sub-region, are at various stages of coping with major structural and attitudinal adjustments.

Some of the smaller SADC armies also remain vulnerable to military instability. The history of coups in Africa reveals no direct correlation between the size of armed forces and military intervention in politics. Because the transition from nondemocratic to democratic rule is often characterized by high levels of internal political conflict and civil strife, the region's embryonic democracies will remain highly susceptible to pressures for military intervention to restore order. In Lesotho, for example, civil–military relations remain volatile; it remains to be seen how the Swazi defense force will react to the mounting pressures for democratization. Zambia and Malawi are also in the process of adjustment to more democratic patterns of civil–military interaction; and the democratic principle of civil supremacy over the military has yet to be institutionalized there.

These conclusions do not imply that no attempt should be made to educate, train, and equip armies for participation in peacekeeping operations until the problems of force transformation and democratization have been resolved. Indeed, such efforts may make a significant contribution to force transformation and regional stability as a whole. However, it is widely accepted that the basis for peacekeeping training is sound general military training, which remains a national responsibility. The importance of this observation cannot be overemphasized; the doctrinal debate on peacekeeping has become increasingly complex, suggesting that the era of the "super soldier" has arrived.

Local attempts to create peacekeeping capabilities should concentrate on the issue of the establishment and maintenance of minimal and appropriate standards of military professionalism in the armed forces. Without concerted development along this dimension, potential peacekeepers will remain potential aggressors. After all, African peacekeepers have not proven immune to violence and corruption.

Prognosis

Although the peace in southern Africa is fragile and characterized by markedly different experiences among the people of the region, it is preferable to the quality of life under conditions of war and armed struggle against oppressive and unrepresentative regimes. Attempts to keep the peace in southern Africa have had mixed results. Even when considered successful, as in Mozambique, an immense developmental challenge remains to be met before the concept of peace becomes really meaningful and sustainable. As Smith has observed, "The most which orthodox peacekeeping can achieve is negative peace—when the guns fall silent, the killing stops and a peace process begins. . . . [I]t is essential for the UN to institutionalize peacekeeping and development as two sides of the same coin." The prospects for achieving the desired levels of development are beyond the scope of this chapter, but they do depend fundamentally upon the maintenance of minimum levels of stability.[21]

The prospects for maintaining such levels of stability in future emergencies caused by violent conflict are clouded by the reluctance of the international community to respond appropriately and adequately to the demands of peacekeeping in Africa. Even where there is ample and vivid warning of an impending human disaster, as in Burundi, little political will exists outside Africa for early action. Nor is there much hope for rapid reaction on the part of the UN. The current standby arrangements still depend on the consent of the troop-contributing countries for participation in particular operations, and their consent will be based on calculations involving their perceived national interests, rather than more altruistic desires to restore peace and security in remote parts of the world.

The OAU is attempting to enhance continental capabilities for keeping the peace, but the progress thus far has been slow and disappointing, much of it achieved only at the level of rhetoric. Although optimism about the prospects of enhancing such capabilities at the subregional level in southern Africa has grown, there is also ample reason for caution when talking of African and southern African capabilities for keeping the peace. Indeed, the secretary general of the OAU sounded the following cautionary note in his opening address to the June meeting of the chiefs of staff:

> While the OAU is considering building such [peacekeeping] capacity, it should be made clear that this new approach must not lead to a sort of marginalization of peace-keeping activities, whereby for example, conflicts in Europe are viewed as the sole responsibility of the Europeans or conflicts in Africa as the sole responsibility of the Africans alone. This goes against the spirit and ideal of the United Nations—its universality and world-wide responsibility for maintaining peace and security. Africa is part and parcel of the international community.[22]

Would it be at all advisable or feasible to pursue strategies and policies aimed at the kind of regional peacekeeping operations associated with the Economic Community of West African States Cease-Fire Monitoring Group (ECOMOG)? Neither Africa nor southern Africa can "go it alone" in providing the stability essential for development. The region simply does not have the means—doctrine, training, trained manpower, finances, or resources. Should the international community attempt to delegate the international role of the UN in peacekeeping to either the OAU or a regional organization such as SADC in the foreseeable future, the result will be entirely predictable. The consequences of such abrogation of responsibility have been aptly illustrated by recent events in Liberia, where peacekeeping, peace enforcement, military intervention, and banditry have become synonymous with one another. Despite the infusion of capacity and resources that South Africa has brought to the region, peacekeeping in Africa by Africans can work only if it occurs in close collaboration and collusion with the UN and the international community. This condition will remain for years to come.[23]

African armed forces should prepare themselves and cooperate with the international community. The only feasible scenario for keeping the peace in Africa is the creation of an internationally sponsored UN standby force in Africa for Africa. Such a force might consist of designated units placed on standby, and trained in their respective countries under UN supervision, for common deployment by the UN, in collaboration with such organizations as SADC or the OAU. Indeed, it seems as though this approach would be a prerequisite for South Africa's involvement in efforts to keep the peace, given the stipulation in the defense white paper that the defense force would participate only in UN-sanctioned operations.[24]

It may be possible, however, to marry the need for enhanced indigenous peacekeeping capabilities and the imperative for continued UN involvement and responsibility. One of the major drawbacks of UN missions in Africa (and elsewhere) has been a lack of consultation between the Security Council and the troop contributors, especially with regard to the formulation and amendment of UN mandates. In March 1996, the Security Council announced a series of procedures to improve these functions. Henceforth, meetings are to be held between members of the Council, troop-contributing countries, and the Secretariat for consultation and exchange of information and views. These meetings will be held as soon as practicable and in good time before the Council takes decisions about the extension and termination of, or significant changes in, the mandate of a particular peacekeeping operation. Furthermore, when the Council considers establishing a new peacekeeping operation, meetings will be held, unless impracticable, with any prospective troop contributors who have been approached by the Secretariat and who have indicated a willingness to contribute to the operation. If these and other consultative procedures take hold, African countries may be able to develop regional and subregional peacekeeping capabilities for utilization within the UN framework. Such an arrangement would preserve many of the benefits of regional peacekeeping (local knowledge and commitment to success), while eliminating its major disadvantages (partiality and lack of major-power support).[25]

In conclusion, the building of effective and sustainable regional peacekeeping capabilities in Africa and southern Africa will take a considerable amount of time, effort, and resources. It will not be achieved merely through the conduct of a few seminars and the introduction or expansion of "UN packages" at various military staff colleges. This last approach may produce some capacity for keeping the peace, but it would be a hollow capacity. What is needed is a more holistic and inte-

grated approach, which encompasses the issues of societal democratization and demilitarization, and the military's adjustment to the resul-
tant (democratic) shifts in the pattern of civil–military relations. If
regional peacekeeping capabilities are not based on firm foundations
of enlightened military professionalism and civic consciousness, the
military will likely remain a major part of the problem of conflict in
Africa, rather than a source of hope for a more peaceful future.

Notes to Chapter 12

1. International Peace Academy (IPA), *Peacekeeper's Handbook* (New York, 1984), 7.

2. *Ibid.*, 22; Boutros Boutros-Ghali, *An Agenda for Peace* (New York, 1992).

3. Michela Wrong, "Fear Drives Africa's Boom Business," *Financial Times*, 8
May 1996; James Kiras, "West Africa," *Peacekeeping and International Relations*,
XXV (1996), 17.

4. All Africa Press Service, 24 Apr. 1996; AP Datastream International
News Wire, "Lessons to be Learned from Rwanda," *International Peacekeeping
News*, II (March/April,1996), 5, 7.

5. Reuter News Reports, "Angola to Disarm Civilians," *ibid.*, 12-13.

6. The cost of an AK-47 was reported by Virginia Gamba, director of the
"Towards Collaborative Peace" project at the Institute of Security Studies (ISS;
formerly the Institute for Defense Policy [IDP]), June 1996.

7. Hobbes quoted in Karl Deutsch, *Politics and Government: How People
Decide Their Fate* (Boston, 1980; 3d ed.), 78.

8. Eric T. Young, "The Development of the FADM in Mozambique: Internal and External Dynamics," *African Security Review*, V (1996), 20-21.

9. Assis Malaquias, "Angola and Mozambique: Lessons Learnt," paper presented at IDP/NUPI seminar, "Beyond the Emergency: Development within UN
Peace Missions," (Pretoria, 1996), 6-7.

10. *Ibid.*, 3.

11. Al J. Venter, "Mercenaries Fuel Next Round in Angolan Civil War,"
Jane's International Defense Review, III (1996), 63.

12. Reuters News Reports, "Angolan Peace Process Lags," *International
Peacekeeping News*, II (March/April, 1996), 13-14.

13. Reuters News Reports, "Angola to Disarm Civilians," *ibid.*, 13; Southern African News Features, 11/96, June 11, 1996.

14. UN, "Report of the Secretary General on the United Nations Angola
Verification Mission," Geneva, February, 7, 1997; Chris McGreal, "Angolan
Troops Join Zaire War," electronic *Mail and Guardian*, 19 Mar. 1997.

15. Reuters News Reports, "UN Failure Helped Rwanda Genocide," *International Peacekeeping News*, II (March/April, 1996), 6.

16. Chris Smith, "Peacekeeping in Africa: A State of Crisis," *Jane's Defense '96: The World in Conflict*, 100.

Chapter VI of the UN Charter deals with "The Pacific Settlement of Disputes." It empowers the Security Council to "investigate any dispute, or any situation which might lead to international friction or give rise to a dispute, in order to determine whether the continuance of the dispute or situation is likely to endanger the maintenance of international peace and security." It emphasizes the primacy of negotiation, mediation, conciliation, arbitration, judicial settlement, or any other means that belligerents might choose to settle their conflicts peacefully. Chapter VI makes no provision for unsolicited intervention. Apart from empowering the Security Council to determine which ongoing disputes endanger peace and security, and to recommend "appropriate" measures to resolve them, it provides a weak and vague basis for the concept and conduct of peace-support operations, authorizing them only with the consent of the parties directly concerned.

Chapter VII concerns "Action with Respect to Threats to the Peace, Breaches of the Peace, and Acts of Aggression." Unlike its precursor, it is essentially coercive, enabling the Security Council to investigate alleged violations and determine how to proceed against the perpetrating *states* to *restore* peace, whether politically, economically, or militarily (Article 42), without the consent of the disputants.

17. Robin Wright, "Christopher Urges Africa to Create Crisis Force," *Los Angeles Times*, 11 Oct. 1996.

18. Tom Woodhouse, "Negotiating the Millennium: Prospects for African Conflict Resolution," *International Peacekeeping News*, II (September/October, 1996), 42.

19. Statements by Salim at a meeting of the chiefs of staff of states belonging to the OAU Central Organ, Addis Ababa, 1996.

20. Communiqué concerning the establishment of the Organ for Politics, Defense, and Security, Gaborone, 1996.

21. Smith, "Peacekeeping," 100.

22. Statement by Salim at a meeting of the chiefs of staff of states belonging to the OAU Central Organ, Addis Ababa, 1996.

23. Jakkie Cilliers and Malan, "A Regional Peacekeeping Role for South Africa: Pressures, Problems, and Prognosis," *African Security Review*, V (1996), 30.

24. *Ibid.*, 31.

25. UN Security Council Press Release, SC/6198, 28 Mar. 1996. For a discussion of the advantages and disadvantages of regional peacekeeping in the southern African context, see Cilliers and Malan, "Regional Peacekeeping," 27-29. See also Jeffrey Herbst, *Securing Peace in Africa,* WPF Reports 17 (Cambridge, Mass., 1998).

About the Authors

Jacklyn Cock is Professor of Sociology, University of the Witwatersrand, Johannesburg. Her research centers on the problem of violence and social inequality in South African society. She has published and co-edited four books, numerous journal articles, chapters in books, reviews, and conference proceedings. She has been a visiting fellow at the Woodrow Wilson School, Princeton University, Oxford University, Rutgers University, and the Institute for Advanced Study, Princeton.

Robert S. Gelbard is President Clinton's special representative for implementation of the Dayton Peace Accords. A career Foreign Service officer, he served as assistant secretary for international narcotics and law enforcement affairs, U.S. Department of State, from 1993 to 1997. He also has served as principal deputy assistant of state for inter-American affairs and ambassador to Bolivia.

Jeffrey Herbst is Associate Professor of Public and International Affairs at Princeton University's Woodrow Wilson School. He has written about the politics of economic and political reform in Africa, the politics of boundaries, and developments in southern Africa. He has taught at the University of Cape Town and the University of the Western Cape.

Mark Malan is senior researcher in the African Security Analysis Program at the Institute for Security Studies (ISS), South Africa. Prior to joining ISS, Malan spent twenty years in the South African army, including five years teaching in the Department of Political Science in the South African Military Academy. He has published widely on issues pertaining to regional security, defense, conflict management, and peacekeeping in Africa.

Katherine Marshall is an official of the World Bank. She was country director for the Southern African Department from 1994 to 1996, and has led World Bank operations in the Sahel and Latin America. She is currently leading World Bank operations in East Asia and the Pacific.

Steven Metz is the Henry L. Stimpson Professor of Military Studies at the U.S. Army War College and research professor in the College's Strategic Studies Institute. He has taught at the Air War College, the U.S. Army Command and General Staff College, and several universities. He has also served as a consultant about U.S. policy in Africa to political organizations and campaigns, and testified before the Senate Africa Subcommittee. He is the author of *Disaster and Intervention in Sub-Saharan Africa: Learning From Rwanda* (1994); *Reform, Conflict, and Security in Zaire* (1996).

Greg Mills is the National Director of the South African Institute of International Affairs (SAIIA). He has taught at the University of the Western Cape and the University of Cape Town. His many journal and popular articles have specialized in security-related and regional-foreign policy analysis. Among his published books at SAIIA are *From Pariah to Participant: South Africa's Evolving Foreign Policy Relations, 1990-1994* (1994); *South Africa and Peacekeeping in Africa* (1995).

Glenn Oosthuysen is a researcher at the South African Institute of International Affairs, Johannesburg, where he works on projects dealing with small-arms proliferation and the illegal-drugs trade in southern Africa. He has a special interest in transnational crime, security, and conflict issues affecting South and southern Africa. He is the author of *Small Arms Proliferation and Control in Southern Africa* (1996).

Robert I. Rotberg is President of the World Peace Foundation of Cambridge, Mass.; Coordinator of Southern African Programs at the Harvard Institute for International Development; and Adjunct Lecturer at Harvard's Kennedy School of Government. He was Professor of Political Science and History, MIT; Academic Vice President, Tufts University; and President, Lafayette College. He is the author or editor of thirty books and many articles, including *Suffer the Future: Policy Choices in Southern Africa* (1980); *South Africa and its Neighbors: Regional Security and Self-Interest* (1985); *Conflict and Compromise in South Africa* (1980); *Namibia: Political and Economic Prospects* (1983); *The Founder: Cecil Rhodes and the Pursuit of Power* (1988).

Mark Shaw is head of the Crime and Policing Program at the Institute for Security Studies in South Africa. He has published extensively on issues relating to crime, intelligence, policing, and security. He chairs a committee appointed by the minister of safety and security to investigate appropriate guidelines to deal with crime in South Africa, 1998 to 2003, and he drafted a white paper about safety and security.

Hussein Solomon is Senior Researcher in the African Security Analysis Program at the Institute for Security Studies, South Africa. He was a research fellow at the Center for Southern African Studies at the University of Western Cape and a lecturer in the Department of Political Science, University of Durban-Westville. His research focuses on southern African regional security, international relations theory, and South African foreign policy.

C.J.D. Venter is currently working for the United Nations drug program in Lusaka, Zambia. He was formerly head of the Organized Crime division in the National Crime Investigation Service of the South African Police Services.

Joan Wardrop is Senior Lecturer in History and Deputy Head (Graduate Studies) in the School of Social Sciences and Asian Languages at Curtin University of Technology, Perth, Western Australia. For the last decade, she has focused on South Africa, in particular, on concepts of the state and relationships between the state and the people.

The World Peace Foundation

THE WORLD PEACE FOUNDATION was created in 1910 by the imagination and fortune of Edwin Ginn, the Boston publisher, to encourage international peace and cooperation. The Foundation seeks to advance the cause of world peace though study, analysis, and the advocacy of wise action. As an operating, not a grant-giving foundation, it provides financial support only for projects which it has initiated itself.

Edwin Ginn shared the hope of many of his contemporaries that permanent peace could be achieved. That dream was denied by the outbreak of World War I, but the Foundation has continued to attempt to overcome obstacles to international peace and co-operation, drawing for its funding on the endowment bequeathed by the founder. In its early years, the Foundation focused its attention on building the peace-keeping capacity of the League of Nations, and then on the development of world order through the United Nations. The Foundation established and nurtured the premier scholarly journal in its field, *International Organization*, now in its fifty-first year.

From the 1950s to the early 1990s, mostly a period of bipolar conflict when universal collective security remained unattainable, the Foundation concentrated its activities on improving the working of world order mechanisms, regional security, transnational relations, and the impact of public opinion on American foreign policy. From 1980 to 1993, the Foundation published nineteen books and seven reports on Third World security; on South Africa and other states of southern Africa; on Latin America, the Caribbean, and Puerto Rico; on migration; and on the international aspects of traffic in narcotics. From 1994 through 1997, the Foundation published books on Europe after the Cold War; on the United States, southern Europe, and the countries of the Mediterranean basin; on reducing the world traffic in conventional arms control; and on Haiti, preventive diplomacy and NGOs, the media and humanitarian crises, and truth commissions.

The Foundation is now focusing most of its energies and resources on the Prevention of Intercommunal Conflict and Humanitarian Crises. This focus proceeds from the assumption that large-scale human suffering, wherever it occurs, is a serious and continuing threat to the peace of the world, both engendering and resulting from ethnic, religious, and other intrastate and cross-border conflicts. The Foundation is examining how the forces of world order may most effectively engage in preventive diplomacy, create early warning systems leading to early preventive action, achieve regional conflict avoidance, and eradicate the underlying causes of intergroup enmity and warfare. It is also concerned with assisting the growth of democracy in selected states like Haiti, Burma, and Sri Lanka, and in all of Africa.

Index

ships" with both government agencies and external organizations in civil society.[10]

The document provides a detailed accurate analysis of the many interconnected factors that have contributed to the growth of crime in South Africa and outlines steps underway in various government departments to counter them. Outside repair of the criminal justice process, three key areas are identified as critical for intervention to reduce crime—environmental design, education, and transnational crime. In addition, the strategy presents eighteen national programs for implementation, involving such plans as improving information systems (poor information transfer being at the heart of the system's problems), empowering and supporting victims, and devising mechanisms to deter organized crime. It also includes various initiatives in line-function departments and provisions for forging partnerships with outsiders.

Notably absent from the list of new programs are specific preventive strategies related to drug use, the proliferation of small arms, and the gang problem in certain parts of the country. Although each is covered directly or indirectly within various sections of the document, it would have been worthwhile to merge current initiatives and develop specific strategies to form two or three additional, conspicuous prevention programs, since these particular criminal activities have the potential to spawn wider forms of criminality.

The issue of increasing drug usage, for instance, is critical. Government response to the drug problem has historically been fragmented and poorly funded, with no coordination between reactive and proactive approaches. What needs to be explored is the establishment of a law-enforcement body separate from the current police and intelligence structures that would provide leadership in the areas of both prevention and enforcement.

It is regrettable that the strategy does not allot more space to initiatives by local government. International experience suggests that the key to crime prevention lies in the cities. The strategy could have advanced the process and stimulated local debate had it emphasized the issue of crime prevention at the metropolitan level. Other countries have established city forums to compare experiences and determine joint guidelines for crime prevention.

Nor have South African city authorities been idle. Many are beginning to work on crime prevention plans and establish local-authority police agencies. But central government has dragged its heels on these developments. No framework yet exists for local government policing or crime-prevention strategies, and, if current developments mean anything, local governments will run ahead of the national authorities in this sphere. Many cities, including crime-ridden Johannesburg, are in the process of formulating plans for city police services designed to supplement the SAPS.

The National Crime Prevention Strategy correctly maintains that local-level initiatives should be able to tailor individual programs for local-level conditions and circumstances. But it is not clear what the consequences will be if local authorities stray outside the vague boundaries delineated by the strategy. The document could have suggested guidelines to contain or, where necessary, focus any such initiatives.

The key to the strategy's success is coordination. Without it, the strategy simply becomes a reflection of a wide variety of programs that might have been possible in one form or the other. A related problem with such a large and complex national initiative is that it is virtually immune to measurement. The danger is that success will be equated with a flurry of activity (in this case, committee meetings) rather than any actual decreases in crime.

The document makes allowance for monitoring departments and programs, but the extent to which the whole enterprise will be subject to review is not clear. Although the difficulty of interpreting crime statistics runs counter to exact prediction, program goals need to be better defined. Despite the fact that it is a guide for implementation, the strategy contains virtually no time frames for the completion of the various initiatives, although some may be forthcoming.

Management is by committee. An interministerial committee, comprised of the ministers of Safety and Security, Defense, Justice, Correctional Services, Welfare, and Intelligence, will supplement the cabinet Committee on Security and Intelligence. It will meet quarterly, or convene on an ad hoc basis if necessary. Under the ministerial committee will be the committee of directors-general, which will also be chaired by the lead department, Safety and Security.

With no deadlines to meet, the committees, which have apparently already assembled, have made little progress. A publicly released set of objectives and deadlines would have provided some basis to judge progress. Without them, the plan could seem like another paper strategy, creating expectations that the government will not be able to honor.

Frustration has already occurred. Media coverage of specific criminal activities has turned the spotlight once again on the issue of crime. Government responses that these activities are just isolated instances or media fabrications fundamentally misunderstand the role of the press. Unless government law-enforcement agencies establish themselves on the ground—in the short term—where most citizens experience crime, no amount of strategies formulated in Pretoria will bring relief. On the contrary, if every fresh outburst of crime provokes only words without visible counteraction, disillusionment with proactive crime prevention, which is indispensable to the long-term solution of disorder in South African society, will grow, further encouraging reactive, self-help, and increasingly violent solutions to crime.

Citizen Responses

The increasing failure of the criminal justice system to deter or punish offenders has led many citizens to take the law into their own hands. None of their options are new; all of them were available in some form under apartheid rule. What is new is the growth of extra-state mechanisms of law and order in conjunction with declining public confidence in the ability of the police to secure a safe environment. Forms of protection vary; the wealthier members of society can afford to contract with the private security sector, whereas those in less fortunate communities are more likely to take their own initiative.

Unlike that in Europe and North America, the South African private security industry has not attracted much study. It has grown rapidly since 1980; it initially expanded at a rate of 30 percent per year, slowing to 10 to 15 percent in the last five years. Since the late 1970s, the estimated annual average growth rate has been 18 percent. The exact value of the industry is difficult to quantify. A recent estimate suggested that the guarding industry alone was worth around R3.6 billion. Private security officers outnumber the public police by about 2 to 1.[11]

The South African security industry shows some unique traits—a mix between sophisticated electronics and the use of armed guards. It is also distinguished by its reliance on the reactive side. Traditionally, both in South Africa and elsewhere, security companies had a proactive function: Guards, modeled on the concept of the "bobby on the beat," patrolled defined areas, but now in South Africa armed response has become more in evidence. Panic buttons relay electronic signals via a control room to security officers patrolling in cars, who perform functions similar to those of the traditional police.

The growth in the South African security industry does not reflect broader trends. Indeed, it seems to be implicated in an inverse relationship with the rest of the economy, tending to thrive in poor economic conditions. During the pre-election months, when most business in the country stagnated, security reflected record growth. It has stabilized to some extent since the 1994 election, but the recent crime wave is boosting the security companies again. Nonetheless, parts of the market, like guarding, are showing more and more signs of saturation.

The development of the private security sector in South Africa has not been untroubled. Attempts to obtain more power for certain kinds of security guards are likely to fall on deaf ears if the consensus is that private security officers are untrained and act unprofessionally. Public perceptions, whether the industry likes it or not, are shaped by individual instances of abuse—for example, the deaths of sixteen people in a stampede caused by security guards armed with electric batons at Tembisa, northeast of Johannesburg in 1996, or the shooting deaths of forty-one alleged burglars over a number of years by "Lious" van Schoor.

The danger of replicating the Tembisa incident is real. Private security companies are operating more and more in the so-called private–public sphere—that is, private property that is open for public usage, such as shopping malls or university campuses. Moreover, the trend of enlisting private police in urban neighborhoods or central business districts is growing. Private firms have been known to handle such public-order activities as clearing squatters.

Heavy dependence on the private security industry does not necessarily release the public police from pressure. The private industry employs mechanisms—guards, alarms, and detection devices—to gather information that can be fed to police. Rather than decreasing